Vanessa Cirannek
Universität Potsdam

Cairoli Lecture Series
Federico Sturzenegger, editor

Laurence J. Kotlikoff, *Generational Policy*

Michael D. Whinston, *Lectures on Antitrust Economics*

Barry Eichengreen, *Global Imbalances and the Lessons of Bretton Woods*

Lectures on Antitrust Economics

Michael D. Whinston

The Cairoli Lectures
Universidad Torcuato
Di Tella

The MIT Press
Cambridge, Massachusetts
London, England

First MIT Press paperback edition, 2008
© 2006 Massachusetts Institute of Technology

All rights reserved. No part of this book may be reproduced in any form by any electronic or mechanical means (including photocopying, recording, or information storage and retrieval) without permission in writing from the publisher.

MIT Press books may be purchased at special quantity discounts for business or sales promotional use. For information, please email special_sales@mitpress.mit.edu or write to Special Sales Department, The MIT Press, 55 Hayward Street, Cambridge, MA 02142.

This book was set in Palatino on 3B2 by Asco Typesetters, Hong Kong and was printed and bound in the United States of America.

Library of Congress Cataloging-in-Publication Data

Whinston, Michael Dennis.
Lectures on antitrust economics / Michael D. Whinston.
   p. cm.
"Based on the 2001 Cairoli lectures" Data sheet.
Includes bibliographical references and index.
ISBN 978-0-262-23256-2 (alk. paper)—978-0-262-73187-4 (pb. : alk. paper)
1. Antitrust law—Economic aspects—United States. I. Title.

HD2758.5.W45 2006
338.8′20973—dc22   2006041955

10 9 8 7 6 5 4

Contents

Series Foreword   vii
Preface   xi

1 Introduction   1

2 Price Fixing   15

3 Horizontal Mergers   57

4 Exclusionary Vertical Contracts   133

Notes   199
References   221
Index   235

Series Foreword

Ricardo Cairoli (1921–1998) was a successful businessman and a committed public official, who, throughout his career devoted himself to enhancing the well-being of Argentina's society. In 1991, he founded Capital Markets Argentina, one of the major independent investment corporations in the country, offering services in brokerage and asset management. Since its inception, the corporation has been involved in numerous philanthropic activities. Currently his wife, Mrs. Haydee Morteo de Cairoli, and his children, Graciela and Pablo, continue to support higher education, sponsoring, among other initiatives, the Capital Markets Corporation Conferences in Business Economics. The conferences are organized by the Universidad Torcuato Di Tella, a private university founded in 1991, which rapidly established itself as a center of excellence for education and research in the social sciences in Latin America. The realization and publication of the conference lectures represents the joint commitment of Capital Markets Argentina and the Universidad Torcuato Di Tella to the advancement of knowledge.

For my father, George Whinston,
and to the memory of my mother,
Joan Aronson Whinston

Preface

This book is based on material I was honored to present as part of the Cairoli Lectures at the Universidad Torcuato Di Tella in Buenos Aires. I appreciated the opportunity to develop further my thoughts about antitrust economics, to interact with the many fine economists and lawyers who attended the lectures, and to meet the wonderfully welcoming Cairoli family. It was my first trip to Argentina, and I look forward to visiting again.

I owe thanks to a variety of individuals and organizations for their contributions toward this book. Michael Black, Patrick Bolton, Dennis Carlton, Richard Caves, Malcolm Coate, Luke Froeb, Rob Gertner, Aviv Nevo, Volker Nocke, Ariel Pakes, Paul Pautler, Craig Peters, Russell Pittman, Rob Porter, Richard Posner, Tom Ross, Ernesto Schargrodsky, Greg Werden, and Abe Wickelgren all helped improve the book by sharing their comments with me. I also thank four anonymous readers for their detailed and insightful suggestions. Fan Zhang, Adam Rosen, and Allan Collard-Wexler provided excellent research assistance. John Covell at the MIT Press helped shepherd the book through the editorial process. Thanks are also due to the NSF and the Searle Foundation for their financial support.

I owe special thanks to three other people. Doug Bernheim and Ilya Segal each have spent countless hours working with me on coauthored projects over the years. Many of those involved issues related to antitrust, and in particular to the vertical contracting issues that I discuss in chapter 4. I've learned a tremendous amount from each of them about that topic, and many more.

My wife, Bonnie Honig, not only provided the usual sorts of spousal support (such as "Get it done already!"), but also was kind enough to read portions of the book and give me some writing tips. I hope the book now shows at least a little of the style that is so evident in her own books.

Finally, I dedicate this book to my father, George Whinston, for his continuing love and support, and to my mother, Joan Aronson Whinston, for having been such a wonderful mother.

MW

1 Introduction

1.1 Aims of the Lectures

Antitrust law plays a prominent role in the business environment of many nations. In any given week the *New York Times* and *Wall Street Journal* usually include at least one, and often several, articles devoted to some aspect of antitrust policy. Will a recently announced merger of two large oil companies cause gasoline prices to rise? Has an important software company violated the antitrust laws by suppressing competition? Did a group of international producers of vitamins conspire to fix prices? Issues like these are featured regularly, not only in American newspapers, but also increasingly around the world.

Antitrust law regulates economic activity. The law's operation, however, differs in important ways from what is traditionally referred to as "regulation." Regulation tends to be industry-specific and to involve the direct setting of prices, product characteristics, or entry, usually after regular, often elaborate hearings. By contrast, antitrust law tends to apply quite broadly, and focuses on maintaining certain basic rules of competition that enable the competitive interaction among firms to produce "good" outcomes. Investigations and intervention are exceptional events, which arise when these basic rules may have been violated.

These lectures are intended to serve as an introduction to the economics behind antitrust law. The lectures do not strive to be comprehensive in their coverage. Rather, I focus selectively on some of the most recent developments in antitrust economics, and on some areas in which I believe important issues require further research. The intended audience is primarily graduate students in economics and practicing economists (both academic and nonacademic) with interests in antitrust policy. My hope, however, is that the book will also find some readers among economically sophisticated antitrust lawyers, especially academic ones. As such, I have tried to confine some mathematics to footnotes and to ensure that the central line of the argument can be followed without necessarily understanding every equation that appears in the body of the text.

The rest of this chapter provides an introduction to the U.S. antitrust laws. The remainder of the book is organized into three chapters. Antitrust analysis can be broken roughly into two categories, one dealing with "collusion" (broadly defined) and the other with "exclusion." In the former category, firms attempt to raise prices through collaboration with rivals, while in the latter category they try to do so through rivals' exclusion. In chapters 2 and 3, I focus on the first type of activity. Chapter 2 discusses price fixing, that is agreements among competitors to restrict output or raise price. Chapter 3 examines horizontal mergers, in which competitors agree to merge their operations. I then shift the focus to exclusionary activities in chapter 4, providing an introduction to the economics of exclusionary vertical contracts.

These three chapters differ significantly from one another in emphasis. Chapter 2, on price fixing, covers what is undoubtedly the most settled area of antitrust. Here I try to unsettle the discourse a bit, suggesting that economists know less about price fixing than they think. In contrast, the analysis of horizontal mergers, which I discuss in chapter 3, is an area of antitrust economics that has seen some of the most significant advances over the last 10–15 years. Here I summarize the main issues in evaluating horizontal mergers, paying particular attention to these recent advances, while also discussing some of the important open questions that remain. Exclusionary vertical contracting, which I discuss in chapter 4, is instead one of the most controversial areas of antitrust. It is also an area in which there has been a good deal of recent theoretical work, and in which currently there is little systematic empirical evidence. Focusing specifically on exclusive contracts, here I aim to explain the source of the controversy and describe these recent theoretical advances. In contrast to chapters 2 and 3, my discussion of empirical evidence here is, of necessity, unfortunately limited.

My selective choice of topics leaves out a number of important issues that a more extended set of lectures ideally would discuss. For example, predatory pricing, collusive facilitating practices, and intrabrand vertical restraints are all interesting and important topics. Likewise, a fuller treatment of exclusionary vertical contracting would consider vertical mergers and tying.

In addition, my focus on the economics of antitrust often allows only passing mention to the legal treatment of these practices. This is in many ways unfortunate. Every student of the subject should read the case law on antitrust. Doing so provides an appreciation for both the economic issues involved in antitrust analysis (even when the court may not have recognized them) and the considerable difficulties involved in formulating effective antitrust laws.[1] I also highly recommend two classic books on antitrust by leading legal scholars, Posner [1976] and Bork [1978], for interesting and often provocative discussions of many of the central issues in antitrust analysis.[2]

Finally, I am also selective geographically. The discussion that follows focuses almost exclusively on the antitrust laws with which I am the most familiar, namely those of the United States. That said, the focus of the lectures is on economics, and the basic principles apply across national boundaries.

1.2 Overview of U.S. Antitrust Law

As a prelude to our discussion, it is useful to begin with a brief overview of the history and content of U.S. antitrust law.[3] The development of the U.S. antitrust laws was sparked by the post–Civil War transformation of the U.S. economy. Two pressures for reform developed during this period. The first came from farmers, upset over a combination of depressed prices for farm products and high rail rates for shipping farm products. These rail rates often were controlled by (legal) rail cartels. The second pressure came from the public's discomfort with the rapidly growing size of modern business. This discomfort was sharpened, in part, by a number of well-publicized business scandals. Together, these pressures led not only to passage of the Sherman Act in 1890, the United States's first antitrust law, but also to the creation of regulatory agencies such as the Interstate Commerce Commission (in 1887).

Sections 1 and 2 of the Sherman Act, shown in figure 1.1, contain its main substantive provisions. (Figure 1.1 summarizes the most important provisions of the U.S. antitrust laws.) An instant's consideration reveals their most

Sherman Act (1890):

Section 1: "Every contract, combination in the form of trust or otherwise, or conspiracy, in restraint of trade or commerce among the several states, or with foreign nations, is hereby declared illegal. . . ."

Section 2: "Every person who shall monopolize, or attempt to monopolize, or combine or conspire with any other person or persons, to monopolize any part of the trade or commerce among the several states, or with foreign nations, shall be deemed guilty of a felony. . . ."

Clayton Act (1914):

Section 2: Prohibits some forms of price discrimination.

Section 3: Prohibits sales based on the condition that the buyer not buy from a competitor where the effect may be "to substantially lessen competition or tend to create a monopoly in any line of commerce."

Section 7: Prohibits mergers where "the effect of such acquisition may be substantially to lessen competition, or to tend to create a monopoly" in any line of commerce.

FTC Act (1914):

Creates the Federal Trade Commission

Section 5: "Unfair methods of competition in or affecting commerce, and unfair or deceptive acts or practices in or affecting commerce, are declared unlawful."

Figure 1.1
U.S. Antitrust Statutes

notable feature: they are very *vague*. Indeed, the Sherman Act's two central sections do little more than authorize the U.S. courts to develop a common law of antitrust to fulfill the statute's intent. As it has been interpreted by the U.S. courts, section 1 applies to a wide range of agreements that may be deemed to reduce competition: price-fixing agreements, horizontal mergers, exclusive contracts, and resale-price-maintenance agreements. Section 2 applies to unilateral actions taken by a dominant firm that may further its market power, such as predatory pricing and product bundling. It makes illegal certain acts of monopolizing, not monopoly itself.

The need for courts to interpret these provisions of the Sherman Act raises the question of Congress's intent. The congressional debates leading to passage of the Sherman Act reflected a number of differing and inherently conflicting goals: promotion of healthy competition, concern for injured competitors, and distrust of large concentrations of economic and political power all make appearances in the debates over the bill. These differing goals have continued to surface in its application ever since. In the last thirty years a number of scholars have made strong appeals for the first of these to be the only goal of antitrust policy (see, for example, Posner [1976] and Bork [1978] for two of the most influential discussions). With the development of a more conservative judiciary since 1980 and increasing infiltration of economics into antitrust analysis, this view seems to be winning the debate.

Even so, the precise formulation of even this economic prescription for "healthy competition" remains unsettled. Bork [1978], for example, argues that the appropriate standard is maximization of aggregate surplus.[4] Certainly, to an economist the thought of designing antitrust policy to maximize aggregate surplus comes naturally and, indeed, much of the economics literature implicitly has taken this to be the appropriate objective for antitrust policy. The basis for this view is the observation that the owners of firms are consumers as well, and the belief that redistribution among consumers should occur through the tax system. Nonetheless, in the absence of perfect lump-sum tax policies, the appropriate weight to be given to consumer-versus-producer surplus gains can depend on distributional objectives.[5] As I note at several points later, which welfare standard is adopted can be critical to the evaluation of contested practices.

Although the U.S. courts have adopted varying and evolving standards in evaluating challenged practices (and are often not very clear on the exact test being applied), at present they seem closest to applying a consumer-surplus welfare standard. Similarly, as we will see in chapter 3, the U.S. enforcement agencies [the U.S. Department of Justice (DOJ) and the Federal Trade Commission (FTC)] seem to adopt essentially this standard in their *Horizontal Merger Guidelines* (although even they are not explicit about it).[6]

The vagueness of the Sherman Act created discontent: those concerned with monopoly power felt that the Act could allow businesses to get away with anticompetitive behavior, while businesses were worried that they could not know precisely which behaviors would be illegal. These concerns were further exacerbated by the Supreme Court's ruling in the *Standard Oil* case [221 U.S. 1 (1911)], in which the Court announced the use of the "rule of reason" in evaluating business practices (a practice's benefits and costs had to be weighed in evaluating the practice). This discontent led, in 1914, to passage of the Clayton Act and the Federal Trade Commission Act.

The Clayton Act named specific practices that would be considered illegal under certain circumstances: certain forms of price discrimination are banned in section 2 of the Act (I do not discuss these issues here), tying and exclusive dealing fall under section 3, and horizontal and vertical mergers fall under section 7.

The Federal Trade Commission Act created the Federal Trade Commission as a specialist agency to enforce the antitrust laws. The central substantive provision guiding the FTC's enforcement actions is section 5. The courts have come to interpret section 5 as applying to anything that is a Sherman Act or Clayton Act violation, but also to somewhat "lesser" acts that violate the "spirit" of those laws.[7] This broader interpretation often has been justified on the basis that the FTC is an administrative authority specializing in these issues (as compared with the judges and juries who must decide cases brought by the DOJ) and that the FTC can impose only what is known as equitable relief for antitrust violations (more on this below).

Finally, there are some special provisions in antitrust law (the Hart-Scott-Rodino Act) requiring that parties to sufficiently large mergers provide notification to the DOJ and the FTC prior to consummating their merger, and giving the agencies a period of time to request information from the parties, and to review and possibly object to the merger. The idea behind this requirement is that it is much easier to prevent a merger before it happens than to "unscramble the eggs" after they have been mixed together.

Sanctions

There are three types of sanctions that can be imposed in U.S. antitrust cases: criminal penalties, equitable relief, and monetary damages. Sherman Act offenses are felonies, and the DOJ (but not the FTC) can seek criminal penalties for them. (Violations of the Clayton and FTC Acts are not crimes.) In practice, criminal penalties are sought only for the most flagrant offenses, which means overt price fixing. These penalties can include both imprisonment and monetary fines. Currently, a violation of the Sherman Act may lead to up to three years in jail for individuals. Monetary fines for Sherman Act violations were historically very small, but have recently increased dramatically. For example, the maximum fine for corporations was $50,000 until it was increased to $1 million in 1974. In 1990 the maximum fine was raised to $10 million. Equally or more important, since 1987 U.S. Sentencing Guidelines have allowed for an alternative fine of either (i) twice the convicted firms' pecuniary gains, or (ii) twice the victims' losses. This alternative was first employed by the DOJ in 1995, and it is what led Archer Daniels Midland to agree to pay a $100 million fine for its role in the recent lysine and citric acid price-fixing conspiracies.[8]

Equitable relief entails undoing the wrong that has occurred. Sometimes this involves forbidding certain actions, sometimes it can involve more affirmative moves to restore competitive conditions such as, for example, divestiture or making certain patents available for license. Both the government and private parties can sue in the federal courts for equitable relief for violations of either the Sherman or Clayton Acts. The result of such a proceeding, should the plaintiff prevail, is a court issued *decree*.[9]

The FTC can also seek equitable relief. Here the procedure is somewhat different and involves a quasi-judicial administrative proceeding within the agency in which the FTC staff and the accused firm(s) present evidence in front of an "administrative law judge." The administrative law judge issues an opinion, which is then reviewed by the commission, consisting of five commissioners appointed by the president for seven-year terms. The commission can approve or change (in any way) the administrative law judge's decision, and it is empowered to issue a "cease and desist" order if it finds that violations have occurred. Like lower court rulings for the DOJ or private party suits, these cease and desist orders can be appealed by the firms to the appellate courts.

Finally, private parties who prove in court that they were injured due to Sherman and Clayton Act offenses can recover treble damages. In addition to providing a means for compensating parties injured by antitrust violations, these penalties help to create an army of private enforcers of the antitrust laws (moreover, an army that is perhaps more aware of when violations are occurring than are the governmental enforcement agencies). For price-fixing violations, for example, damages are equal to the amount of the overcharge arising from the conspiracy.[10]

It is of interest to note that monetary damages for Sherman Act price-fixing violations may, in some circumstances, be less effective at deterring illegal behavior than one might initially expect. The reason, as noted by Salant [1987] and Baker [1988], is that buyers who know that they might collect damages may factor this in when they calculate the effective price they are paying. If so, this increases buyers' willingness to pay, which counteracts—sometimes completely—the direct deterrence effect of damages on the sellers' pricing incentives.

To be more specific, suppose that there is a group of firms that, absent collusion, would set price equal to their marginal cost c. Let t denote the damage multiple, let $\phi(p, t)$ be the probability of successful detection and prosecution given p and t (we expect this probability to increase as the price and damage multiple increase, so that $\phi_p(p,t) \geq 0$ and $\phi_t(p,t) \geq 0$), and let $x(\cdot)$ be the demand function. The joint monopoly price p^m maximizes $(p-c)x(p)$.

Consider a single period model in which the firms first set prices and make sales, and then at the end of the period any collusive activity that occurred during the period may be detected and prosecuted. Suppose that the firms secretly collude and set price equal to $p > c$. Then the effective (net of damages) price to a (risk neutral) buyer who might collect damages equal to $t(p-c)$ is $p^*(p,t) = p - \phi(p,t)t(p-c)$. Buyers will therefore buy $x(p^*(p,t))$ units from the cartel, and so the cartel's expected profit is

$$\Pi(p,t) = (p-c)x(p^*(p,t)) - \phi(p,t)t(p-c)x(p^*(p,t))$$
$$= (p^*(p,t) - c)x(p^*(p,t)).$$

The cartel's profit maximizing choice is clearly to set p such that $p^*(p,t) = p^m$, the monopoly price, if this possible. Figure 1.2a depicts such a case. In such a circumstance, the cartel's output and expected profit are *completely unaffected* by the possibility of damages. In contrast, if there is no p such that $p^*(p,t) = p^m$, as in figure 1.2b, then the cartel chooses p to maximize the effective price $p^*(p,t)$. In this case, damages lower the effective price paid by consumers.[11] For example, if the probability of detection $\phi(\cdot)$ depends only on t, then the cartel can achieve an effective price of p^m if $t\phi(t) < 1$. But if $t\phi(t) \geq 1$, then the best the cartel can do is set p equal to c, so that damages fully deter inefficient pricing.

This simple model makes an interesting observation but probably paints an overly negative picture of the effectiveness of private damages in preventing collusive pricing

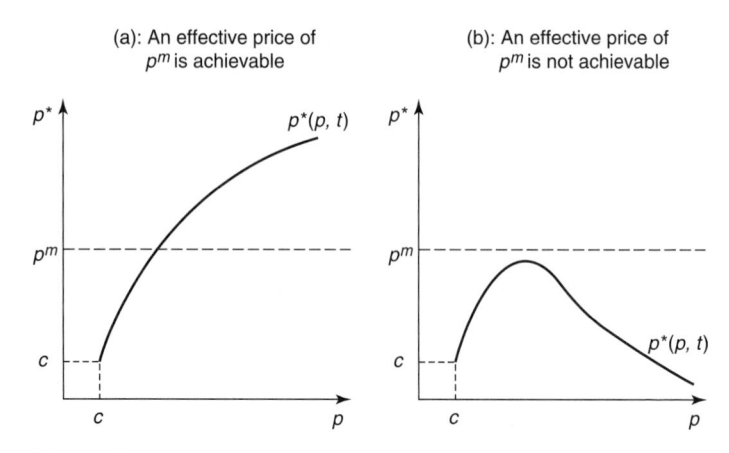

Figure 1.2
The effective (net of damages) price when buying from a cartel

since it omits a number of ways in which private damages may lead to more efficient behavior. First, when damages do lower the expected profit to colluding, they also reduce the likelihood of the cartel forming in the first place. Second, suppose that the cartel faces other penalties $K > 0$ (either fines or jail time) so that its payoff is $\Pi(p,t) - \phi(p,t)K$. In this case, if a greater damage multiple t increases the responsiveness of the detection probability to price (that is, if $\phi_{pt}(\cdot,\cdot) > 0$), then it will always lead the cartel to set a lower effective price. Similarly, suppose that we instead consider a multiperiod model. For example, imagine that there are two periods of potential collusion. If collusion in period 2 can occur only if collusion is not detected in period 1, the cartel suffers a loss of, say, $K > 0$ if collusion is detected in period 1. Then, just as when the cartel faces other penalties, a higher damage multiple will lower the first period cartel price if $\phi_{pt}(\cdot,\cdot) > 0$. In addition, a new effect arises in the dynamic setting: here, as long as

$\phi_t(\cdot,\cdot) > 0$, damages increase expected welfare by causing the cartel to end more quickly. Finally, in many cases, buyers will actually be unaware that collusion is taking place, in which case increasing t can be shown (even in the static model) to necessarily reduce the price charged while the cartel is active.[12]

1.3   Looking Ahead

In the next three chapters, we will look at three central topics in antitrust: price fixing, horizontal mergers, and exclusionary vertical contracts. In each case (albeit to varying degrees), economists have made substantial progress in understanding the economic issues involved. Yet, at the same time, some very substantial challenges remain. These challenges are both theoretical and empirical in nature. Moreover, to improve antitrust law and its administration, our economic understanding will need to be joined with an appreciation for issues of judicial procedure. This will not be an easy task. My hope is that this book can help point the way.

2 Price Fixing

2.1 Introduction

In this chapter, we begin our discussion of antitrust economics by looking at what many consider its most central element: its ban on "price fixing"—that is, agreements among competitors regarding their prices or outputs.[1] The prohibition on price fixing is one part of antitrust law that is regarded with approval even by those generally skeptical of government competition policy. Nonetheless, some significant and challenging questions remain unanswered. In fact, this least controversial area of antitrust may well be the one for which economists have the least satisfactory theoretical models of how the illegal activity—talking about prices (and reaching an "agreement")—matters. Moreover, the empirical evidence concerning price fixing's actual effects is surprisingly limited and mixed in its findings. Before coming to those points, though, I start by reviewing the legal treatment of price fixing.

2.2 Price Fixing and the per se Rule

A short summary of U.S. law in this area always reads "price fixing is per se illegal." That means that if a firm engages in "price fixing"—say, by meeting with its competitor at the Golden Fleece Motel and agreeing on the prices they will charge—it will be found guilty without any inquiry into the actual anticompetitive effects, or procompetitive benefits, of the agreement. This per se rule contrasts with the rule-of-reason approach adopted in most other areas of antitrust, in which these benefits and costs are said to be weighed explicitly.[2]

This seemingly straightforward rule masks, however, a more complex reality. This complexity is both legal and economic in nature. On the economic side lies the fact that nearly every price fixer has a reason why their particular price-fixing scheme is in fact good for society (or, at least, it seems so at times). For an example of such human ingenuity, one need not look beyond one of the earliest antitrust cases to come before the Supreme Court after the passage of the Sherman Act. In 1897 the Court was faced with the *Trans-Missouri* case [166 U.S. 290 (1897)], in which eighteen railroads west of the Mississippi River had formed an association to set railroad rates. In the lower courts the railroads had argued that their agreement was not illegal because their rates were reasonable and, absent the agreement, ruinous competition would ultimately lead to monopoly and consequently to higher prices.

Can this ruinous competition argument be dismissed as being simply illogical and preposterous? Like many proposed justifications for price-fixing arrangements, the answer is in fact no. The railroad industry is one of high fixed costs and an oligopolistic structure. It is well-understood by now that the number of firms that unfettered competition can support in a market need not be efficient in such cases (see, for example, Mankiw and Whinston [1986]). The Trans-Missouri Freight Association's ruinous competition argument can be viewed as saying exactly this: that unrestricted oligopolistic competition would lead to too few firms (namely, one firm) relative to what is socially efficient. In such cases, it is possible that an inducement to entry in the form of cartelized prices could actually raise social welfare.

To see a simple example, suppose we have an industry with demand function $x(p) = 2 - p$, marginal costs of 1, and an entry cost of $\frac{1}{16}$ in which, absent an ability to price fix, entry of a second firm would result in Bertrand competition (and hence a price of 1). In that case, only one firm will enter and the price will be $\frac{3}{2}$, the monopoly price. This monopolist's profit is then $\frac{1}{4} - \frac{1}{16} = \frac{3}{16}$, and consumers enjoy a surplus of $\frac{1}{8}$. Hence, aggregate surplus equals $\frac{5}{16}$.

Suppose, instead, that firms are allowed to talk about pricing and that this allows duopolists to raise the price to $\frac{5}{4}$ (that is, despite being allowed to discuss pricing, they fail to sustain the full monopoly price). If so, a duopolist's gross profit (before entry costs) will instead be $\frac{3}{32}$ and so a second firm will enter. With two firms in the market, the price cost margin will be $\frac{1}{4}$ instead of $\frac{1}{2}$ and consumer surplus increases to $\frac{9}{32}$. Since aggregate profits are $\frac{3}{16} - \frac{2}{16} = \frac{1}{16}$, aggregate surplus rises from $\frac{5}{16}$ to $\frac{11}{32}$. Thus, both consumers and society as a whole are better off in this example when this type of communication is allowed.

Of course, collusion need not have increased welfare in the *Trans-Missouri* case. For example, if the duopolists could collude perfectly, charging the monopoly price, then allowing collusion in the example above would have led to socially costly entry and no reduction in price. Moreover, theory tells us that at least in the case of homogeneous products, we should typically expect *too much* entry from the perspective of aggregate welfare in the absence of a conspiracy (for a precise statement of these conditions, see Mankiw and Whinston [1986]). In such cases, allowing price fixing would worsen this problem. (And, as long as free entry holds profits to exactly zero, any reduction in aggregate surplus must imply as well a reduction in consumer surplus.)[3]

The Supreme Court refused to consider the defendant railroads' justification in the *Trans-Missouri* case. If valid arguments for price-fixing conspiracies are possible, why would a sound competition policy not consider these possible benefits? The answer is that while possible, they appear improbable, and a sound policy must also consider the costs of administration. If nearly every firm caught engaging in price fixing can come up with some theoretical argument that its price fixing is socially beneficial, and if actually measuring the social benefits and costs of a particular price-fixing conspiracy is very difficult (as it certainly is), price-fixing cases will be extended and costly affairs indeed (good for economists and lawyers, but bad for everyone else). Moreover, if our sense is that in most cases we will reject such claims because socially beneficial price-fixing conspiracies are rare, then it makes sense to refuse to listen to and evaluate these claims despite their theoretical possibility—that is, to have a per se rule. As George Stigler [1952] noted early in his career, "Economic policy must be contrived with a view to the typical rather than the exceptional, just as all other policies are contrived. That some drivers can safely proceed at eighty miles per hour is no objection to a maximum-speed law."

This justification of the per se rule is really nothing more than an application of optimal statistical decision making. The importance of administrative costs for the design of optimal antitrust policy has not been adequately recognized in the academic economics and legal literatures. In the economics literature, it is common for a journal article that shows that a particular practice could either raise or lower welfare to conclude that this implies that the practice should be accorded a rule of reason standard. As the foregoing discussion suggests, such a conclusion makes little sense. In the legal literature, there appears to be surprisingly little formal application of the theory of optimal statistical decision making to the issue of optimal legal rules.[4]

While a per se rule simplifies judicial administration, legal complexities still arise whenever the courts are called upon to decide whether a novel set of facts should in fact be called "price fixing." Historically, this categorization process has seemed in many cases to take on a particularly semantic nature (as in, do the words "price fixing" describe this behavior?).[5] The real issue is whether the practice seems to be one for which a per se approach seems appropriate. Of course, for this, at least a quick look at the underlying economic facts is necessary. That is, although perhaps paradoxical from a semantic perspective, to decide to treat a defendant's behavior as a per se violation (for which the court supposedly does not listen to justifications), a court must give at least some consideration to possible justifications.

In this regard, the per se rule is perhaps best thought of as a very fast rule of reason analysis, in which the court first takes a quick look to see whether further analysis is appropriate. This is an approach that is fully in line with the theory of optimal statistical decision making. Moreover, although the courts struggled with this issue for a long time, it is a view that they have widely adopted in recent years.[6]

2.3 Effects of the Ban on Price Fixing

Theory of Price Fixing

The Sherman Act's ban on price fixing helps prevent anticompetitive collusive pricing in two ways. The first, although rarely explicitly discussed, is critical: it makes any formal contract among competitors regarding the prices they will charge unenforceable.[7] The second is more commonly acknowledged: the Sherman Act prohibits firms from talking and reaching an "agreement" about prices, outputs, or market division.[8] What is not usually recognized is how little formal economic theory says about the manner in which this second prohibition prevents anticompetitive pricing and improves welfare.

A first problem, of course, concerns the law's focus on "agreement," whose meaning can be difficult to pin down. For example, imagine a scenario in which two firms sit down at a table with each declaring in sequence, "I am morally opposed to price fixing, but tomorrow I will set my price equal to 100." Should such unilateral speech be treated differently than if they instead each said "I'll set my price equal to 100 if you do"? And does that differ from the situation in which firm 1 says "Let's set our prices equal to 100 tomorrow," and firm 2 replies "I agree"? Perhaps there is a difference (certainly the law often believes there is, not only in reference to the Sherman Act, but also in areas such as contract law), but economists have essentially nothing to say about this.

With this first problem granted, what does economics have to say about the effects of the act of talking itself? Modern economic theory tells us that oligopolists who seek to come to an agreement to sustain high prices but who cannot sign binding agreements (note here the effect of the first critical role of the Sherman Act) face two principal problems: an *incentive problem* and a *coordination problem*. The incentive problem can be formally stated as follows: To be credible, any agreement must be a subgame perfect Nash equilibrium. If it were not, then some party to the agreement would find it profitable to cheat. But note that this is exactly the same condition that economic theory uses to identify the set of outcomes that are sustainable without any direct communication, that is, through *"tacit"* collusion. So if the Sherman Act's prohibition on talking helps prevent high prices, it must be because it worsens the oligopolists' coordination problem.

The coordination problem arises because typically there are *many* possible subgame perfect Nash equilibrium outcomes. One of these is always the purely noncooperative (that is, static) outcome: if each firm expects all other firms to be noncooperative, it will be optimal for that firm to be noncooperative as well. Frequently, however, a range of more cooperative outcomes is possible, including in some cases the joint monopoly solution. Notably, however, economic theory has relatively little to say about the process of coordination among equilibria. It is natural to think that talking may help with this coordination, but exactly to what degree and in what circumstances is less clear.

The most relevant work in economic theory concerning this coordination issue is the literature on "cheap talk" about intended play in games.[9] "Cheap talk" is speech that has no direct payoff consequences. When an oligopolist tells his competitor that he will raise his price tomorrow if his competitor also does so, this talk is cheap. One possible outcome is always that cheap talk is regarded by everyone as

	Player 2	
	L	R
U	8,8	−10,7
D	7,−10	5,5

Player 1 labels rows; Player 2 labels columns.

Figure 2.1
A two-player coordination game

meaningless (this is the so-called "babbling equilibrium"). Nonetheless, cheap talk about intended play may sometimes be meaningful and alter players' actions. This is so because should those that hear it believe it and respond to it in favorable ways, those who speak it can have incentives to speak informatively. What the literature on cheap talk about intended play has struggled with is the question of the exact circumstances in which we should expect it to be believed.

Consider, for example, the two-player coordination game depicted in figure 2.1. Here player 1 chooses U or D, while player 2 chooses L or R. Each pair of choices leads to a pair of payoffs (u_1, u_2), where u_i is player i's payoff. There are two Nash equilibria: (U,L) and (D,R). The former is better for both players than the latter. However, for player 1, choosing U is very risky: unless he is very confident that player 2 will play L, player 1 should play D. Similarly, L is very risky for player 2.

Suppose that before the game is played player 1 can say, "I will play U" or "I will play D," or can remain silent. One view is that we should expect the players to successfully coordinate on (U,L) because "I will play U" is a message that, if believed by player 2, creates an incentive for player 1 to act as he claims. Hence, one could argue, player 2 will believe such a claim. On the other hand, observe that player 1 would like player 2 to play L *regardless* of what he intends to play. This fact leads some game theorists to argue that in the above game player 2 might not believe player 1's claim that he will play U. Oligopoly settings are similar to this situation since a firm will always want to convince its rival to behave cooperatively (in its price or output choice) regardless of its own actual intentions. The main difference, and complication, is that in oligopoly settings firms may wish to communicate about their intended dynamic strategies, rather than about simple actions.[10]

There has been some experimental work examining when cheap talk about intentions matters for play in games. Much of this work has concerned play of static coordination games, although some has considered repeated oligopoly games. The results appear mixed. In some cases, cheap talk matters quite a bit and leads to significant coordination by the players. In other cases, it appears to make little difference. Also, the type of communication that is most useful varies across games—sometimes one-sided communication is better than two-sided, sometimes the reverse. Likewise, it can matter whether communication is unregulated or tightly structured. Holt [1993] and Crawford [1998] survey this work.[11] Unfortunately, there does not yet appear to be a consensus in the experimental literature about the exact circumstances and manner in which cheap talk about intended play matters. (Moreover, there is also the question of whether the results of these experiments, usually with college students as subjects, are indicative of the actual market behavior of businessmen and women.)

While relatively little is known about how cheap talk about intentions affects oligopolistic coordination, the economic theory literature has had more to say about a different role for cheap talk: communication about private information. The literature has studied extensively the problem faced by a cartel whose members' costs are privately observed and may differ at any given point in time. (For example, highway construction firms may differ in their costs of doing a particular job because of their current inventory of jobs and other factors.) Such a cartel faces an *information revelation problem*, in addition to the incentive and coordination problems discussed earlier. A profit-maximizing cartel wants to allocate a sale to the firm whose cost is currently the lowest, and may also want to make its current price depend upon this firm's cost level. However, when each firm's cost is known only by that firm, a cartel's members will be tempted to misrepresent their cost levels in an attempt to gain a larger market share.

This problem was studied initially in a series of papers using static-mechanism design models (Roberts [1985], Cramton and Palfrey [1990], McAfee and McMillan [1992], and Kihlstrom and Vives [1992]). In those papers, the firms each announced their cost "type" and were assigned an output or price. It was simply assumed that firms would abide by these assigned prices or outputs and that the cartel could coordinate on the most profitable mechanism. Hence, the incentive and coordination problems were assumed away to focus solely on the information revelation problem. The papers then addressed whether the cartel could achieve its full information outcome, and the form of the optimal mechanism. The papers differed in their assumptions in several respects: whether transfers were allowed, the set of possible cost types, and the nature of any individual rationality constraints imposed.

More recently, Athey and Bagwell [2001] imbed this type of mechanism-design framework in a dynamic model (see also Athey, Bagwell, and Sanchirico [2004]). There are two key differences from the previous static models. First, Athey and Bagwell reintroduce the incentive problem by requiring that firms have incentives not to deviate from their assigned prices. This additional constraint can in some cases affect the cartel's optimal policies. Second, even when monetary transfers across firms are prohibited, firms have the ability to use future play as a transfer mechanism by shifting future market shares in response to firms' current efficiency claims.[12]

One notable feature of these information revelation settings (whether static or dynamic) is that allowing collusion has the potential to improve aggregate welfare by increasing productive efficiency, since the cartel will try to assign sales to the member with the lowest cost.

A second role for communication of private information in oligopolies arises when firms have different information about how likely it is that some cartel members have cheated previously. Papers by Compte [1998] and Kandori and Matsushima [1998] show how firms can coordinate collective punishments for deviators using public claims about the signals they privately observe.[13]

While these contributions have significantly increased understanding of how talk can be used to reveal information in collusive oligopolies, the literature on communication of private information has yet to show clearly how the ability to talk changes oligopoly outcomes relative to a scenario where talk is prohibited. For example, in the Athey and Bagwell [2001] model, firms are unable to either signal or split market shares in the case in which they are not allowed to talk. How talk matters in the absence of these restrictions is not clear. The Compte [1998] and Kandori and Matsushima [1998] papers, on the other hand, do not show what happens in the absence of communication. More importantly, while communication to reveal private information may well be of some importance, communication to improve coordination seems a much larger part of most price-fixing conspiracies.

It is in some sense paradoxical that the least controversial area of antitrust is perhaps the one in which the basis of the policy in economic theory is weakest. Of course, most economists are not bothered by this, perhaps because they believe (as I do) that direct communication (and especially face-to-face communication) often will matter for achieving cooperation, and that procompetitive benefits of collusion are both rare and difficult to document. Nonetheless, it would be good if economists understood better the economics behind this belief. Moreover, as we will see in section 2.4, such an understanding could also help guide enforcement efforts.

Evidence on the Effects of Price Fixing

If formal economic theory is surprisingly silent about the effects of the Sherman Act's ban on firms' communications and agreements about prices, perhaps existing empirical work offers strong support for the view that preventing oligopolists from talking has a substantial effect on the price they charge? In fact, the existing published literature

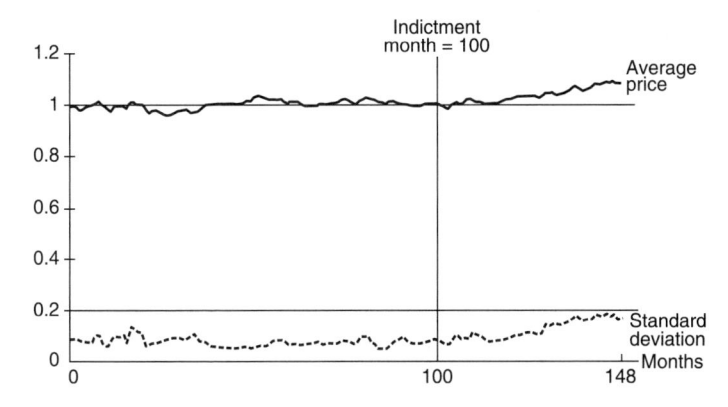

Figure 2.2
Effect of price-fixing indictments on prices (Sproul [1993])

offers less evidence for this proposition than one might expect.

Sproul [1993], for example, examines 25 of the approximately 400 cases in which individuals or firms were indicted for price fixing from 1973 to 1984 (these 25 cases were the ones in which the necessary data were available). For each case, he constructs a "predicted price" based on a regression of the product's price on related prices for the period prior to the indictment.[14] He then examines the ratio of the actual price to the predicted price in the period following the indictment. Figure 2.2 shows the average effect he observes. (In constructing the figure, the underlying series for the 25 products are aligned so that in each case the indictment occurs in "month 100.")

If anything, prices seem to rise (relative to the predicted price) after the indictment. Examining the price changes following other important events—the date the government believed the conspiracy to have ended, the date government penalties were imposed, or the date civil penalties were imposed—does not change this basic conclusion, as panels (a)–(c) in figure 2.3 show.[15]

Certainly, there is little in Sproul's study to suggest that a government price-fixing enforcement action leads to any significant reductions in price. One serious concern with Sproul's study, however, is that his price data often come from the Bureau of Labor Statistics (BLS) price indices that may include many products other than the specific product that is the focus of the indictment. If so, the effects of ending a conspiracy could be lost in the noise from other price movements. Likewise, several of Sproul's cases are gasoline price-fixing cases for which he uses a citywide average price. Whether these are, in fact, problems is hard to tell from the information in Sproul's article.

A study that examines the issue at a much more disaggregated level using price data that are at an appropriate level of aggregation is Block, Nold, and Sidak [1981] (henceforth, BNS). BNS examine prices in sixteen local (city-level) bread markets from 1965 to 1976. During this period the DOJ prosecuted a number of bread producers for price fixing. BNS construct what they call a "mark-up" measure for these local bread markets from the fitted values of the regession

$$p_{it} = IC_{it} + \sum_j \beta_j w_{ijt} + \varepsilon_{it}, \tag{2.1}$$

where p_{it} is a citywide BLS retail price index for bread, IC_{it} is the cost of ingredients in market i in year t (derived using a standard recipe for bread), and w_{ijt} is the cost of non-ingredient input j (electricity, natural gas, or labor) in market i in year t. BNS then define the mark-up to be

Price Fixing

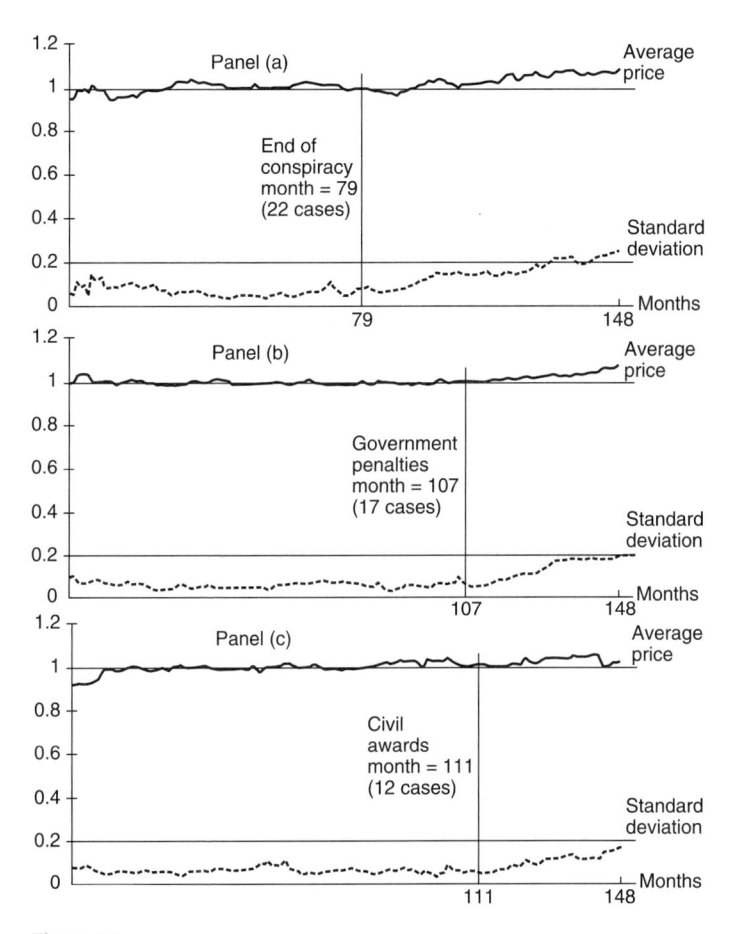

Figure 2.3
Effects on prices of ending a conspiracy, imposing government penalties, and awarding civil damages (Sproul [1993])

$$M_{it} = \frac{p_{it} - \hat{p}_{it}}{\hat{p}_{it}}. \tag{2.2}$$

(It should be noted that this variable is better thought of as the deviation from the sample average cost-adjusted price of bread than as a mark-up. For example, if all markets set the same mark-up over costs in every period, this measure would be identically zero.) BNS then regress this mark-up measure on measures of antitrust enforcement in the first-difference form

$$\Delta M_{it} = \alpha_0 \cdot \Delta Budget_t + \alpha_1 \cdot DOJREG_{it} + \alpha_2 \cdot DOJREM_{it} + u_{it}, \tag{2.3}$$

where $\Delta Budget_t$ is the change in the DOJ's Antitrust Division budget in year t, $DOJREG_{it}$ takes the value of 1 for city i in year t if a different city in the same region had a price-fixing enforcement action against the bread industry in year $t-1$, and $DOJREM_{it}$ takes the value of 1 for city i in year t if there was a price-fixing enforcement action against the bread industry in city i in year $t-1$. The first column of numbers in table 2.1 shows the result of this regression (t-statistics are in parentheses). The regressions whose results are reported in the next two columns include measures of price changes in the food sector ($\Delta FOODM$) and general manufacturing ($\Delta GENM$) to control for unrelated factors affecting bread prices.

Increases in the Antitrust Division budget, price-fixing enforcement actions in neighboring cities, and price-fixing enforcement actions in a given city all are found to lower prices. But the effects on price appear small. An enforcement action in a given city is found to lower the price in the next year and ensuing years by 4.6% (of the predicted price $\hat{p}$). Certainly this represents a relatively small effect on price.[16,17]

Table 2.1
Estimated effects of changes in DOJ enforcement on changes in markups in the bread industry

Independent variables	(1)	(2)	(3)
Δ BUDGET	−.015[a]	−.024	−.020
	(−2.68)	(−4.06)	(−3.65)
DOJREG	−.026	−.025	−.027
	(−2.21)	(−2.09)	(−2.26)
DOJREM	−.046	−.046	−.044
	(−2.32)	(−2.41)	(−2.32)
Δ FOODM		+.058	
		(2.33)	
Δ GENM			−.010
			(−1.60)
Constant	.013	.014	.017
R^2	.082	.113	.101
F-statistic	6.04 (3, 204)	6.47 (4, 203)	5.68 (4, 203)

Source: Block, Nold, and Sidak [1981].
Notes: Each regression is based on 208 observations.
[a] This coefficient is estimated in per million dollars.

Other studies that show small effects of price-fixing enforcement on pricing are Stigler and Kindahl [1970, 92], Feinberg [1980], and Choi and Philippatos [1983].

How can we interpret these results that show little or no reductions in price following a price-fixing enforcement action? One possibility is that talking does not matter much because conspiracies simply may be hard to police and maintain without the ability to have binding agreements. Another possibility is that talking does not matter much because firms may be able to collude effectively even without the ability to talk. Still a third possibility is that talking may matter a great deal for increasing prices, but firms may simply ignore the risks of being caught, even after having been caught once. In any of these three cases, there may not be much to gain from the ban on talking.

It is also possible that talking has some procompetitive price-reducing effects that fully or partially offset any tendency toward higher prices. Sproul [1993], for example, argues that many price-fixing conspiracies may be engaged in socially beneficial activities that reduce costs and, hence, prices (perhaps by allocating output more efficiently across firms, as discussed above). McCutcheon [1997] suggests another possibility: the Sherman Act's ban on talking may make collusion *easier* because it makes renegotiation of planned punishments more difficult. Certainly these last two possible explanations would be consistent with the view that the Sherman Act's ban on talking was doing more harm than good.

Yet, there are several reasons why those studies could be missing some of the price-reducing effects of the ban on talking. The first is an issue with measurement: it may be that firms who have been engaged in price fixing are able to maintain high prices for a period of time even after they are no longer talking.[18] If so, those studies simply may have missed the effect by not considering a period long enough after the enforcement event. A second reason is that cartels that talk may be relatively ineffective now because of conspirators' fear of investigation and detection. If so, those studies may not give us a good sense of what prices would be without any form of price-fixing enforcement. Third, firms may take the probability of detection as unchanged even after being caught. If so, their behavior will not change after an indictment, even if the prospect of being caught does affect the extent to which they engage in price fixing.

In addition, a number of studies—including several recent ones—do provide evidence of more substantial elevations in price because of price-fixing conspiracies. Porter and Zona [1999] examine bidding behavior at procurement auctions for school milk in Ohio from 1980 to 1990. The data were collected as part of a case brought by the attorney general of Ohio against thirteen Ohio dairies as a result of the 1993 confessions of two dairies operating in the southwestern part of the state (who testified that they had rigged bids with other firms in the area). As a measure of the effect of the conspiracy on prices, Porter and Zona conduct a regression analysis in which they regress the winning bid on various measures of the contract terms requested by the school district (for example, was a cooler to be provided? straws?), various measures of the costs of the potential bidders (for example, the distance between the school district and the closest and second-closest milk plants), and a function of two measures of competition: (i) the inverse of the Herfindahl-Hirschman Index derived from firms' shares of milk processing plants within seventy-five miles of the school district (the number of "equivalent firms") and (ii) the *change* in the *effective* Herfindahl-Hirschman Index because of the presence of any defendant firms with plants within seventy-five miles of the school district, denoted as *Delta* (that is, the amount the index changes when one treats the conspiring firms as a single firm).

Columns (a)–(c) of table 2.2 show for each year the estimated coefficients on variables that include Delta—Delta itself, the square of Delta (labeled $Delta^2$), and an interaction term between Delta and the inverse of the Herfindahl-Hirschman Index. Column (d) shows the average percentage effects on price in each year that are implied by those estimated coefficients for school districts in southwestern Ohio.[19] They average to a 4.6% price elevation over the ten-year time period. Weighting instead by the different

Table 2.2
The effect of price-fixing on the price paid for school milk

School year	Estimated delta coefficient	Estimated delta^2 coefficient	Estimated interaction coefficient	Estimated average effect	Estimated effect conditional on incumbency
	(a)	(b)	(c)	(d)	(e)
1980–1981	−.00140	−.00150	.00163	3.0%	3.2%
1981–1982	.01304	.01167	.00103	11.3%	40.2%
1982–1983	.02731	.00225	.00098	8.6%	23.2%
1983–1984	.02995	−.00970	.00156	4.5%	1.1%
1984–1985	.02147	.00106	.00199	6.7%	19.7%
1985–1986	.02684	−.00230	.00122	5.4%	11.5%
1986–1987	.02425	.00173	.00130	6.5%	20.5%
1987–1988	.00368	.02901	.00060	3.3%	49.0%
1988–1989	−.02270	.03636	.00229	2.9%	29.4%
1989–1990	−.04940	.01340	.00410	−1.6%	3.4%
1990–1991	−.02010	−.01260	.00634	−0.3%	−8.3%

Source: Porter and Zona [1999].

number of auctions in the different years, and excluding three years in which the cartel was said to have broken down (1983–1984, 1989–1990, and 1990–1991), the average is 6.5%.

Although a 6.5% elevation is not large, two points should be noted. First, Porter and Zona have some direct information on the firms' costs. While the bid predicted for a nondefendant dairy that is twenty miles from the school district is between 12.5 and 13.0 cents per half-pint carton (depending on the model used), variable costs are roughly 10 cents per carton. The 6.5% price increase therefore represents roughly a 30% increase in the mark-up over costs. Assuming no reduction in quantities purchased (school demand for milk is in fact very inelastic), the percentage increase in profits because of collusion is substantial even if the price elevation is not. Second, this 6.5% is an average over districts in which defendants did and did not have market power. Column (e) of table 2.2 shows the average percentage increase in price in each year because of the conspiracy when attention is limited to southwestern districts in which one of the defendants was an incumbent in the previous year, as these were likely to be markets in which the defendants jointly had greater market power. The average price increases in each year for those markets are substantially larger, ranging as high as 49% and averaging roughly 24.6% over the eight years in which the cartel was effective.

Another study showing substantial effects of price fixing in procurement auctions is Froeb, Koyak, and Werden [1993]. They examine the effect of a proven conspiracy among bidders in U.S. Department of Defense procurement auctions for frozen perch (a type of fish). They fit a reduced-form pricing model from the postconspiracy period and project back into the conspiracy period to get "no-conspiracy" predicted prices (also known as "but for" prices) for the earlier conspiracy period. Doing so, they find an estimated price elevation of 27.3% over the entire conspiracy period.

Kwoka [1997] studies a long-lasting conspiracy among bidders in real estate auctions in Washington, DC. Kwoka is able to get an estimate of the cartel overcharge (since Kwoka examines a buyer cartel, this is the amount that bids were reduced) by comparing the price paid by the cartel in the auction to the price at which the item was sold later in a postauction "knock-out auction" among the cartel members.[20] From this comparison, Kwoka estimates an overcharge of roughly 32%.

Howard and Kaserman [1989] examine the effects of a price-fixing conspiracy among firms bidding on city sewer construction contracts. The evidence in the case indicated that at one point the firms became frightened of being discovered (because of federal criminal investigations in the road paving business) and ceased their collusive activity. This allowed Howard and Kaserman to compare bidding on seven rigged and thirty-nine nonrigged jobs. They estimate an overcharge of roughly 40% because of price fixing.

These four studies focus on auction settings in which collusion may be relatively easy (government procurement auctions in Porter and Zona [1999], Froeb, Koyak, and Werden [1993], and Howard and Kaserman [1989]; an oral ascending auction in Kwoka [1997]). Some recent highly publicized international cartels have provided evidence of substantial price increases in nonauction settings (Connor [2001a], Griffin [2001]).

One such conspiracy was the highly publicized lysine cartel, which fixed prices from 1992–1995. Lysine is a feed ad-

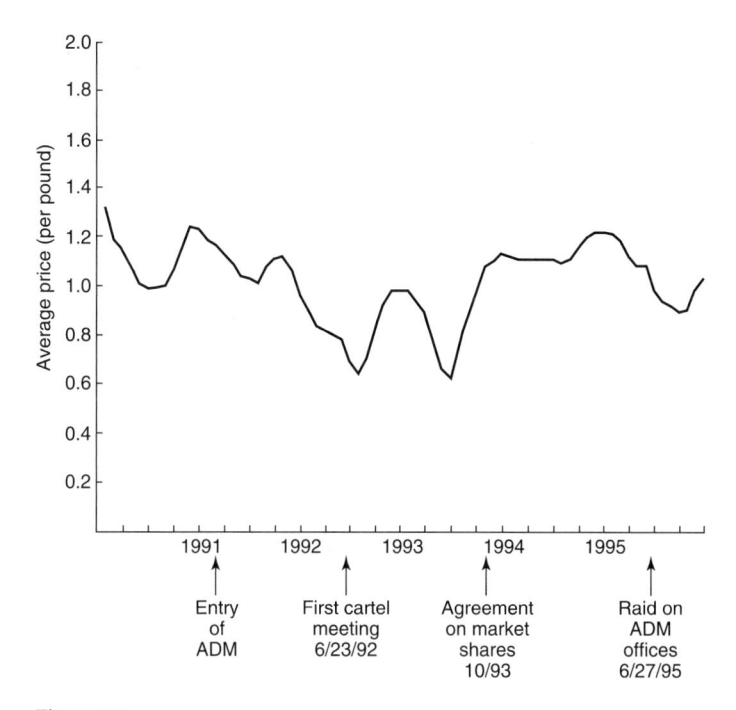

Figure 2.4
Price of lysine, January 1990–December 1995

ditive that promotes the growth of lean muscle in animals. Figure 2.4 shows the price of lysine from January 1990–December 1995 (drawn using data in White [2001]). Prior to 1991, the lysine industry involved a small number of firms, all foreign. Then, in early 1991, Archer Daniels Midland (ADM) entered the industry with a new production facility. This facility massively increased industry capacity from 390 million pounds to 640 million pounds a year. By mid-1992, with this plant still producing at only 40% of its capacity, lysine prices had fallen dramatically, to the point where

ADM no longer was covering its variable costs. The cartel formed in June of 1992 with an agreement to raise prices from their 69 cent level to over 1 dollar. Prices rose, but then in early 1993 adherence to the cartel agreement began to unravel. In October 1993, the cartel reached a new agreement fixing market shares, after which prices stabilized at a high level. Then, in June 1995, the FBI raided ADM headquarters, ending the conspiracy.

Judging exactly how much of the lysine price increase was because of the conspiracy requires disentangling the regular seasonal cycle in lysine prices (which decline in summer and rise each fall, with the notable exception of 1994 during the conspiracy) and also determining what prices would have been without the conspiracy. A plaintiff's witness in the case estimates the overcharge at 17% (Connor [2001a, 264]; see also Connor [2001b] and White [2001]).

Overall, then, the published evidence on the effect of price-fixing conspiracies is somewhat mixed. Given the fact that significant damage awards in price-fixing cases are a relatively common occurrence, and those are by law based on evidence regarding the overcharge resulting from the conspiracy, it is surprising how limited the published literature is that documents significant effects of price fixing.[21] It would be good to see more of this evidence documented in print (in refereed settings). Also, to the extent that the mixed empirical evidence reflects a real diversity of effects, it would be useful to learn something about the factors associated with greater price increases from price fixing.

2.4 Detecting Price Fixing

In many cases direct evidence that a price-fixing conspiracy exists may not be available (for example, evidence of meetings at which prices to be charged were agreed to), but we may want to draw indirect inferences from other evidence. There are two principal reasons why we might wish to do so. First, an enforcement agency may be interested in using various indicia to guide their enforcement efforts. With these in hand, certain industries might be targeted for more in-depth investigation in a search for direct evidence of a price-fixing conspiracy. Second, a court (or jury) in a price-fixing case may be faced with a fact pattern in which there is no "smoking gun"—that is, no direct evidence that any discussions took place—and may need to decide based on indirect evidence whether to find the defendants guilty. The question in both cases is what kinds of evidence we should interpret as increasing the likelihood that a price-fixing conspiracy is taking, or has taken, place? The economics and legal literatures have focused on two types of evidence, *structural* evidence and *behavioral* evidence.

Structural Evidence

Structural evidence focuses on characteristics of the industry and its product(s). The most well-known paper on this issue is Hay and Kelley [1974]. They discuss various structural factors that might be expected to influence the likelihood of the firms in an industry engaging in price fixing, and then they document the characteristics of the industries in which the DOJ has found price fixing to have occurred.

At a very rudimentary level, we can expect the likelihood of price fixing to be increasing in the net benefit of engaging in it, including the expected costs of the conspiracy being detected and successfully prosecuted, which might be written as

$$\pi(\text{talk}) - \pi(\text{do not talk}) - E(\text{costs}). \tag{2.4}$$

We can divide the factors that might be expected to affect this net benefit into three categories:

(i) Factors that affect the potential size of $\pi(\text{talk}) - \pi(\text{do not talk})$.

Here we capture the difference between the most profitable outcome possible for the firms (the best possible subgame perfect Nash equilibrium) and the worst. Put simply, if this difference is small, say because there is very little ability to sustain positive profits in an industry, then there is little reason to attempt to fix prices given the potential criminal penalties that could result. One set of factors affecting this potential difference relates to the incentives to cheat. These factors make it harder to sustain any given increase in price above the noncooperative level. Industry characteristics that affect this would include

• the level of concentration in the industry (greater concentration makes sustaining a given supracompetitive price easier; see Tirole [1988, 247–248]),

• the degree of observability of firms' prices (lesser observability, including more noisy signals of price cuts, make sustaining a given supracompetitive price harder; see Stigler [1964] and Green and Porter [1984]),

• the lumpiness of demand (lumpy demand makes sustaining a collusive scheme more difficult; see Tirole [1988, 248]),

• the levels of capacity in the industry (both the level of aggregate capacity and its distribution can matter, although the effect is not necessarily monotonic; see Brock and Scheinkman [1985] and Compte, Jenny, and Rey [2002]).

Another set of factors that affect this potential difference relates to the extent to which a given price increase raises profits. These include, for example, market size (doubling market demand at each price doubles the potential gains from price fixing if costs exhibit constant returns to scale) and the elasticity of demand.[22]

(ii) Factors that affect the amount of the potential gain that is actually realized by talking.

Many of the factors discussed by Hay and Kelley fall into this category. In Hay and Kelley's discussion, they focus on how a given factor affects the ease of coordination with explicit collusion. The difficulty, however, is that most of the factors that one might think of here have theoretically ambiguous effects because a factor that makes coordination easier is likely to make coordination easier *both* when firms talk and when they do not. For example, when there are more firms in an industry, coordination is likely to be harder *both* with talking and without; when the products are more homogeneous in the sense that there are fewer of them, their characteristics are unchanging, and so on, coordination is likely to be easier *both* when talking and when not; and when the firms are more symmetric, coordination is likely to be easier, *both* with talking and without. What determines how a given factor affects the incentive to engage in price fixing is the extent to which it makes coordination relatively easier when firms talk than when they do not. In essence, Hay and Kelley's discussion assumes that firms are very unlikely to coordinate successfully without explicit communication, so that only changes in the ease of coordinating with explicit communication matter. However, as we saw in section 2.3, relatively little is currently known about this issue.[23]

(iii) Factors that affect the expected costs of price fixing.

The first factor that affects the expected costs of collusion is simple: the severity of punishments. Unfortunately, this will not typically vary across industries (at least within a country). However, a number of factors can be expected to affect the likelihood of detection and are likely to vary across industries. Here we can include the number of necessary participants (more participants is generally thought to make it more likely that some participant will either inform the authorities or tell someone else who will inform the authorities), the sophistication of buyers (if they know the costs of production, they are more likely to know when price levels or increases are not justified and may then perform their own private investigation), the importance of the product to buyers (greater importance increases buyers' incentive to monitor and investigate privately), and factors that increase the required number of meetings such as the number of products or product characteristics over which agreement must be reached.[24] In addition, there may be costs of price fixing unrelated to detection and punishment, including costs of meetings, bargaining, and monitoring. These costs are likely to increase, for example, with the number of participants.

Hay and Kelley present a summary of successful criminal price-fixing cases brought by the DOJ from 1963 to 1972.[25] Altogether they find sixty-five such cases (a summary of these cases can be found in the appendix of the Hay and Kelley paper). The conspiracies were detected in a variety of ways. Of the forty-nine cases for which Hay and Kelley know how the conspiracy was detected, twelve were uncovered as a result of a grand jury investigation in another case; ten were because of a complaint by a competitor (a somewhat puzzling fact, perhaps indicating that the firms were engaged in exclusionary behavior as well); seven were because of a customer complaint; six were because of a complaint by a local, state, or federal agency; and three were because of a complaint by current or former employees. (The remaining cases were detected in various ways, with each method of detection accounting for one or two cases.)

One of Hay and Kelley's most striking conclusions is that these cases were weighted heavily toward highly concentrated markets. Table 2.3 summarizes the distributions of the number of conspirators for the sixty-two cases in which this information was available and the four-firm market concentration ratio for the fifty cases in which this information was available.[26] Of the fifty latter cases, twenty-one involved a market with a four-firm concentration ratio over seventy-five (42%), and thirty-eight of the fifty involved a market with a four-firm concentration ratio over fifty (76%). In comparison, Scherer and Ross [1990] report that the population distribution of concentration among four-digit manufacturing industries in 1982 had only 5.1% of the industries with concentration over eighty, and 17.6% with concentration over sixty.[27] This finding must be considered with some care. Since we are observing a sample of successfully prosecuted conspiracies, the selection process that determines which conspiracies are detected matters here. However, since it seems more likely that conspiracies involving many firms will be detected (and Hay and Kelley report that conspiracies involving many firms did not last long before being detected), these concentration numbers may actually be downward biased relative to the true population distribution of concentration for markets with conspiracies.[28] Table 2.3 also reveals that almost all conspiracies involving a large number of firms involved a formal trade association. What is less clear from these statistics is

Table 2.3
The distribution of conspirators, market concentration, and trade association involvement in successful DOJ price-fixing cases 1963–1972

Number of conspirators	2	3	4	5	6	7	8	9	10	11–15	16–20	21–25	>25	Total
Number of cases	1	7	8	4	10	4	3	5	7	5	2	—	6	62
Trade association involvement	—	—	1	—	4	1	—	1	3	1	1	—	6	18

	Concentration ratios				
Concentration (percentage)	0–25	25–50	51–75	76–100	Total
Number of cases	3	9	17	21	50

Source: Hay and Kelley [1974].

whether there is a reduced likelihood of price fixing at the very highest levels of concentration (for example, once there are only two or three firms).

In other dimensions, Hay and Kelley find that nearly all of the cases involve products that are homogeneous across firms and that a majority of the cases involve a conspiracy that was organized in response to price wars or a "lack of discipline" in the market. In addition, it was often the case that when members of an industry in one local market were found to be colluding, the members in other markets were as well, lending support to the view that there are structural factors that affect the likelihood of collusion. Relative to our discussion in section 2.3 concerning interpretations of findings of small effects from price-fixing enforcement actions, it is noteworthy that Hay and Kelley also observe that an industry that was prosecuted successfully once often was prosecuted successfully again later.

Finally, thinking about the incentives for firms to engage in price fixing has some potentially interesting implications for interpreting empirical results on price fixing's effects. Specifically, as penalties for price fixing become more severe, the level of effectiveness at which firms find price fixing to be worthwhile should increase. Since U.S. price-fixing penalties have increased markedly over time, especially after the passage of the U.S. Sentencing Guidelines, we might expect more recent price-fixing conspiracies to have greater price effects. The evidence we reviewed in section 2.3 seems to show some of this pattern.

Behavioral Evidence

One might also hope to draw inferences about the likelihood of price fixing from evidence of firms' behavior. Can observation of firms' behavior be used to infer the existence of a price-fixing conspiracy? What if all firms charge the same price? How about the same very high price? What if they all follow the prices announced by firm A, the largest firm in the industry? What if they, in other ways, seem to behave "cooperatively"? The difficulty we run into with all of these ideas is the same difficulty we ran into earlier: formal economic theory tells us that any outcome that is possible with talking is also possible without it.[29] If we are to draw an inference then, it must be because we think that certain types of behaviors are nonetheless more likely when firms are able to explicitly coordinate. But, as we have seen, formal economic theory currently offers little help on this point.

Intuition suggests that we might in some cases be inclined to draw an inference of price fixing. Suppose, for example, that we observe complicated parallel behavior: each of ten firms charge 19.174 per unit on Friday and all simultaneously (that is, without first observing other firms doing so) change to 20.343 on Monday morning. Suppose further that there has been no sudden change in demand and no change in the price of any significant input. Finally, suppose that the profit loss from being the *only* firm to charge the higher price is severe, making a unilateral price increase quite risky for a firm, as in the game depicted in figure 2.1. It is certainly possible that such behavior could result without any communication. But it appears unlikely, even if this can unfortunately be said at present mostly at an intuitive, rather than at a formal theoretical level.[30]

Economists' efforts at providing evidence of conspiracy instead typically focus on identifying whether firms have been exhibiting "cooperative" behavior. In the simplest form of this work, an economist charged with convincing a judge or jury that a conspiracy has taken place (or an economist at the DOJ or FTC looking for evidence of a conspiracy) would look at whether prices were high relative to costs compared to other similar markets or time periods. More generally, an economist might look for any differences in behavior across markets, time periods, or firms (that is, suspected conspirators versus nonconspirators).

Two interesting attempts to look for cooperative behavior in the context of procurement auctions appear in a pair of papers: Porter and Zona [1993] and [1999]. Both papers attempt to identify cooperative behavior in a subset of firms known to have colluded by looking for differences in behavior from a control group comprised of the other firms in the market. (The idea is that if the tests work in these cases, then one might feel confident in using them when one suspects collusion may be taking place.)

In the Porter and Zona [1999] study of school milk procurement auctions discussed in section 2.3, they look at two features of a firm's behavior: its decision of whether to bid and its decision of how much to bid conditional on submitting a bid. The explanatory variables include the procurement specifications as well as the firm's cost position absolutely and relative to other firms. Figures 2.5 and 2.6 depict how these two decisions depend on distance for "competitive" firms (those not accused of price fixing) based on the results of their estimations. (The three curves in each figure correspond to the results for their "base" model and two models that include fixed effects for different bidders and for different bidders and different school districts, respectively.) The likelihood of bidding declines sharply with the distance to the school district, while bid levels increase with this distance. In contrast, Porter and Zona show that suspected members of the cartel display radically different behavior. For example, their bids instead often *decrease*

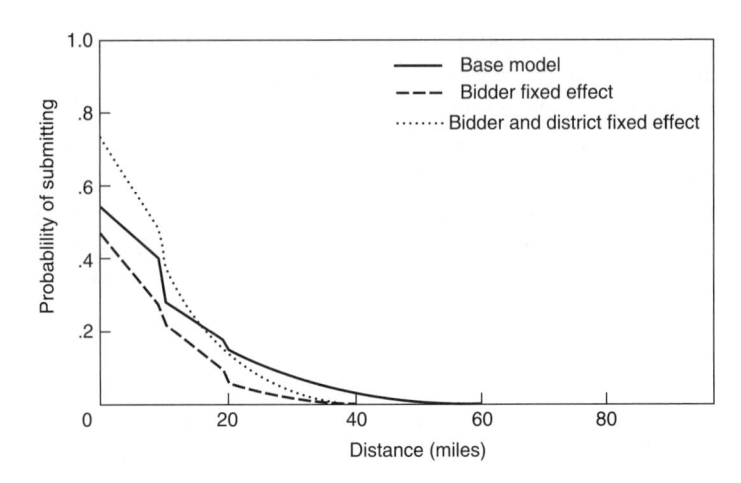

Figure 2.5
Predicted probability of submitting a school milk bid by distance from district for competitive firms (Porter and Zona [1993])

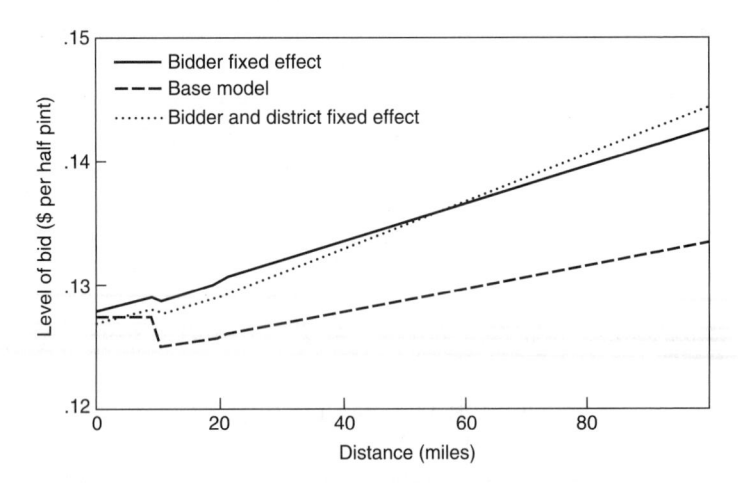

Figure 2.6
Predicted level of school milk bid (conditional on bidding) by distance from district for competitive firms (Porter and Zona [1993])

with distance since they bid competitively when they bid in auctions that are far away and not covered by the cartel agreement.

Porter and Zona [1993] studies procurement auctions for highway paving jobs on Long Island, New York from April 1979 through March 1985. In contrast to the school milk study, here no characteristics of the job are available in their data. Hence, comparing bid levels across jobs is not feasible. Instead, Porter and Zona make use of a clever insight: if the suspected firms are engaged in a price-fixing scheme whereby they designate one bidder as the serious bidder and the rest as "phantom" bidders, then the determinants of the lowest cartel bid might be quite different than those for all other cartel bids (the former should be based on costs, the latter may not be), while the determinants of bids for all competitive firms should be the same. They examine this idea by focusing on the ranking of bids within a job. Specifically, let X_i denote observable factors affecting the costs of firm i doing the project (such as the number of jobs the firm currently is handling) and assume as do Porter and Zona that we can write a firm's bid function as an increasing function $b(X_i\beta + \varepsilon_i)$. With just two firms, for example, we can write the probability that firm i bids less than firm j as

$$\Pr(b_i < b_j) = \Pr(\varepsilon_j - \varepsilon_i \leq (X_i - X_j)\beta).$$

As Porter and Zona observe, if r_n is the identity of the nth highest bidder from among a set of N firms, then we can write

$$\Pr(r_1, \ldots, r_N | \beta) = \Pr(r_1 | \beta) \cdot \Pr(r_2, \ldots, r_N | r_1, \beta).$$

Now, if firms are behaving noncooperatively, we should get the same estimates of β from either trying to explain the identity of the low bidder from among a group of N

Table 2.4
Rank-based estimates of bid determinants for competitive firms in highway paving jobs

	All ranks (1)	Low ranks (2)	Higher ranks (3)
Observations	244	75	169
Log likelihood	−291.4	−89.85	−199.4
UTIL	−.0070	.0161	−.0552
	(.1)	(.1)	(.3)
UTILSQ	.0986	.0534	.1596
	(.8)	(.3)	(1.0)
NOBACK	−.0283	.0089	−.0454
	(1.0)	(.2)	(1.3)
CAP	−1.888	−1.641	−2.100
	(3.8)	(2.4)	(3.0)
CAPSQ	6.869	6.517	7.020
	(3.9)	(2.6)	(2.9)
ISLAND	−.0182	−.0759	.1016
	(.3)	(.9)	(.9)

Source: Porter and Zona [1993].
Note: Absolute values of t-statistics are displayed in parentheses.

firms using the probability model $\Pr(r_1|\beta)$, or explaining the ordering of the other $N-1$ firms using the probability model $\Pr(r_2,\ldots,r_N|r_1,\beta)$. Porter and Zona estimate these two models for competitive firms and suspected cartel firms separately. Table 2.4 shows the results for competitive firms. Column (1) reports parameter estimates based on explaining the ranks of all bids according to the model $\Pr(r_1,\ldots,r_N|\beta)$, column (2) is based on explaining the identity of the lowest bidder using the model $\Pr(r_1|\beta)$, and column (3) is based on explaining the ranking of all but the lowest bid using the model $\Pr(r_2,\ldots,r_N|r_1,\beta)$. The parameter estimates are very similar in columns (2) and (3) (compare the coefficients on the capacity utilization variables

Table 2.5
Rank-based estimates of bid determinants for suspected cartel firms in highway paving jobs

	All ranks (1)	Low ranks (2)	Higher ranks (3)
Observations	85	50	35
Log likelihood	−73.97	−44.58	−24.92
UTIL	.0429	.2107	.2310
	(.3)	(1.0)	(.6)
UTILSQ	−.0112	−.1128	−.4300
	(.1)	(.6)	(.9)
CAP	.4306	1.101	−2.537
	(.9)	(1.3)	(1.6)
CAPSQ	−.8473	−1.904	3.861
	(.9)	(1.2)	(1.4)

Source: Porter and Zona [1993].
Note: Absolute values of t-statistics are displayed in parentheses.

CAP and CAPSQ, which are the only statistically significant variables); one cannot reject the hypothesis that the parameters are the same. In contrast, we see in table 2.5 that the estimates for explaining the lowest bidder from among the cartel firms are very different from those explaining the ranks of the other cartel bids. Here one can reject the estimates being the same at a 94% confidence level.

This is a very nice exercise, but a few caveats are worth mentioning. First, Porter and Zona impose fairly strong functional-form restrictions in their estimation. Second, cooperation could take forms that would not be detectable by this test. For example, firms could collude simply by agreeing to behave as if their costs were inflated by some fixed percentage. By doing so they would be indistinguishable from firms that are behaving noncooperatively. Third, for the reasons we have discussed previously, the methods in these papers cannot eliminate the possibility that the behavior in question arises without any explicit communication having occurred.

The courts have struggled with this inference issue, and their decisions often appear rather confused both in terms of their goal and how they try to achieve it. Sometimes a court has said that they are trying to infer an express agreement but has used criteria that do not make any sense, such as mere evidence that behavior is interdependent. At other, less frequent, times the courts have seemed to say that the occurrence of an express agreement is not even necessary for finding a violation if behavior is sufficiently cooperative—some form of "conscious parallelism" would do.[31]

2.5 Antitrust Policy Toward Tacit Collusion

The discussion at the end of section 2.4 raises a significant question: Why should we require an express agreement to find firms guilty of a violation of the Sherman Act? That is, can we not apply the Sherman Act's prohibition on conspiracies in restraint of trade to include tacit "conspiracies"—that is, tacit collusion? Leaving aside issues of the original intent of the statute, what should we think of such a policy?

It is sometimes argued that a good reason for limiting application of the Sherman Act to express agreements is that it is hard to describe what it is we would be telling oligopolists to do otherwise. Can we tell them "Do not tacitly collude"? Or "Do not make your pricing decisions with regard to what your rivals do"? Are they not just acting rationally when they make these decisions? And would it be fair to send managers to jail for failing to follow such vague prescriptions? It is also sometimes argued that to apply the Sherman Act to tacit collusion would involve the courts in an ongoing process akin to price regulation of industries.

Donald Turner, who provided the most forceful articulation of these arguments, concluded that the elimination of tacit collusion was best left out of section 1 enforcement (Turner [1962]). Instead, Turner argued for a policy of restructuring highly concentrated markets through divestiture (under either section 2 of the Sherman Act or new legislation) to address the underlying structural causes of tacitly collusive behavior [Turner (1969)]. This view was also adopted by the well-known *Neal Report* [1968].

A different approach has been championed by Posner [1976, 2001]. Posner takes issue with the underlying premise that the "rationality" of oligopolistic pricing precludes antitrust limits on oligopolists' pricing practices. After all, does the threat of traffic tickets not alter the behavior of "rational" drivers of automobiles? Posner proposes then that the DOJ and FTC be able to seek monetary penalties if they prove that an industry was engaged in tacit collusion.

Each of these proposals avoids the problem of continuing price regulation of the industry, and neither involves jail sentences as a possible penalty, but each also has its problems. Regarding Turner's (and the *Neal Report*'s) proposal, Posner [2001], for example, devotes an entire chapter to arguing that, historically, structural divesture under the antitrust laws (in response to mergers or monopolization) has been slow, costly, and of minimal benefit. Moreover, the need to consider any possible efficiency losses (because of losses of economies of scale or otherwise) often may make restructuring proceedings difficult and costly affairs.

Posner's proposal, on the other hand, suffers from a vagueness about exactly what is to be considered "tacit collusion." It seems to require that courts draw an inference that firms are using dynamic strategies (for example, not undercutting the market price because of concerns over rivals' responses or responding to rivals' price cuts by starting a price war) to be guilty of "tacit collusion." High prices from static Cournot competition, for example, seem not to qualify. But, in the real world firms' strategies are dynamic for many reasons: they respond to customers showing them a lower price received from a rival, they set prices given demand that is itself often dynamic in nature, and they respond to rivals' previous long-lived investments. Any such determination by a court seems likely to be fraught with difficulty.

One can also think of some other possible approaches: perhaps the trigger for structural intervention or monetary penalties could be evidence of high price-cost margins, rather than either high concentration (which need not always lead to high margins) or "tacitly collusive" behavior. This has the advantage of focusing directly on the ultimate welfare concern. Moreover, if structural remedies are to be imposed, perhaps significant weight should be given to the ease with which such divestitures could be carried out.

Yet, these ideas, too, are not without their problems. First, economists are able to determine margins only imperfectly in many cases. False positives are a real danger here, although as our empirical techniques improve (and they recently have been improving rapidly), this should become less of a problem. Second, there is an important issue of ex ante incentives that our discussion has ignored so far. Firms will naturally avoid placing themselves in positions that trigger antitrust intervention, whether monetary damages or restructuring, and this may lead them to shy away from cost reductions or product improvements that might improve their margins.

These issues are clearly difficult ones. The last extended public discussion of them occurred some thirty years ago. They largely were forgotten after the 1970s in the general move away from confidence in activist government intervention in the economy. Recently they have begun to receive some attention once again.[32]

3 Horizontal Mergers

3.1 Introduction

In this chapter our attention turns to horizontal merger policy. The Sherman Act's prohibition on "contracts, combinations, and conspiracies in restraint of trade," whose application to price fixing we discussed in chapter 2, also applies to horizontal mergers. In addition, section 7 of the Clayton Act includes a more specific prohibition on mergers whose effect may be "substantially to lessen competition, or to tend to create a monopoly."

While both horizontal mergers and price fixing may help firms raise price (mergers even more effectively than price fixing), there is an important difference: mergers are much more likely to lead to significant efficiency improvements. This makes the balancing of anticompetitive price effects and procompetitive efficiency effects central to merger analysis.

Despite the potential for merger-related efficiencies, from the 1950s through the 1970s the U.S. courts were extremely hostile toward horizontal mergers, often condemning them in markets that were and would remain unconcentrated.[1] Since 1980, however, with a more conservative judiciary and an increasing influence of economic reasoning, horizontal merger policy has become much more permissive. During this same period, there has also been substantial progress in economists' ability to analyze proposed horizontal mergers. In what follows we will review this progress while also noting some of the significant open questions that remain.

3.2 Theoretical Considerations

The Williamson Trade-off

The central issue in the evaluation of horizontal mergers lies in the need to balance any reductions in competition against the possibility of productivity improvements arising from a merger. This trade-off was first articulated in the economics literature by Williamson [1968], in a paper aimed at getting efficiencies to be taken seriously. This "Williamson trade-off" is illustrated in figure 3.1.

Suppose that the industry is initially competitive, with a price equal to c. Suppose also that after the merger, the marginal cost of production falls to c' and the price rises to p'.[2] Aggregate social surplus before the merger is given by area ABC, while aggregate surplus after the merger is given by area ADEF. Which is larger involves a comparison between the area of the shaded triangle, which is equal to the deadweight loss from the postmerger supracompetitive pricing, and the area of the shaded rectangle, which is equal to the merger-induced cost savings. If there is no improvement in costs, then the area of the rectangle will be zero and the merger reduces aggregate surplus; if there is no increase in price, then the area of the triangle will be zero, and the merger increases aggregate surplus. Williamson's main

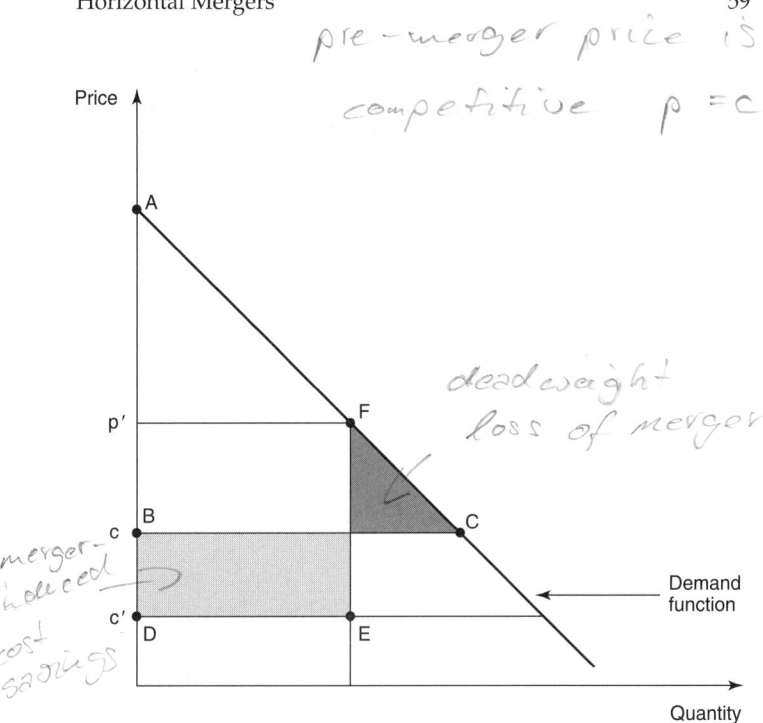

Figure 3.1
The Williamson trade-off

point was that it does not take a large decrease in cost for the area of the rectangle to exceed that of the triangle: put crudely, one might say that "rectangles tend to be larger than triangles." Indeed, in the limiting case of small changes in price and cost, differential calculus tells us that this will always be true; formally, the welfare reduction from an infinitesimal increase in price starting from the competitive price is of second-order (that is, has a zero derivative), while the welfare increase from an infinitesimal decrease in cost is of first-order (that is, has a strictly positive derivative).

Four important points should be noted, however, about this Williamson trade-off argument. First, a critical part of the argument involves the assumption that the premerger price is competitive; that is, equal to marginal cost. If, instead, the premerger price p exceeds the premerger marginal cost c then we would no longer be comparing a triangle to a rectangle, but rather a trapezoid to a rectangle (see figure 3.2) and "rectangles aren't bigger than trapezoids;" that is, even for small changes, both effects are of first-order.[3] Put simply, when a market starts off at a distorted

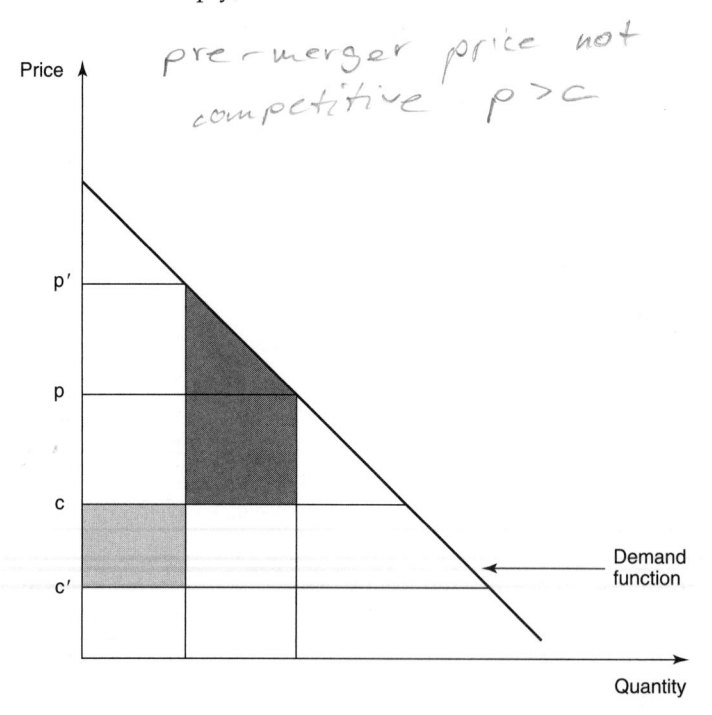

Figure 3.2
The Williamson trade-off when the premerger price exceeds marginal cost

supracompetitive price, even small increases in price can cause significant reductions in welfare.

Second, the Williamson argument glosses over the issue of differences across firms by supposing that there is a single level of marginal cost in the market, both before and after the merger. However, since any cost improvements are likely to be limited to the merging firms, it *cannot* be the case that this assumption is correct both before and after the merger, except in the case of an industry-wide merger. More importantly, at an empirical level, oligopolistic industries (that is, those in which mergers are likely to be scrutinized) often exhibit substantial variation in marginal cost across firms. The import of this point is that a potentially significant source of welfare variation arising from a horizontal merger is entirely absent from the Williamson analysis, namely the welfare changes arising from shifts of production across firms that have differing marginal costs; so-called, "production reshuffling." We will explore this point in some detail shortly.

Third, the Williamson analysis takes the appropriate welfare standard to be maximization of aggregate surplus. But, as we discussed in chapter 1, a question about distribution arises with the application of antitrust policy. Although many analyses of mergers in the economics literature focus on an aggregate surplus standard, current U.S. law as well as the DOJ and FTC *Horizontal Merger Guidelines* (which we discuss in section 3.3) are probably closest to a consumer surplus standard.[4,5] If so, then no trade-off needs to be considered: the merger should be allowed if and only if the efficiencies are enough to ensure that price does not increase.

Finally, the Williamson argument focuses on price as the sole locus of competitive interaction among the firms. In practice, however, firms make many other competitive decisions, including their choices of capacity investment, R&D, product quality, and new product introductions. Each of these choices may be affected by the change in market structure brought about by a merger. We return to this point at the end of this section.

Formal Analysis of the Welfare Effects of Mergers

Careful consideration of these issues requires a more complete model of market competition. Farrell and Shapiro [1990] provide such an analysis for the special case in which competition takes a Cournot form. (For related analyses, see Levin [1990] and McAfee and Williams [1992].) They investigate two principal questions: First, under what conditions are cost improvements sufficiently great for a merger to reduce price? As noted earlier, this is the key question when one adopts a consumer surplus standard. Second, can the fact that proposed mergers are profitable for the merging parties be used to help identify mergers that increase aggregate surplus? In particular, one difficult aspect of evaluating the aggregate welfare impact of a merger involves assessing the size of any cost efficiencies. The merging parties always have an incentive to overstate these efficiencies to help gain regulatory approval (or placate shareholders), and these prospective claims are hard for the DOJ or FTC to verify. But since only the merging parties realize these efficiency gains, it might be possible to develop a *sufficient* condition for a merger to enhance aggregate surplus that does not require investigation of claimed efficiencies by asking when the merger has a positive net effect on parties other than the merging firms.

Consider the first question: When does price decrease as a result of a merger in a Cournot industry? To be specific, suppose that firms 1 and 2 contemplate a merger in an N-

firm industry and, without loss of generality, suppose that their premerger outputs satisfy $\hat{x}_1 \geq \hat{x}_2 > 0$. Following Farrell and Shapiro, we assume that the equilibrium aggregate output increases if and only if, given the premerger aggregate output of nonmerging firms $\hat{X}_{-12}$, the merger causes the merging firms to want to increase their joint output. The following two assumptions are sufficient (although not necessary) for this property to hold:[6]

(A1) The industry inverse demand function $P(\cdot)$ satisfies $P'(X) + P''(X)X < 0$ for all aggregate output levels X.

(A2) $c_i''(x_i) > P'(X)$ for all output levels x_i and X having $x_i \leq X$, and for all i.

Letting $\hat{X}$ be the aggregate premerger output in the market, the premerger Cournot first-order conditions for these two firms are

$$P'(\hat{X})\hat{x}_1 + P(\hat{X}) - c_1'(\hat{x}_1) = 0 \tag{3.1}$$

$$P'(\hat{X})\hat{x}_2 + P(\hat{X}) - c_2'(\hat{x}_2) = 0. \tag{3.2}$$

Adding these two conditions together we have

$$P'(\hat{X})(\hat{x}_1 + \hat{x}_2) + 2P(\hat{X}) - c_1'(\hat{x}_1) - c_2'(\hat{x}_2) = 0. \tag{3.3}$$

Now suppose that the merged firm's cost function will be $c_M(\cdot)$. Assuming that the merged firm's profit function is concave in its output [which is also implied by (A1) and (A2)], its best response to $\hat{X}_{-12}$ is greater than the sum of the two firms' premerger outputs $\hat{x}_1 + \hat{x}_2$ if and only if

$$P'(\hat{X})(\hat{x}_1 + \hat{x}_2) + P(\hat{X}) - c_M'(\hat{x}_1 + \hat{x}_2) > 0, \tag{3.4}$$

or, equivalently [using (3.3)], if

$$c_2'(\hat{x}_2) - c_M'(\hat{x}_1 + \hat{x}_2) > P(\hat{X}) - c_1'(\hat{x}_1). \tag{3.5}$$

Since $c_1'(\hat{x}_1) \leq c_2'(\hat{x}_2) < P(\hat{X})$ [this follows from the premerger first-order conditions (3.1) and (3.2) and the fact that $\hat{x}_1 \geq \hat{x}_2 > 0$], this can happen only if

$$c_M'(\hat{x}_1 + \hat{x}_2) < c_1'(\hat{x}_1). \tag{3.6}$$

Condition (3.6) is a stringent requirement. It says that for price to fall the merged firm's marginal cost at the premerger joint output of the merging firms must be below the marginal cost of the more efficient merger partner. To better understand this condition, suppose that the merged firm has the *same* marginal cost as the more efficient merger partner (at the premerger output levels) and think about each of their incentives to increase output marginally. A marginal increase in output has the same incremental cost and is also sold at the same price for the two firms. However, the accompanying reduction in the market price is more costly for the merged firm than it would be for the more efficient merger partner because the merged firm sells more. Since the more efficient merger partner did not find it worthwhile to further increase its output before the merger, neither will the merged firm. Hence, for the merged firm to increase its output above the premerger level, it must have a lower marginal cost than the more efficient merger partner.

From condition (3.6), we can see that some kinds of mergers can *never* reduce price. First, as is no surprise, a merger that reduces fixed, but not marginal, costs cannot lower price. For example, imagine that before the merger each of the merging firms has cost function $c(x) = F + cx$, while the cost function of the merged firm is $c_M(x) = F_M + cx$, where $F_M < 2F$. By (3.6), this merger cannot reduce price.

More interesting, however, a merger that involves "no synergies"—that is, whose only efficiencies involve a reallocation of output across the firms so that

$$c_M(x) = \min_{x'_1, x'_2}[c_1(x'_1) + c_2(x'_2)] \quad \text{s.t.} \quad x'_1 + x'_2 = x, \tag{3.7}$$

also will not result in a lower price. To see why, consider the simple case where the merging firms have increasing marginal costs. If, after the merger, both merger partners' plants remain in operation, efficient production rationalization involves equating the marginal costs of the two firms. This must result in the merged firm's marginal cost lying between the marginal costs of the two merger partners. Hence, condition (3.6) cannot be satisfied in this case. If, on the other hand, one of the merger partner's plants is shut down after the merger to save on fixed costs, then the other plant will be producing more than its premerger level. Since marginal costs are increasing, (3.6) once again cannot hold. More generally, Farrell and Shapiro show that a merger that involves no synergies must raise price whenever (A1) and (A2) hold.[7]

Let us now turn to the second question by supposing that the merger does increase price. Under what circumstances does it nevertheless increase aggregate surplus? To see this, suppose that firms in set I contemplate merging. Let x_i denote firm i's output and let $X_I = \sum_{i \in I} x_i$. Now consider the effect of a small reduction in the output X_I of the merging firms, say $dX_I < 0$ (by our previous assumptions, if price is to increase—and hence aggregate output is to decrease—it must be that the output of the merging firms falls), and the accompanying reduction in aggregate output $dX < 0$. Let dx_i and dp be the corresponding changes in firm i's output (for $i \notin I$) and the price.

The key step in Farrell and Shapiro's analysis is their use of the presumption that proposed mergers are profitable for the merging firms.[8] If this is so, then we can derive a *sufficient condition* for the merger to increase aggregate surplus based on the *external effect* of the merger on nonparticipants; that is, on consumers and the nonmerging firms. Specifically, the welfare of nonparticipants is given by

$$E = \int_{P(X)}^{\infty} x(s)\,ds + \sum_{i \notin I}[P(X)x_i - c_i(x_i)]. \tag{3.8}$$

If a privately profitable merger increases E, then it increases aggregate surplus.

To examine the effect of the merger on E, Farrell and Shapiro study the external effect of a "differential" price-increasing merger. That is, they examine the effect on E of a small reduction in output by the merging parties, $dX_I < 0$, along with the accompanying differential changes in the outputs of rivals, dx_i for $i \notin I$. These changes dx_i arise as the nonmerging firms adjust their optimal outputs given the reduction in the merged firms' output $dX_I < 0$. Under Farrell and Shapiro's assumptions, these changes reduce the overall output in the market: $dX = dX_I + \sum_{i \notin I} dx_i < 0$. Totally differentiating (3.8) we see that their effect on E is

$$dE = -\hat{X}P'(\hat{X})\,dX + \sum_{i \notin I}\hat{x}_i P'(\hat{X})\,dX + \sum_{i \notin I}[P(\hat{X}) - c_i'(\hat{x}_i)]\,dx_i. \tag{3.9}$$

The first two terms in (3.9) are, respectively, the welfare loss of consumers and welfare gain of the nonmerging firms because of the price increase. The former is proportional to consumers' total purchases $\hat{X}$, while the latter is proportional to the nonmerging firms' total sales $\sum_{i \notin I} \hat{x}_i$. The third term in (3.9) is the change in the nonmerging firms' profits because of production reshuffling. Combining the first two terms and replacing the price-cost margin in the third term using the first-order condition for the nonmerging firms we can write:

$$dE = -\hat{X}_I P'(\hat{X})\, dX + \sum_{i \notin I}[-P'(\hat{X})\hat{x}_i]\, dx_i \qquad (3.10)$$

$$= -P'(\hat{X})\, dX \left[\hat{X}_I + \sum_{i \notin I} \hat{x}_i \left(\frac{dx_i}{dX}\right)\right] \qquad (3.11)$$

$$= -P'(\hat{X})\hat{X}\, dX \left[s_I + \sum_{i \notin I} s_i \left(\frac{dx_i}{dX}\right)\right], \qquad (3.12)$$

where s_i is firm i's premerger market share (s_I is the collective market share of the firms in set I), and $\frac{dx_i}{dX}$ is the (differential) change in nonmerging firm i's output when industry output changes marginally.[9] Thus, $dE \geq 0$ if and only if

$$s_I \leq -\sum_{i \notin I} s_i \left(\frac{dx_i}{dX}\right). \qquad (3.13)$$

Farrell and Shapiro establish conditions under which signing this differential effect at the premerger point is sufficient for signing the global effect.[10] Note one very important aspect of condition (3.13): it establishes that a merger is welfare enhancing without the need to quantify the efficiencies created by the merger since the sign of the external effect is purely a function of premerger market shares and the nonmerging firms' reactions to the merging firms' output reduction.

As one example, consider a situation with a (weakly) concave inverse demand function $[P''(\cdot) \leq 0]$ and constant returns to scale for the nonmerging firms. We then have

$\frac{dx_i}{dX} = -\left[1 + \frac{P''(X)x_i}{P'(X)}\right] \leq -1$ for all i, and so the external effect dE is nonnegative when

$$s_I \leq \sum_{i \notin I} s_i \left(1 + \frac{P''(X)x_i}{P'(X)}\right) = (1 - s_I) + \frac{P''(X)X}{P'(X)} \sum_{i \notin I} (s_i)^2,$$

or

$$s_I \leq \frac{1}{2}\left\{1 + \frac{P''(X)X}{P'(X)} \sum_{i \notin I} (s_i)^2\right\}. \tag{3.14}$$

Since, $P''(\cdot) < 0$, this condition holds whenever the merging firms have a share below $\frac{1}{2}$.[11]

As another example, consider a situation with linear inverse demand function $P(X) = a - X$ in which the cost function for a firm with k units of capital is $c(x, k) = \frac{1}{2}\left(\frac{x^2}{k}\right)$. (A merger of two firms with k_1 and k_2 units of capital results in a merged firm with $k_1 + k_2$ units of capital.) Farrell and Shapiro show that in this case the external effect is nonnegative if

$$s_I \leq \left(\frac{1}{\varepsilon}\right) \sum_{i \notin I} (s_i)^2; \tag{3.15}$$

that is, if the share of the merging firms is less than an elasticity-adjusted Herfindahl-Hirschman Index of the nonmerging firms.

Observe that in these two examples the external effect is more likely to be positive when the merging firms are small and the nonmerging firms are large. This is so because of two effects. First, there is less of a welfare reduction for consumers and the nonmerging firms in aggregate resulting from a given price increase when the output of the merging firms is low (to first-order, this welfare reduction for consumers and nonparticipating firms is proportional to the output of the merging firms, X_I). Second, after the merger, the output of the nonmerging firms increases. Since in the Cournot model larger firms have lower marginal costs in equilibrium [this follows from (3.1) and (3.2)], the effect of this reshuffling of production on nonmerging firms' profits is more positive when the nonmerging firms are large. It is also noteworthy that the external effect is more likely to be positive when the shares of the nonmerging firms are more concentrated.[12]

Conditions (3.14) and (3.15) are simple conditions that require only readily available data on premerger outputs and, for condition (3.15), the market demand elasticity.[13] However, the precise forms of these tests are very special and depend on having a great deal of a priori information about the underlying demand and cost functions. For more general demand and cost specifications, condition (3.13) requires that we also know the slopes of the nonmerging firms' best-response functions [in order to know $\left(\frac{dx_i}{dX}\right)$]. These slopes are significantly more difficult to discern than are premerger outputs and the elasticity of market demand.

Several further remarks on the Farrell and Shapiro method are in order. First, using the external effect to derive a sufficient condition for a merger to be welfare enhancing depends critically on the assumption that proposed mergers are privately profitable. To the extent that agency problems may lead managers to "empire build" to the detriment of firm value, this assumption may be inappropriate.[14]

Second, this approach also relies on the assumption that all of the private gains for the merging parties represent social gains. If, for example, some of these gains arise from tax savings or represent transfers from other stakeholders in the firm this assumption would be inappropriate (see Werden [1990], Shleifer and Summers [1988]).

Third, Farrell and Shapiro use the assumption that the merger is profitable in only a limited way. By asking when the external effect is positive, they provide a sufficient condition for a merger to increase aggregate surplus that requires no consideration at all of efficiencies. More generally, an antitrust authority that cannot verify claimed efficiencies directly might use the fact that a merger is profitable to update its beliefs about the extent of likely efficiencies. It could then ask whether the merger results in an increase in expected aggregate surplus given this updated belief.

Fourth, the Farrell and Shapiro analysis is based on the strong assumption that market competition takes a form that is described well by the Cournot model, both before and after the merger. Many other forms of price/output competition are possible, and—as mentioned when discussing the Williamson trade-off—important elements of competition may occur along dimensions other than price/quantity. There has been no work that I am aware of extending the Farrell and Shapiro approach to other forms of market interaction. The papers that formally study the effect of horizontal mergers on price and welfare in other competitive settings (for example, Deneckere and Davidson [1985] and some of the papers discussed in the next part of this section) all assume that there are no efficiencies generated by the merger.[15]

Finally, there is some evidence that the efficiency consequences of production reshuffling that the theory focuses on may be important in practice. Olley and Pakes [1996], for example, study the productivity of the telecommunications equipment industry following a regulatory decision in 1978 and the break up of AT&T in 1984, both of which facilitated new entry into a market that essentially had been a (Western Electric) monopoly. They document that productivity varied greatly across plants in the industry. More significantly from the perspective of the Farrell and Shapiro model, Olley and Pakes show that there was a significant amount of inefficiency in the allocation of output across plants in the industry once market structure moved away from monopoly.[16]

Mergers in a Dynamic World
One of the notable aspects of the Farrell and Shapiro model is its static nature. A number of interesting and important issues arise when one thinks of mergers in a more dynamic context. Many of these issues have received only limited attention.

Repeated Interaction In simple static-pricing models such as Farrell and Shapiro's Cournot model, mergers necessarily raise price in the absence of any merger-induced efficiencies [under assumptions (A1) and (A2)]. This need not be true when firms interact repeatedly and tacit collusion is a possibility. (In antitrust lingo, a merger's effects on tacit collusion are referred to as "coordinated effects," in contrast to the "unilateral effects" it has on static-pricing incentives.) In such cases, as Davidson and Deneckere [1984] note, mergers can be a double-edged sword: they reduce the merging firms' direct incentives for cheating on tacit agreements, but they may also raise the profits of firms when collusion breaks down, and thus indirectly increase the temptation to cheat, especially for nonmerging firms. Compte, Jenny, and

Rey [2002], for example, consider the effects of horizontal mergers on price in a repeated Bertrand model with capacity constraints and asymmetrically-positioned firms. In such models, capacity limitations affect both the incentive to undercut the equilibrium price (more capacity allows a greater increase in sales) and also the ability to punish deviators who undercut. Mergers, which result in the consolidation of the capacities of the merging firms, may or may not result in higher prices. Compte, Jenny, and Rey investigate which mergers lead to higher prices and which lead to lower ones. Focusing on a specific class of equilibria (in which firms maintain the same market share in price wars as in collusive states), they show that when small firms have enough capacity that strong punishment is possible regardless of the merger, a merger that increases the size of the largest firm improves the ability to maintain the monopoly price. When, instead, small firms have more limited capacity, such a merger reduces this ability.

Durable Goods The Farrell and Shapiro analysis focuses on nondurable goods. Many mergers, however, occur in durable-goods industries. Two issues arise when merging firms operate in a durable-goods market. First, consumers' abilities to delay their purchases in anticipation of future price reductions affect the ability to exercise market power. As emphasized by Coase [1972], this may mitigate—sometimes completely—the ability of a durable good monopolist to earn positive profits. On the other hand, consumers' abilities to delay their purchases may make tacit collusion among durable good oligopolists *easier* by reducing the sales enjoyed by a deviating seller. This occurs because consumers who anticipate that a price war is about to break out will delay their purchases. Indeed, Gul [1987] and Ausubel and Deneckere [1987] show that in some cases durable good oligopolists may be able to sustain a higher price than can a durable good monopolist.

The second issue concerns the welfare costs of horizontal mergers that do increase market power. Carlton and Gertner [1989] point out that used goods may constrain the pricing of even a monopolist whose market power is not otherwise constrained by the factors noted by Coase. Indeed, when new goods depreciate in quantity but not in quality (so that used goods may be combined to yield equivalent consumption value to new goods) and the market is initially at a competitive steady state, even a newly formed monopolist will not be able to raise price above the competitive level until the current stock of used goods depreciates. If it depreciates slowly, or if entry is likely to occur before too long, then even a merger to monopoly will have small welfare effects.[17]

Entry In Farrell and Shapiro's analysis, the set of firms is fixed. In most market settings, however, merging firms need to worry about the possibility of new entry following their merger. This can affect both the set of proposed mergers and their welfare consequences.

The possibility of postmerger entry reduces the set of profitable mergers. It also affects the average characteristics of profitable mergers. Werden and Froeb [1998], for example, in their exploratory study of mergers and entry, observe that mergers that lead to entry are rarely profitable in the absence of efficiency improvements. Thus, the set of profitable mergers when entry is possible is likely to be more heavily weighted toward mergers that reduce costs.

Consider now how the possibility of entry affects the welfare evaluation of mergers. If we are interested in a consumer surplus standard, the possibility of new entry increases the likelihood that a given merger will lower price. If we are interested in an aggregate surplus standard, however, the possibility of entry need not make a given merger more attractive. To see why, consider the standard two-stage model of entry with sunk costs (as in Mankiw and Whinston [1986]; see also, Mas-Colell, Whinston, and Green [1995], chapter 12). For simplicity, also imagine that competition takes a Cournot form, that firms have identical constant returns to scale technologies, and that the merger creates no improvements in efficiency. In this setting, the short-run result of two firms merging is an elevation in price, while the long-run effect (once entry can occur) is the entry of exactly one additional firm and a return to the premerger price. However, in this setting, we know that entry incentives are generally excessive (see Mankiw and Whinston [1986]): too many firms enter the industry in a free-entry equilibrium. This implies that the merger's effect on aggregate surplus is *worse* when entry is possible than when it is not.

We will see in section 3.3 that easy entry conditions tend to make the DOJ and FTC more receptive to a merger. If the goal were to maximize aggregate surplus, would such a presumption make sense given the above observation? One reason it might is related to Farrell and Shapiro's idea of conditioning on a proposed merger being profitable. In particular, if easier entry causes profitable mergers to involve, on average, greater efficiencies, then mergers that are proposed in markets with easy entry may nonetheless be more likely to increase aggregate surplus (and consumer surplus, too).

Endogenous Mergers There is a fairly large amount of literature that tries to endogenize the set of mergers that will occur in a market in the absence of any antitrust constraint (see, for example, Mackay [1984], Kamien and Zang [1990], Bloch [1996], Yi [1997], Gowisankaran and Holmes [2004]). One key observation in this literature is that an unregulated merger process may stop far short of full monopolization. The reason is a "hold-out" problem: if potential acquirees anticipate that the acquirer will be purchasing other firms, and thereby raising the market price, they may insist on such a high price for their own firm as to make their acquisition unprofitable. Indeed, in some cases, this may mean that no mergers occur at all.[18]

This literature has some potentially important implications for Farrell and Shapiro's analysis of the welfare effects of proposed horizontal mergers. For example, observe that when Farrell and Shapiro assume that a proposed merger is profitable for the merging parties they do this under the assumption that this merger is the only merger that can happen. In a dynamic context in which other mergers may follow the currently proposed merger (or, may occur if it is *not* consummated), what it means for a merger to be "profitable" is that the merger must increase the sum of the two firms' values. This is not the same as saying that the merger is profitable in the absence of other mergers. Moreover, the external effect of the merger may differ markedly from Farrell and Shapiro's calculation of the change in E. For example, it may include changes in the amounts that non-merging firms are paid later when they themselves are acquired.

This literature also suggests that there may be some subtle effects from a change in the DOJ and FTC's rules for blocking mergers. Such a change may not have only a direct effect through the change in treatment for certain mergers, but also may change the set of permissible mergers that are actually proposed.

Other Competitive Variables Focusing on dynamics, one can begin to consider other, more long-run aspects of competition among firms, such as capacity investment, R&D, and new product development. In principle, a merger's effect on welfare may be as much or more through changes in these dimensions than through changes in prices/outputs. Some progress on these issues has been made through the use of computational techniques. Berry and Pakes [1993], for example, discuss simulations of a dynamic-oligopoly model with capacity investment in which a merger's long-run effects on profitability and welfare through changes in investment indeed swamp its static price/output competition effects. Further work along these lines can be found in Gowrisankaran [1999], who also attempts to endogenize the merger process itself.

Multimarket Contact Finally, in a dynamic world in which tacit collusion is possible, a merger may affect pricing in a market not only by changing within-market concentration, but also by changing the extent to which multiproduct firms compete against one another in multiple markets. Bernheim and Whinston [1990], for example, show theoretically that, in some cases, multimarket contact can improve firms' abilities to sustain high prices by pooling the incentive constraints that limit tacit collusion. Some evidence of multimarket-contact effects is provided by Phillips and Mason [1992] and Evans and Kessides [1994]. The latter study provides evidence that the price increases that arose from a series of horizontal mergers in the U.S. airline industry in the 1980s were to a significant degree because of multimarket-contact effects.

3.3 The DOJ/FTC Merger Guidelines

The DOJ and FTC have periodically issued guidelines outlining the method they would follow for evaluating horizontal mergers. The most recent *Horizontal Merger Guidelines* were issued jointly in 1992, with a revision to the section on efficiencies in 1997.[19] The *Guidelines* first took a form resembling their present one in the early 1980s. The changes to the *Guidelines* introduced at that time dramatically increased the level of economic sophistication in horizontal merger review.

In practice, the approach followed by the DOJ and FTC in their merger reviews has an enormous effect on the set of mergers that are actually consummated. Antitrust cases are extremely expensive affairs. As a result, once the DOJ or FTC announce that they will seek to block a merger, few firms decide to incur the costs required to fight in court.

The merger analysis described in the *Guidelines* consists of four basic steps:

(1) Market definition

(2) Calculation of market concentration and concentration changes

(3) Evaluation of other market factors

(4) Procompetitive justifications

Market Definition

For simplicity suppose that the two merging firms produce widgets. The DOJ and FTC will first ask the following question:

Would a hypothetical profit-maximizing monopolist of widgets impose at least a small but significant and non-transitory increase in the price of widgets given the premerger prices of other products?

In practice, a "small but significant and non-transitory increase in price" (the "SSNIP test") is usually taken to be 5% of the premerger price. If the answer to this question is yes, then widgets is the relevant market. If the answer is no, then the agencies add the next closest substitute product (the product that would gain the most sales as a result of a 5% increase in the price of widgets) and ask the question again for this new larger potential market. This process continues until the answer to the question is yes. The idea is to arrive at a "relevant market" of products in which a merger potentially could have an anticompetitive effect.

In this example, the two firms were both producing the homogeneous product widgets. Sometimes they will be producing imperfect substitutes, say widgets and gidgets (or products sold in imperfectly overlapping geographic areas). The DOJ and FTC will start by asking the same question for each of these products separately. The merger is "horizontal" if this leads to a market definition in which the two products are both in the same market.

So far we have assumed that the merging firms each produce a single product. In many cases, however, they will be multiproduct firms. The DOJ and FTC will follow the same procedure for each product they produce.

The market definition procedure described in the *Guidelines* makes a number of seemingly arbitrary choices to resolve potential ambiguities (and in some cases leaves these ambiguities unresolved). For example, consider the 5% price increase test. If an oil pipeline buys oil on one end, transports it, and sells it at the other, is the "price" the total price charged for the oil at the end, or is it the net price for the transportation provided? Note that if oil is supplied competitively, then the basic economic situation is not affected by whether the pipeline buys oil and sells it to consumers, or charges oil companies for transportation with the oil companies selling delivered oil to consumers. Yet, which price is chosen matters for the *Guidelines'* market-definition procedure. The *Guidelines* explicitly discuss this example, and opt for the net price of transportation. In contrast, in discussing retail mergers, the *Guidelines* opt for looking at the increase in retail prices, rather than the (implicit) net price of retail services. As another example, should the test be that the hypothetical monopolist raises price on all products by at least 5%, or that it does so for at least one of them? Here the *Guidelines* require that at least one price including one of the products of the merging parties increase by at least this amount. It is in some sense difficult to know what is the "right" way to resolve these (and other) ambiguities because the *Guidelines'* procedure— while intuitive—is not based directly on any explicit model of competition and welfare effects.

Calculating Concentration and Concentration Changes

Once the DOJ or FTC has defined the relevant market, the next step is to calculate the pre- and postmerger concentration levels. To do so, the DOJ and FTC will include all firms that are producing currently as well as all likely "uncommitted entrants;" that is, firms that could and would readily and without significant sunk costs supply the market in response to a 5% increase in price. Premerger shares are then calculated for each of these firms, usually on the basis of sales, although sometimes based on production, capacity (or, more generally, asset ownership), or (when uncommitted entrant responses are important) likely sales shares in response to a hypothetical 5% price increase. Using these premerger shares, say $(s_1,\ldots,s_N)$, the DOJ and FTC then calculate the following concentration measures:

Premerger Herfindahl-Hirschman Index: $HHI_{pre} = \sum_i (s_i)^2$.

Postmerger Herfindahl-Hirschman Index:

$$HHI_{post} = \sum_i (s_i)^2 - (s_1)^2 - (s_2)^2 + (s_1 + s_2)^2$$

$$= \sum_i (s_i)^2 + 2s_1 s_2.$$

The Change in the Herfindahl-Hirschman Index:

$\Delta HHI = HHI_{post} - HHI_{pre} = 2s_1 s_2$.

The levels of these measures place the merger in one of the following categories:

HHI_{post} < 1000: These mergers are presumed to raise no competitive concerns except in exceptional circumstances.

HHI_{post} > 1000 and < 1800: These mergers are unlikely to be challenged if the change in the Herfindahl-Hirschman Index is less than 100. If it exceeds 100, then the merger "potentially raises significant competitive concerns," depending on consideration of other market factors.

HHI_{post} > 1800: These mergers are unlikely to be challenged if the change in the Herfindahl-Hirschman Index is less than 50. If it is between 50 and 100, then the merger "potentially raises significant competitive concerns," depending on consideration of other market factors. If the change exceeds

100, it is presumed that the merger is likely to be anticompetitive without evidence showing otherwise.

Recalling that in a symmetric oligopoly the Herfindahl-Hirschman Index is equal to 10,000 divided by the number of firms in the market, an index of 1000 corresponds to 10 equal-sized firms; an index of 1800 corresponds to 5.6 equal-sized firms. A change of 100 in the Herfindahl-Hirschman Index would be caused by the merger of two firms with roughly a 7% share; a change of 50 would be caused by the merger of two firms with a 5% share.

Actual enforcement practice has been more lenient than these numbers may suggest. This is because of, in part, the DOJ and FTC's consideration of other market factors and procompetitive justifications, to which we now turn.

Evaluation of Other Market Factors

Calculation of premerger concentration and its change because of the merger is only the starting point of the DOJ and FTC's investigations. After calculating these concentration figures, the DOJ and FTC consider a number of other factors affecting the likely competitive impact of the merger. These include:

Structural factors affecting the ease of sustaining collusion (tacit or explicit) These include factors such as homogeneity of products, noisiness of the market, and others that were discussed in chapter 2. Generally, the DOJ and FTC are more concerned about mergers in markets in which tacit or explicit collusion is easier to sustain. One might wonder, however, whether mergers in markets in which collusion is easier should necessarily be of greater concern. After all, relatively little competitive harm can come from a merger in a market in which it is already easy for the firms to sustain the joint monopoly outcome. Put differently, the question is whether a merger will increase prices. Market conditions that make collusion easier need not make the price effect of a merger larger (recall the discussion in section 2.3).

Evidence of market performance Although not explicitly mentioned in the *Guidelines*, the DOJ and FTC often consider empirical evidence showing how the level of concentration in such a market affects competitive outcomes. We will discuss this type of evidence further in section 3.4.

Substitution patterns in the market The DOJ and FTC will ask whether the merging firms are closer substitutes to each other than to other firms in the market. This is a way to avoid discarding important information about substitution patterns, as might occur by simply calculating concentration figures.

Substitution patterns between products in and out of the market The DOJ and FTC will ask whether there is a large degree of differentiation between the products just "in" and just "out" of the market. This is, in a sense, a way of softening the edges of the previous determination of the relevant market; that is, it is a way of making the "in-or-out" decision regarding certain products less of an all-or-nothing proposition.

Capacity limitations of some firms in the market Here the aim is to avoid the loss of important information about the competitive constraint provided by the merging firms' rivals that might occur from a simple calculation of market concentration. If a rival is capacity constrained, one would expect it to be less of a force in constraining any postmerger price increase. Also, as discussed in section 3.2, capacity constraints can affect the degree to which the merger facilitates tacit or explicit collusive pricing.

Ease of Entry Here the DOJ and FTC will consider the degree to which conditions of easy entry might preclude anticompetitive effects arising from the merger. The question they ask is whether, in response to a 5% price increase, entry would be likely to occur within two years that would drive price down to its premerger level. As we have discussed in section 3.2, this makes sense with a consumer surplus welfare standard, but there is a question about how the ease of entry should affect merger analysis if instead the goal is to maximize aggregate surplus.

Procompetitive Justifications
The principal issue here is the consideration of efficiencies. The DOJ and FTC typically adopt a fairly high hurdle for claimed efficiencies because it is relatively easy for firms to claim that efficiencies will be generated by the merger, and relatively hard for antitrust enforcers to evaluate the likelihood that these efficiencies will be realized. As we discussed in chapter 1, how efficiencies should be factored into the analysis of a merger depends on the welfare standard adopted by the agencies. The 1997 revisions to the DOJ and FTC *Guidelines*, while somewhat ambiguous, lean toward the position that the efficiencies need to be sufficient to keep consumer surplus from decreasing for a merger to be approved.[20] With such a consumer surplus standard, for example, reductions in fixed costs do not help a merger gain approval; only reductions in marginal costs matter. In contrast, until recent court decisions, Canada's Competition Act adopted an aggregate surplus standard by asking whether efficiency gains outweigh any reduction in consumer surplus because of higher prices.

Regardless of whether a consumer or aggregate surplus standard is followed, the efficiencies that are counted must be efficiencies that could not be realized easily by less restrictive means, such as through individual investments of the firms, through joint production agreements, or through a merger that includes some limited divestitures.

One concern in mergers that claim significant operating efficiencies (say through reductions in manpower or capital) is whether these reductions alter the quality of the products produced by the firms. For example, in a recent merger of two Canadian propane companies having roughly a 70% share of the overall Canadian market, the merging companies proposed consolidating their local branches, reducing trucks, drivers, and service people. These would be valid efficiencies if the quality of their customer service did not suffer, but if these savings represent instead a move along an existing quality-cost frontier, they would not be valid efficiencies from an antitrust standpoint.

3.4 Econometric Approaches to Answering the *Guidelines'* Questions

There are two principal areas in which econometric analysis has been employed in applying the DOJ and FTC *Guidelines*. These are in defining the relevant market and in providing evidence about the effects of increased concentration on prices.

Defining the Relevant Market

Suppose that we have a collection of substitute products (goods $1, \ldots, N$) that include the products of the merging firms. To answer the *Guidelines'* market-definition question we want to study whether a hypothetical profit-maximizing monopolist of some subset of these products would raise price by at least 5%, taking the prices of other firms as fixed (at their premerger levels). We can do this if we know the demand and cost functions for these products, and the premerger prices of all N products.

To answer the *Guidelines'* question, we must first estimate the demand functions for these products. The simplest case to consider arises when we are considering a hypothetical monopolist of a single homogeneous product, say widgets, which is differentiated from the products of all other firms. In this case, we only need to estimate the demand function for widgets, which is given by some function $x(p, q, y, \varepsilon)$, where p is the price of widgets, q is a vector of prices of substitute products, y is a vector of exogenous demand shifters (for example, income, weather, and so on), and ε represents (random) factors not observable by the econometrician. For example, a constant elasticity demand function (with one substitute product and one demand shifter) would yield the estimating equation

$$\ln(x_i) = \beta_0 + \beta_1 \ln(p_i) + \beta_2 \ln(q_i) + \beta_3 \ln(y_i) + \varepsilon_i, \qquad (3.16)$$

where i may indicate observations on different markets in a cross section of markets or on different time periods in a series of observations on the same market.[21] Several standard issues arise in the estimation of equation (3.16). First, as always in econometric work, careful testing for an appropriate specification is critical. Second, it is important to appropriately control for the endogeneity of prices: the price of widgets p is almost certain to be correlated with ε because factors that shift the demand for widgets but are unobserved to the econometrician will, under all but a limited set of circumstances, affect the equilibrium price of widgets.[22] The most common direction for the bias induced by a failure to properly instrument in estimating equation (3.16) would be toward an underestimation of the elasticity of demand because positive shocks to demand are likely to be positively correlated with p.[23] Observe, however, that if we were to estimate instead the inverse demand function

$$\ln(p_i) = \bar{\beta}_0 + \bar{\beta}_1 \ln(x_i) + \bar{\beta}_2 \ln(q_i) + \bar{\beta}_3 \ln(y_i) + \varepsilon_i, \quad (3.17)$$

then since the equilibrium quantity x is also likely to be positively correlated with ε, we would expect to underestimate the *inverse* demand elasticity—that is, to *overestimate* the demand elasticity. (Indeed, the difference between these two estimates of the demand elasticity is one specification test for endogeneity.) This observation leads to what might, in a tongue-in-cheek manner, be called the *Iron Law of Consulting*: "Estimate inverse demand functions if you work for the defendants and ordinary demand functions if you work for the plaintiffs." What is needed to properly estimate either form are good cost-side instruments for the endogeneous price/quantity variables; that is, variables that can be expected to be correlated with price/quantity but not with demand shocks.

Matters can become considerably more complicated when the product set being considered includes differentiated products. If the number of products in the set is small, then we simply can expand the estimation procedure just outlined by estimating a system of demand functions together. For example, suppose that we are considering a hypothetical monopolist of widgets and gidgets, and that there is a single substitute product. Then, in the constant elasticity case, we could estimate the system

$$\ln(x_{wi}) = \beta_{10} + \beta_{11} \ln(p_{wi}) + \beta_{12} \ln(p_{gi})$$
$$+ \beta_{13} \ln(q_i) + \beta_{14} \ln(y_i) + \varepsilon_{1i}, \quad (3.18)$$

$$\ln(x_{gi}) = \beta_{20} + \beta_{21} \ln(p_{gi}) + \beta_{22} \ln(p_{wi})$$
$$+ \beta_{23} \ln(q_i) + \beta_{24} \ln(y_i) + \varepsilon_{2i}. \tag{3.19}$$

The main difficulty involved is finding enough good instruments to identify the effects of the prices p_w and p_g separately. Usually one will need some variables that affect the production cost of one product and not the other (or at least that differ significantly in their effects on the costs of the two products).

As the number of products being considered expands, however, estimation of such a demand system will become infeasible because the data will not be rich enough to permit separate estimation of all of the relevant own- and cross-price demand elasticities among the products (which increase in the square of the number of products). In the past, this was dealt with by aggregating the products into subgroups (for example, premium tuna, middle-line tuna, and private-label tuna in a merger of tuna producers) and limiting the estimation to the study of the demand for these groups (the prices used would be some sort of price indices for the groups). Recently, however, there has been a great deal of progress in the econometric estimation of demand systems for differentiated products. The key to these methods is to impose some restrictions that limit the number of parameters that need to be estimated, while not doing violence to the data.

Two primary methods have been advanced in the literature to date. One, developed by Berry, Levinsohn, and Pakes [1995], models the demand for the various products as a function of some underlying characteristics (see also Berry [1994]).[24] For example, in the automobile industry that is the focus of their study, cars' attributes include length, weight, horsepower, and various other amenities.

Letting the vector of attributes for car j be a_j, the net surplus for consumer i of buying car j when its price is p_j is taken to be the function

$$u_{ij} = a_j \cdot \beta_i - \alpha_i p_j + \xi_j + \varepsilon_{ij}, \tag{3.20}$$

where β_i is a parameter vector representing consumer i's weights on the various attributes, α_i is consumer i's marginal utility of income, ξ_j is a random quality component for car j (common across consumers) that is unobserved by the econometrician, and ε_{ij} is a random consumer/car-specific shock that is unobserved by the econometrician and is independent across consumers and cars. The parameters β_i and α_i may be common across consumers, may be modeled as having a common mean and a consumer-specific random element, or (if the data are available) may be modeled as a function of demographic characteristics of the consumer.[25] The consumer is then assumed to make a choice among discrete consumption alternatives, whose number is equal to the number of products in the market.

Berry, Levinsohn, and Pakes [1995], Berry [1994], and Nevo [2000a, 2000b, 2001] discuss in detail the estimation of this demand model including issues of instrumentation and computation. The key benefit of this approach arises in its limitation of the number of parameters to be estimated by tying the value of each product in the market to a limited number of characteristics. The potential danger, of course, is that this restriction will not match the data well. For example, one model that is nested within equation (3.20) is the traditional logit model (take β_i and α_i to be common across consumers, assume that $\xi_j \equiv 0$, and take ε_{ij} to have an extreme value distribution). This model has the well-known Independence of Irrelevant Alternatives (IIA) property, which implies that if the price of a good increases, all consumers who switch to other goods do so in proportion to these goods' market shares.[26] This assumption is usually at odds with actual substitution patterns. For example, it is common for two products with similar market shares to have distinct sets of close substitutes. Berry, Levinsohn, and Pakes discuss the example of a Yugo and a Mercedes (two cars) having similar market shares, but quite different cross-elasticities of demand with a BMW. If the price of a BMW were to increase, it is likely that the Mercedes's share would be affected much more than the share of the Yugo.[27] A good deal of work in this literature has focused (successfully) on how to estimate versions of this model that have richer substitution patterns than the logit model. For example, by allowing consumers to differ in their β_i coefficients, the model generates more reasonable substitution patterns, since the second choice of a consumer who chooses a BMW (and, hence, is likely to value highly horsepower and luxury) is much more likely to be a Mercedes than a Yugo because a Mercedes's characteristics are more similar to the characteristics of a BMW than are a Yugo's.

The second method is the multistage budgeting procedure introduced by Hausman, Leonard, and Zona [1994] (see also Hausman [1996]). In this method, the products in a market are grouped on a priori grounds into subgroups. For example, in the beer market that these authors study, beers are grouped into the categories of premium beers, popular-price beers, and light beers. They then estimate demand at three levels. First, they estimate the demand within each of these three categories as a function of the prices of the within-category beers and the total expenditure on the category, much as in equations (3.18) and (3.19). Next, they estimate the expenditure allocation among the three categories as a function of total expenditures on beers and price indices for the three categories. Finally, they estimate a demand function for expenditure on beer as a function of an overall beer price index.

In this method, the grouping of products into categories (and the separability and other assumptions on the structure of demand that make the multistage budgeting approach valid) restricts the number of parameters that need to be estimated. This allows for a flexible estimation of the substitution parameters within groups and in the higher-level estimations. On the other hand, the method does impose some strong restrictions on substitution patterns between products in the different (a priori specified) groups. For example, the substitution toward products in one group (say, premium beers) is independent of which product in another group (say, popular-price beers) has experienced a price increase.

To date there has been very little work evaluating the relative merits of these two approaches. One such study is Nevo [1997], who compares the two methods in a study of the ready-to-eat cereal industry. In that particular case, he finds that the Berry, Levinsohn, and Pakes characteristics approach works best (the multistage budgeting approach produces negative cross-price elasticities for products like Post's and Kellogg's raisin bran cereals that are almost surely substitutes), but it is hard to know at this point how the two methods compare more generally.

The second step in answering the *Guidelines'* market definition question is estimation of firms' cost functions. This can, in principle, be accomplished directly by estimating cost functions, or indirectly by estimating either production functions or factor demand equations. Like estimation of demand, these methods all must confront endogeneity issues; selection issues can also arise.[28] One additional problem with the cost side, however, is often a lack of necessary data. The output and price data needed for demand estimation tend to be more readily available than the cost or input information needed to determine a firm's cost function.

Without the ability to directly estimate firms' cost functions, we can still estimate marginal costs if we are willing to assume something about firms' behavior. For example, suppose we assume that firms are playing a static Nash (differentiated product) pricing equilibrium before the merger and that each firm i produces a single product before the merger.[29] Then we can use the fact that the firms' prices satisfy the first-order conditions

$$(p_i - c_i'(x_i(p)))\frac{\partial x_i(p_i, p_{-i})}{\partial p_i} + x_i(p) = 0 \quad \text{for } i = 1, \ldots, N \tag{3.21}$$

to derive that

$$c_i'(x_i(p)) = p_i + \left[\frac{\partial x_i(p_i, p_{-i})}{\partial p_i}\right]^{-1} x_i(p) \quad \text{for } i = 1, \ldots, N. \tag{3.22}$$

This gives us an estimate of firms' marginal costs if we are willing to assume that marginal costs are approximately constant in the relevant range.[30]

Given estimated demand and cost functions for the products controlled by the hypothetical monopolist, and the premerger prices of other products, one can compute the hypothetical monopolist's profit-maximizing prices and compare these to the premerger prices of these products to answer the *Guidelines'* 5% price increase market-definition question.

The econometric tools to estimate demands and costs, particularly in an industry with extensive product differentiation, are fairly recent. Moreover, time is often short in these investigations. As a result, a number of simpler techniques often have been applied to try to answer the *Guidelines'* market-definition question. The simplest of these involve a review of company documents and industry marketing studies, and informally asking customers about their likelihood of switching products in response to price changes. These methods, of course, are likely to produce at best a rough sense of the degree of substitution between products.[31]

Two other methods involve examining price correlations among a set of products and, for cases in which the issue is geographic market definition, looking at patterns of transshipment. Both of these have serious potential flaws, however.

To consider the use of price correlations, imagine that we have two cities, A and B, that are located 100 miles apart. City B has a competitive widget industry that produces widgets at a cost per unit of c_B. There is a single widget producer in city A who has a cost per unit of c_A. These costs are random. The demand at each location i is $x_i(p) = \alpha_i - p$ and there is a cost t of transporting a widget between the cities.

Imagine, first, that the transport cost is infinite, so that the markets are in fact completely distinct. Then the price in market A will be $p_A^m = (\alpha_A + c_A)/2$ and the correlation between the prices in market A and market B will be

$$\frac{cov(p_A, c_B)}{\sqrt{var(p_A)var(c_B)}} = \frac{\frac{1}{2}cov(\alpha_A, c_B) + \frac{1}{2}cov(c_A, c_B)}{\sqrt{var(p_A)var(c_B)}}. \quad (3.23)$$

If, for example, α_A is fixed and $c_A = c_B \equiv c$, then the correlation will equal 1 (perfect correlation) even though the markets are completely distinct. (This is just the case of a common causal factor, in this case the level of marginal cost.)

Suppose instead that t is random, that $\alpha_A = 1$ and $c_A = c_B \equiv c$, and that for all realizations of t we have $(c+t) < \frac{1}{2}$. In this case, the price in market B fully constrains the price in market A so that $p_A = c + t$. If t and c are independently distributed, then the correlation between the prices in the two markets is

$$\frac{cov(c+t,c)}{\sqrt{var(c)+var(t)}\sqrt{var(c)}} = \frac{var(c)}{\sqrt{var(c)+var(t)}\sqrt{var(c)}}. \quad (3.24)$$

Hence, if $var(c)$ is small, the correlation between the prices will be nearly zero, despite the fact that market A is fully constrained by the competitive industry in market B. On the other hand, if the variance of t is instead small, then the correlation will be close to 1. Yet—and this illustrates the problem—whether it is $var(c)$ or $var(t)$ that is small has no bearing on the underlying competitive situation.

A problem with looking at transshipments is also illustrated by this last case since no transshipments take place in equilibrium despite the fact that market A is fully constrained by market B.

Evidence on the Effects of Increasing Concentration on Prices

In the consideration of "other factors," one type of evidence that one or both sides in horizontal merger cases often present is evidence of the effects of concentration on prices. These studies typically follow the "structure-conduct-performance" paradigm of regressing a measure of performance—in this case price—on one or more measures of concentration and other control variables.³² A typical regression seeking to explain the price in a cross section of markets $i = 1, \ldots, I$ might look like

$$p_i = \beta_0 + w_i \cdot \beta_1 + y_i \cdot \beta_2 + CR_i \cdot \beta_3 + \varepsilon_i, \tag{3.25}$$

where w_i are variables affecting costs, y_i are variables affecting demand, and CR_i are measures of the level of concentration (the variables might be in logs, and both linear and nonlinear terms might be included). In the most standard treatment, these variables all are treated as exogenous causal determinants of prices in a market. As such, and given the mix of demand and cost variables included in the regression, it has become common to refer to the regression results as "reduced form" estimates, with the intention of distinguishing them from "structural" estimates of demand and supply relationships (see, for example, Baker and Rubinfeld [1999]). Given the results of regression (3.25), the impact of the merger on price is typically predicted from (3.25) using pre- and postmerger measures of concentration, where postmerger concentration is calculated by assuming that the merged firms' postmerger share is equal to the sum of their premerger shares (for example, that the HHI changes from HHI_{pre} to HHI_{post}).

Regressions such as these have seen wide application in horizontal merger cases. In the FTC's challenge of the Staples/Office Depot merger, for example, this type of regression was used by both the FTC and the defendants.³³ In that merger the focus was on whether these office "superstores" should be considered as a distinct market (or "submarket") or whether these stores should be viewed as a small part of a much larger office-supply market. The parties used this type of regression to examine the determinants of Staples's prices in a city.³⁴ In that case, an observation of the dependent variable was the price of a particular Staples store in a particular month; the concentration measures included both a measure of general concentration in the office-supply market and measures of whether there were office-supply superstores within the same metropolitan statistical areas and within given radiuses of the particular Staples store.

As another example, when the Union Pacific Railroad (UP) sought to acquire the Southern Pacific Railroad (SP) in 1996 shortly after the merger of the Burlington Northern Railroad (BN) and the Sante Fe Railroad (SF), many railroad routes west of the Mississippi River would go from being served by three firms to being served by two firms in the event of the merger, and some would go from being served by two firms to one firm. The merging parties claimed that SP was a "weak" railroad, and that it did not have a significant competitive effect on UP in any market in which BN/SF was already present. To bolster this claim, the merging parties conducted this type of study of UP's prices, where the concentration variables included separate dummy variables indicating exactly which competitors UP faced in a particular market.[35]

Although this method has provided useful evidence in a wide range of cases, it can suffer from some serious problems. A first problem has to do with the endogeneity of concentration. In fact, (3.25) is *not* a true reduced form. A true reduced form would include only the underlying exogenous factors influencing market outcomes and not concentration, which is an outcome of the competitive process.[36] Indeed, in many ways equation (3.25) is closer to estimation of a supply relation, in the sense discussed in Bresnahan [1989]. To see this, consider the case in which demand takes the constant elasticity form $X(p) = Ap^{-\eta}$, all firms are identical with constant unit costs of c, and firms play a static Cournot equilibrium. Then we can write an active firm's first-order condition as

$$p = c - P'(X)x_i = c + \frac{s_i}{\eta}p = c + \frac{H}{\eta}p, \quad (3.26)$$

where $P(\cdot)$ is the inverse demand function and s_i is firm i's market share, which, given symmetry, equals the Herfindahl-Hirschman Index, which I denote here by H. As in Bresnahan [1989], we can nest this model and perfect competition by introducing a conduct parameter θ and rewriting (3.26) as

$$p = c + \theta\frac{H}{\eta}p.$$

Thus,

$$p = \left(\frac{\eta}{\eta - \theta H}\right)c, \quad (3.27)$$

where the term in parentheses represents the proportional mark-up of price over marginal cost. Taking logarithms, we can write (3.27) as

$$\ln(p) = \ln(c) + \ln(\eta) - \ln(\eta - \theta H). \quad (3.28)$$

Suppose that marginal cost takes the form $c = \bar{c}e^{\varepsilon}$, where ε is an unobservable cost component and $\bar{c}$ is either observable or a parameter to be estimated. Then (3.28) becomes

$$\ln(p) = \ln(\bar{c}) + \ln(\eta) - \ln(\eta - \theta H) + \varepsilon, \quad (3.29)$$

which has a form very close to (3.25), the main difference being the interaction between the concentration variable H and the demand coefficient η. Estimating equation (3.25) might then be considered a linear approximation to this supply relation.

The problem in estimating (3.29) is that, because of its endogeneity, H is likely to be correlated with the cost shock ε, causing least squares estimation to produce inconsistent (in other words, biased) parameter estimates. Specifically, since the number of firms in a market is determined by the profitability of entry, H will be related to the level of costs in the market. To derive consistent parameter estimates in this case we need to find instrumental variables that are correlated with H but not with the unobserved costs ε. Possibilities include the "market size" variable A, and measures of the cost of entry.

Even if we can find such instruments, however, the model we used to derive equation (3.29) assumed that firms are symmetric. This is problematic, since (aside from a Cournot industry with identical constant returns to scale firms) either the premerger or the postmerger situation is likely to be asymmetric. When we allow for asymmetries, however, a firm's supply relation is unlikely even to take a form like (3.25), in which rivals' prices or quantities affect the firm's pricing only through a concentration measure like H. If so, (3.25) will be misspecified.

Another potential problem with using estimates of (3.25) to predict merger-induced price changes arises because of unobservable strategic choices by firms. For example, firms often will make strategic decisions that affect costs, such as conducting R&D or investing in capacity. These decisions, say k, typically will depend on the degree of competition in a market; that is, in a sample of markets they may be described by some function $k^*(H, \cdot)$. Looking back at equation (3.29), if k is unobserved by the econometrician, it will end up in the unobserved cost term ε. Since $k^*(\cdot)$ depends on H, this induces a correlation between ε and H that cannot readily be instrumented for, because variables that are correlated with H almost always will be correlated with k and hence with ε. Thus, even if firms are symmetric and H really is exogenous in our sample of markets, our parameter estimates will be inconsistent.

Is this a problem? One might argue that the answer is no. After all, if H is really exogenous, then the least squares estimates still tell us the expectation of price conditional on H (and observable demand and cost factors). Since this is what we really want to know—the total effect of a change in H on price, including any effects due to induced changes in k—perhaps we are fine? The problem is that this is true only if the merger will change the strategic choices k in accord with the function $k^*(H, \cdot)$ that holds in the data. This may or may not be the case. For example, $k^*(H, \cdot)$ may reflect the long-run equilibrium choice of k given H, but k may be very different from this in the short- and medium-run after the merger.

For instance, consider the UP/SP example. One important factor for the determination of prices on a route is the level of aggregate capacity available on that route (such as tracks, sidings, and yards); higher capacity is likely to lead to lower prices, all else equal. In the premerger data, this aggregate capacity level is likely to be correlated with the number and identity of competitors on a route. For example, aggregate capacity probably is larger when more firms are present. Hence, in a regression that includes the number of firms on a route, but not capacity, some of the effect that is attributed to an increase in concentration likely results from the fact that, across the sample of markets, higher concentration is correlated with lower capacity levels. But in a merger, while the number of firms will decrease on many routes, the level of capacity on these routes may well remain unchanged (at least in the short run). If so, the regression would predict too large an elevation in price following the merger.

Finally, with asymmetric firms the endogeneity of H also causes a problem when we turn to using the estimates for predicting the price change because of a merger. The actual postmerger equilibrium level of H is unlikely to equal HHI_{post}, the level calculated by simply assuming that the postmerger share of the merged firms is equal to the sum of their premerger shares. Indeed, in the Cournot model we know that (without synergies) H will *not* be equal to HHI_{post}, since the merged firms' combined share will fall. As one simple example, in the case of an N-firm symmetric Cournot industry with constant returns to scale, the postmerger Herfindahl-Hirschman Index will be $1/(N-1)$, while $HHI_{post} = 2/N$. We can deduce the true merger-induced change in concentration if we have structural estimates of demand and supply relations. But, as we will see in the next section, if we have estimates of these relations we also can use them to directly predict postmerger prices, and so there would not be much point to using (3.25).

Given the relative ease and widespread use of this method, one might hope that it gives at least approximately correct answers despite these problems. It would be good to know more than we now do about whether this is right.[37]

3.5 Breaking the Market-Definition Mold

When they were introduced, the *Guidelines* greatly improved the agencies' analysis of proposed horizontal mergers. At the same time, we have seen that their market-definition based process, while intuitive, is not based on any explicit model of competition and welfare effects. Given this fact, it is natural to ask whether there are other techniques that do not require this type of market definition exercise and examination of concentration changes. In this section, we examine three alternative techniques that economists have proposed for evaluating the likely effects of a merger. These are merger simulation, residual demand estimation, and the event study approach. Of these, merger simulation methods seem particularly promising.

Merger Simulation

If we are really going the route of estimating demand and cost functions to answer the *Guidelines'* market-definition question (as discussed in the first part of section 3.4), why not just examine the price effects of the merger directly using these estimated structural parameters? That is, once we estimate a structural model of the industry using premerger data, we can *simulate* the effects of the merger. Doing so, we also can avoid a costly debate over what should be "in" and "out" of the "market."

Conceptually, simulating the price effects of a merger is simple: given demand and cost functions for the various products in the market and an assumption about the behavior of the firms (existing studies typically examine a static simultaneous move price choice game), one can solve numerically for the equilibrium prices that will emerge from the postmerger market structure. For example, if firms 1 and 2 in a three-firm industry merge, the equilibrium prices (p_1^*, p_2^*, p_3^*) in a static simultaneous price choice game will be such that after the merger (p_1^*, p_2^*) maximizes the merged firm's profit given p_3^*; that is (the notation follows that in the discussion of differentiated product demand systems in section 3.4),

(p_1^*, p_2^*) solves $\max_{p_1,p_2} \sum_{i=1,2} [p_i x_i(p_1, p_2, p_3^*, q, y)$

$$- c_i(x_i(p_1, p_2, p_3^*, q, y))],$$

while p_3^* maximizes the profit of the third firm given (p_1^*, p_2^*), that is

p_3^* solves $\max_{p_3} p_3 x_3(p_1^*, p_2^*, p_3, q, y) - c_3(x_2(p_1^*, p_2^*, p_3, q, y))$.

Given explicit functional forms for the demand and cost functions, fixed-point algorithms (or, in some cases, explicit solutions using linear algebra), can be used to find post-merger equilibrium prices. (More detailed discussions of the method can be found in Hausman, Leonard, and Zona [1994], Nevo [2000b], and Werden and Froeb [1994].) Going one step further, one also can ask how large a marginal cost reduction must arise from the merger to prevent consumer surplus from falling (or, with an aggregate surplus standard, what combinations of fixed and marginal cost reductions are necessary to prevent aggregate surplus from falling). With the recent advances in estimating structural models, this approach is gaining increasing attention.

There are, however, three important caveats regarding this method. First, correct estimation of demand is essential for the quality of any predictions through simulation. Demand estimates will be more reliable when the simulation does not have to rely on out-of-sample extrapolation; that is, when the merger does not cause prices to move outside the range of prior experience.

Second, a critical part of the simulation exercise involves the choice of the postmerger behavioral model of the industry. One can base this behavioral assumption on estimates of behavior using premerger data, a technique that has a long history in the empirical industrial-organization literature (see, for example, Bresnahan [1987, 1989] and Porter [1983]).[38] A serious concern, however, is that the firms' behavior may *change* as a result of the merger. For example, the reduction in the number of firms could cause an industry to go from a static equilibrium outcome (say, Bertrand or Cournot) to a more cooperative tacitly collusive regime. In principal, this too may be something that we can estimate if we have a sample of markets with varying structural characteristics. But, to date, those attempting to conduct merger simulations have not done so.

Third, as previously discussed, pricing is likely to be only one of several important variables that may be affected by a merger. Entry, long-run investments in capacity, and R&D may all be altered significantly by a merger. The empirical industrial-organization literature is just beginning to get a handle on these dynamic issues. To date, no actual merger simulation has included them. Nonetheless, dynamics is a very active area of research, and it may not be long before this begins to happen.

In recent work, Peters [2003] evaluates the perfomance of these simulation methods by examining how well they would have predicted the actual price changes that followed six airline mergers in the 1980s. The standard merger-simulation technique, in which price changes arise from changes in ownership structure (given an estimated demand structure and inferred marginal costs) produces the price changes shown in table 3.1 in the column labeled "Ownership change."[39] The actual changes, in contrast, are in the last column of the table, labeled "Actual %Δp". While the merger simulation captures an important element of the price change, it is clear that it predicts the price changes resulting from the various mergers only imperfectly. For ex-

Table 3.1
Simulated and actual price changes from airline mergers

Merger	Component effects of average percent relative price change in overlap markets					
	# of markets	Ownership change	Observed changes	Change in μ	Change in c	Actual %Δp
NW-RC	78	19.8	−1.4	0.9	−10.1	7.2
TW-OZ	50	20.8	−2.2	−0.8	−1.0	16.0
CO-PE	67	6.4	0.7	0.2	20.5	29.4
DL-WA	11	7.6	−1.5	−0.5	6.0	11.8
AA-OC	2	4.7	−3.6	−1.8	7.6	6.5
US-PI	60	12.7	2.0	−1.9	6.7	20.3

Source: Peters [2003].

ample, the US Air-Piedmont merger (US-PI) is predicted to lead to a smaller price increase than either the Northwest-Republic (NW-RC) or TWA-Ozark (TW-OZ) mergers, but the reverse actually happened.

Peters next asks how much of this discrepency can be accounted for by other observed changes that occurred following the merger, such as changes in flight frequency or entry, by including these observed changes in the postmerger simulation. The column labeled "Observed changes" in table 3.1 reports the answer. As can be seen there, these observed changes account for little of the difference.[40]

Given this negative answer, Peters then looks to see whether changes in unobserved product attributes (such as firm reputation or quality, denoted by μ in the table) or in marginal costs (denoted by c in the table) can explain the difference. The changes in unobserved product attributes can be inferred, using the premerger estimated demand coefficients, by solving for the levels of these unobserved attributes that reconcile the postmerger quantities purchased with the postmerger prices. Given the inferred postmerger unobserved product attributes, Peters can solve for the Nash equilibrium prices that would obtain were product attributes to have changed in this way, assuming that marginal costs remained unchanged. (Observe that since the postmerger unobserved product attributes are obtained entirely from the demand side, these computed equilibrium prices need not equal the actual postmerger prices.) As can be seen in the column labeled "Change in μ," this accounts for little of the difference between predicted and actual prices.

Finally, Peters can infer a change in marginal cost by calculating the levels of marginal costs that would make the computed Nash equilibrium prices equal to the actual postmerger prices. (This is done by including all of the previous changes, including the inferred changes in unobserved product attributes μ, and solving for marginal costs using the Nash equilibrium pricing first-order conditions, as in the discussion of econometric approaches to market definition in section 3.4.) The price change in the column labeled "Change in c" reports the size of the change if these marginal cost changes are included in the simulation, omitting the product attribute changes. As can be seen in the table, the changes because of changes in c represent a large portion of the discrepency between the initial simulation and the actual price changes.

It should be noted, however (as Peters does), that an alternative interpretation of these results is that it was firm conduct rather than marginal costs that changed postmerger. For example, this seems most clear in the case of the Continental-People Express (CO-PE) merger, where the acquired airline was suffering serious financial difficulty prior to the merger. In that case, prices undoubtedly increased not because of a true marginal cost change, but rather because of a change in the previously distressed firm's behavior. Changes in behavior may have occurred in the other mergers as well. At the very least, however, Peters's study suggests directions that are likely to be fruitful in improving prospective analyses of mergers.

It seems clear that as techniques for estimating structural models get better, merger simulation will become an increasingly important tool in the analysis of horizontal mergers. How quickly this happens, however, and the degree to which it supplants other techniques, remains to be seen. My sense is that it is likely that before too long these techniques, and their further refinements, will constitute the core of merger analysis, at least for cases in which data and time limitations are not too severe.

Residual Demand Estimation

Another technique that does not follow the *Guidelines'* path, but that also avoids a full-blown structural estimation, is the residual demand function approach developed by Baker and Bresnahan [1985]. Specifically, Baker and Bresnahan propose a way to determine the increase in market power from a merger that involves separately estimating neither the cross-price elasticities of demand between the merging firms' and rivals' products nor cost function parameters. As Baker and Bresnahan [1985, 59] put it:

Evaluating the effect of a merger between two firms with $n - 2$ other competitors would seem to require the estimation of at least n^2 parameters (all of the price elasticities of demand), a formidable task.... That extremely difficult task is unnecessary, however. The necessary information is contained in the slopes of the two single-firm (residual) demand curves before the merger, and the extent to which the merged firm will face a steeper demand curve.... The key to the procedures is that the effects of all other firms in the industry are summed together.... This reduces the dimensionality of the problem to manageable size; rather than an n-firm demand system, we estimate a two-firm residual demand system.

To understand the Baker and Bresnahan idea, it helps to start by thinking about the residual demand function faced by a single firm (that is, its demand function, taking into account rivals' reactions), as in Baker and Bresnahan [1988]. Specifically, consider an industry with N single-product firms and suppose that the inverse demand function for firm 1 is given by

$$p_1 = P_1(x_1, x_{-1}, z), \qquad (3.30)$$

where x_1 is firm 1's output level, x_{-1} is an $(N-1)$ vector of output levels for firm 1's rivals, and z are demand shifters. To derive the residual inverse demand function facing firm 1, Baker and Bresnahan posit that the equilibrium relation between the vector x_{-1} and x_1 given the demand variables z and the cost variables w_{-1} affecting firms $2, \ldots, N$ can be written as

$$x_{-1} = B_{-1}(x_1, z, w_{-1}). \qquad (3.31)$$

For example, imagine for simplicity that there are two firms in the industry ($N = 2$). If equilibrium output levels are determined by either a static simultaneous choice quantity game or by a Stackleberg game in which firm 1 is the leader, then (3.31) is simply firm 2's best-response function. Substituting for x_{-1} in (3.30) we can then write firm 1's residual inverse demand function as

$$p_1 = P_1(x_1, B_{-1}(x_1, z, w_{-1}), z) \equiv R_1(x_1, z, w_{-1}). \tag{3.32}$$

For example, in the simple case in which z and w_{-1} are both scalar variables, we might estimate this in the simple constant-elasticity form:

$$\ln(p_{1i}) = \gamma_0 + \gamma_1 \ln(x_{1i}) + \gamma_2 \ln(z_i) + \gamma_3 \ln(w_{-1,i}) + \varepsilon_i. \tag{3.33}$$

Baker and Bresnahan would then look to the estimate of γ_1, the quantity elasticity of the residual inverse demand function, as a measure of the firm's market power.[41]

Note that since x_1 typically will be correlated with ε, we will require an instrument for x_1. Moreover, since the rivals' cost variables w_{-1} are already in the estimating equation (3.33), this will need to be a cost variable that affects *only* firm 1, say w_1. Unfortunately, such an instrument is often hard to find.

Figure 3.3 depicts the idea of what identifies the residual demand function $R_1(\cdot)$. Imagine that firms other than firm 1 produce a homogeneous product, that firm 1's product may be differentiated, and that the N firms compete by simultaneously choosing quantities. By holding fixed the demand variable z and the cost variables w_{-1} for firm 1's rivals, the estimating equation (3.33) effectively holds fixed the rivals' aggregate best-response function, which is labeled as $\bar{B}_{-1}(\cdot)$ in figure 3.3.[42] A shift in the cost variable for firm 1 from w_1' to $w_1'' < w_1'$ shifts firm 1's best-response function outward as depicted in figure 3.3. This increases x_1 from x_1' to x_1'' and reduces the sum of the rivals' joint output X_{-1}. The slope of the residual demand function is then equal to the ratio of the resulting change in firm 1's price to the change in its quantity. For example, if rivals have constant returns to scale and act competitively, and if firm 1's product is not differentiated from its rivals' products, then $\bar{B}_{-1}(\cdot)$ will be a

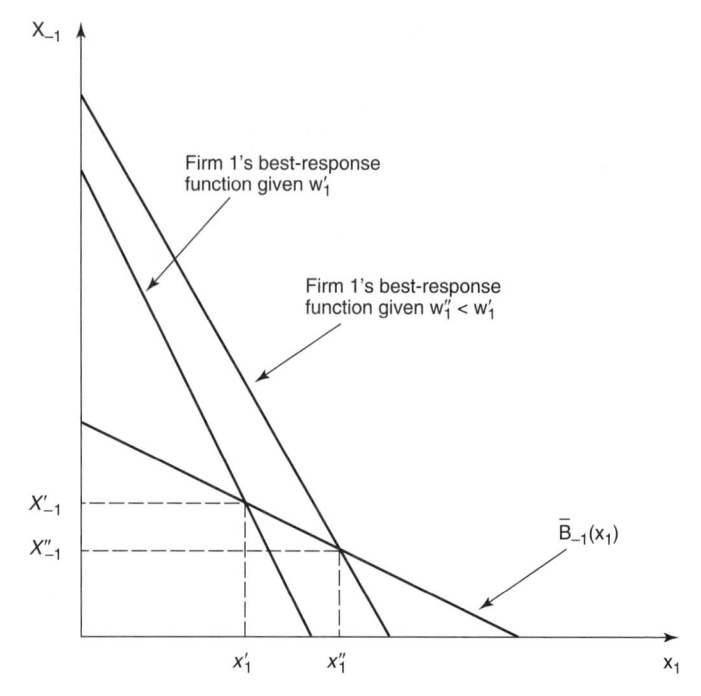

Figure 3.3
Idea behind the Baker-Bresnahan residual demand function estimation

line with slope -1, and the coefficient γ_1 estimated in equation (3.33) will be zero since any increase in firm 1's output will be met by a unit-for-unit decrease in its rivals' output.

While clever, there are at least two serious potential problems with this approach in addition to the difficulty of finding suitable instruments. First, the "equilibrium relation" between firm 1's output x_1 and its rivals' outputs x_{-1} may not take the form in (3.31). For example, if there are two firms ($N = 2$) and outputs are determined via a Stackleberg game with *firm 2* as the leader, then firm 2's output will depend on all of the variables that affect firm 1's best-response function (that is, including w_1), not just on (x_1, z, w_2).

Second, unless firm 1 is *actually* a Stackleberg leader, the output chosen by firm 1 in equilibrium will *not* be the solution to $\max_{x_1}[R_1(x_1, z, w_{-1}) - c_1]x_1$. For example, if outputs actually are determined in a simultaneous (Cournot) quantity choice game, the residual demand function derived from this procedure will not have any direct correspondence to the actual price-cost margins in the market.

Baker and Bresnahan's procedure for evaluating a merger expands on this idea. Imagine, for simplicity, an industry in which initially there are three firms, and suppose that firms 1 and 2 will merge and that firm 3 will remain independent (the idea extends again to any number of independent firms). Now suppose that the inverse demand functions for firms 1 and 2 are

$$p_1 = P_1(x_1, x_2, x_3, z) \tag{3.34}$$

and

$$p_2 = P_2(x_1, x_2, x_3, z). \tag{3.35}$$

As before, suppose that firm 3's best-response function is

$$x_3 = B_3(x_1, x_2, z, w_3). \tag{3.36}$$

Substituting as before we can write:

$$p_1 = R_1(x_1, x_2, z, w_3) \tag{3.37}$$

$$p_2 = R_2(x_1, x_2, z, w_3). \tag{3.38}$$

Equations (3.37) and (3.38) give the residual inverse demands faced by merged firms 1 and 2, taking into account firm 3's reactions to their price choices. Given estimates of these equations, Baker and Bresnahan propose evaluating the merger by computing the percentage price increase for each of the merging firms caused by a 1% reduction in *both* of their outputs, and comparing this to the two merging firms' single-firm residual inverse demand elasticities (as derived here); if these elasticities are much greater in the former case, they conclude that the merger increases market power.

Unfortunately, this method for evaluating postmerger market power suffers from the same problems as in the single-firm case. Moreover, an additional problem emerges with the method Baker and Bresnahan use to compare pre- and postmerger market power: since both of the merging firms could not have been Stackleberg leaders prior to the merger, the single-firm residual inverse demand elasticities clearly are not directly related to premerger markups.[43]

Taken together, these various problems make the residual-demand approach less useful than merger simulation.

Event-Study Approach

A third empirical technique that does not follow the *Guidelines'* method, examines the effect of a merger without *any* kind of structural estimation. The simple idea, originating in Eckbo [1983] and Stillman [1983], is as follows: A merger that will raise the prices charged by the merging firms is good for rivals, while one that will lower these prices is bad for them. Hence, we should be able to distinguish these two cases by looking at rivals' stock-price reactions to the merger announcement and any subsequent enforcement actions. (Eckbo and Stillman looked at these reactions for a number of mergers and found no positive effects on rivals, and therefore concluded that most mergers are not anticompetitive.)

Although a simple technique (it uses the standard event-study method), it has a number of potential pitfalls. The first has to do with the power of the test. McAfee and Williams [1988], for example, examine what they argue was an "obviously anticompetitive merger" and find no evidence of statistically significant positive stock-price reactions by rivals. They argue that the problem is that the rivals may be large firms with highly variable stock returns so that the power of the test may be low; that is, we should not take the lack of statistically significant reactions in rivals' stock prices to mean that the merger will not raise prices.

Another issue has to do with what the literature calls "precedent effects." If a merger is announced, this may convey information about market (or regulatory) conditions more generally. For example, consider the announcement of an efficiency-enhancing merger. This announcement may indicate not only that the merged firms' costs will fall, but also that the other firms in the industry are likely to follow their example by merging themselves. Typically, the resulting reduction in all firms' costs will lead to both lower prices and higher profits. Thus, the informational content of this announcement—what it says about likely future mergers and their effects—will lead rivals' stock prices to *increase* upon announcement of this price-reducing merger.[44]

In the other direction, there is a possibility that a merger that increases the size of a firm could also increase the likelihood of anticompetitive exclusionary behavior. For example, in a "deep pocket" model of predation in which the size of a firm's asset holdings affects its ability to predate on rivals (for example, Benoit [1984], Bolton and Scharfstein [1990]), a merger might increase the likelihood that rivals are preyed upon. This could lead to negative returns for rival stock values from announcement of a price-increasing merger.

These interpretational difficulties can be substantially avoided by looking instead at *customer* stock prices as done by Mullin, Mullin, and Mullin [1995]. Doing so allows one to look directly at the stock market's expectation of the changes in price (as well as any nonprice dimensions of buyer surplus such as quality) arising from the merger. Mullin, Mullin, and Mullin study the United States Steel (USS) dissolution suit that was filed in 1911. They begin by identifying thirteen potentially significant events in the history of the case, and then narrow their focus to five events by restricting attention to those events that caused a statistically significant movement in USS's stock price. The five events are described in table 3.2, which also indicates with a (+) or a (−) whether the event is associated with an increase or a decrease in the probability of dissolution.

They then examine the effects of these events on the stock market values of four sets of firms: steel industry rivals, railroads, the Great Northern Railway, and street railway companies. Examining steel industry rivals follows the Eckbo-Stillman method.[45] Railroads and street rail companies, in contrast, were both customers of USS, in that they bought significant quantities of steel.[46] The event responses of these groups to the five events are shown in table 3.3, which also shows the response of USS to each event.[47] As can be seen in the table, the responses of steel industry rivals are generally insignificant. The railroad stocks, however, respond to these events in a statistically and economically significant way, and in a direction that suggests that dissolution of USS would lower steel prices. Indeed, since steel represented only 10% of railroad costs, the 2% value reduction that railroads felt in response to the *USRUMOR* event would correspond to a 20% reduction in the expected

Table 3.2
Event descriptions

Variable		Description
USSRUMOR	(+)	Wall Street reacts to rumors that U.S. Steel will voluntarily dissolve and the following day the *New York Times* reports that U.S. Steel and the Department of Justice (DOJ) are negotiating the voluntary dissolution. Neither the DOJ nor U.S. Steel comments on these reports initially. September 20–21, 1911.
USSDEN	(−)	U.S. Steel announces that it is not contemplating dissolution and believes that it is not guilty of antitrust violations. September 26, 1911.
DISSUIT	(+)	The DOJ files the dissolution suit against U.S. Steel. On the same day, U.S. Steel officially announces that it will cancel the Great Northern lease and lower the freight rates on iron ore as had been previously reported. October 26, 1911.
SCTREARG	(−)	The Supreme Court orders reargument in several large antitrust cases before it, including the U.S. Steel case. May 21, 1917.
SCTDEC	(−)	The Supreme Court affirms the district court decision in U.S. Steel's favor. March 1, 1920.

Source: Mullin, Mullin, and Mullin [1995].

cost of steel if the probability of the dissolution went from 0 to 1 as a result of this news, and even more otherwise.

Two further points are also worth noting. First, while Mullin, Mullin, and Mullin found significant effects on customers, it should be noted that finding no statistically significant customer stock-price response to a merger's announcement may not indicate the absence of a price effect: If customers are themselves producers, any price increases may be fully passed on to final consumers. In addition, as

Table 3.3
Average estimated event responses

Event	Steel rivals	Railroads	Street rails
USSRUMOR	.00374	.02033	
	(.1782)	(3.0246)	
USSDEN	.00903	−.01320	
	(.4316)	(−1.9742)	
DISSUIT	−.03532	.01260	
	(−1.6874)	(1.8828)	
SCTREARG	.06233	−.01860	
	(1.7707)	(−.7394)	
SCTDEC	.04260	−.02858	−.02551
	(1.3366)	(−1.7453)	(−.3533)

Source: Mullin, Mullin, and Mullin [1995].
Note: *t*-statistics are in parentheses.

noted in the McAfee-Williams critique, the power of such a test may be low. Second, similar kinds of tests could also be run, looking instead at effects on firms that produce complements to the products of the merging firms.

Any suggestion that an antitrust authority should primarily rely on event-study analyses presumes that stock market participants are able to forecast the competitive effects of mergers more accurately (and faster) than is the agency, perhaps a questionable assumption.[48] Less extreme is the idea that an antitrust authority might use event-study evidence as just one source of information, perhaps as a check on its own internal analysis and any opinions obtained directly from industry and stock market participants.

3.6 Examining the Results of Actual Mergers

All of the foregoing discussion has focused on a *prospective* analysis of horizontal mergers. It is natural to ask, however, what we know, looking *retrospectively*, about their *actual* effects. Such analyses can be useful for at least two reasons. First, they can guide our priors about the likelihood of mergers being anticompetitive or efficiency-enhancing (ideally, as a function of their characteristics). Second, we can use this information to assess how well various methods of prospective merger analysis perform, as the Peters [2003] paper discussed in section 3.5 does for merger simulation.

Unfortunately, the economics literature contains remarkably little of this kind of analysis. In the remainder of the chapter, I discuss some studies that have looked at either price or efficiency effects in actual mergers (none look at both). This is clearly an area that could use more research.[49,50]

Price Effects

A small number of studies have analyzed the effects of actual mergers on prices. Many of these have focused on the airline industry, where a number of high-profile mergers occurred in the mid-1980s and price data are publicly available because of data reporting regulations. Borenstein [1990] studies the effects of the mergers of Northwest Airlines (NW) with Republic Airlines (RC) and Trans World Airlines (TW) with Ozark Airlines (OZ) in 1985 and 1986. In both cases, the merging airlines had their major hub at the same airport: Minneapolis served as the hub for both NW and RC; St. Louis was the hub for TW and OZ.[51] Both mergers began in 1985 with final agreements reached in the first quarter of 1986, and received regulatory approval (from the Department of Transportation) in the third quarter of 1986. Table 3.4 shows the average "relative prices" before and after the mergers for four categories of markets, defined by whether both merging firms were active competitors in the

Table 3.4
Merging airlines' price changes at their primary hubs

	Other firms	Mkts	Relative prices[a]			Av. change[a]
			1985	1986	1987	1985–1987
NW & RC	Yes	16	3.1 (2.8)	0.2 (4.5)	10.1[d] (5.9)	6.7 (4.3)
NW or RC	Yes	41	14.3[b] (2.6)	21.2[b] (3.5)	19.9[b] (2.8)	6.0[c] (2.6)
NW & RC	No	11	15.2[d] (8.2)	32.1[b] (10.3)	37.8[b] (7.5)	22.5[b] (5.2)
NW or RC	No	16	27.0[b] (6.7)	36.6[b] (9.5)	39.4[b] (7.1)	12.0[c] (5.5)
Total		84	14.7[b] (2.3)	21.5[b] (3.3)	24.1[b] (2.7)	9.5[b] (2.1)
TWA & OZ	Yes	19	−1.3 (6.1)	−2.7 (4.0)	3.2 (4.6)	4.6 (7.5)
TWA or OZ	Yes	29	10.5[c] (4.0)	4.7 (4.2)	5.7 (4.4)	−3.0 (3.1)
TWA & OZ	No	9	39.6[b] (7.5)	55.5[b] (13.2)	27.4[b] (2.4)	−5.8 (6.4)
TWA or OZ	No	10	56.0[b] (12.0)	61.4[b] (11.8)	33.5[b] (8.1)	−12.3[c] (4.0)
Total		67	17.8[b] (4.0)	17.9[b] (4.6)	12.1[b] (3.0)	−0.0 (3.5)

Source: Borenstein [1990].
Notes:
[a] Shown in percent.
[b] Significant at 1-percent level (two-tailed test).
[c] Significant at 5-percent level (two-tailed test).
[d] Significant at 10-percent level (two-tailed test).

market before the merger (that is, each firm having at least a 10% market share on the route prior to the merger and shown in the first column of the table) and by whether they faced any competition before the merger (whether there were "Other firms" in the market is shown in the second column of the table). The "Relative prices" columns record for the third quarters of 1985, 1986, and 1987 the average over markets in the respective category of the percentage difference between the average price for the merging firms in that market and the average price for a set of markets of a similar distance (throughout the table, standard errors are in parentheses). The "Av. change" over 1985–1987 is the average over markets in the respective category of the percentage difference between the 1987 "relative price" in the market and the 1985 "relative price."[52]

The results in table 3.4 reveal very different experiences following the two mergers. Prices increased following the NW-RC merger, but not following the TW-OZ merger. Looking at the different categories in the NW-RC merger, (relative) prices increased by 22.5% on average in markets which were NW and RC duopolies prior to the merger.[53] It is also noteworthy that prices also increased on routes in which NW and RC did not compete prior to the merger. This could reflect a price-constraining effect of potential entry prior to the merger, increased market power arising from domination of the hub airport after the merger, or, in the case of markets in which they faced competitors, the effects of increased levels of multimarket contact with competitor airlines. Borenstein also notes that the prices of other airlines on these routes displayed a pattern very similar to the pattern seen for the merging firms in table 3.4.

Kim and Singal [1993] expand on Borenstein's analysis by examining the price changes resulting from fourteen airline mergers that occurred from 1985 to 1988. Table 3.5 depicts the average of the changes in the relative prices for routes served by the merging firms compared to all other routes of similar distance. The table is divided horizontally into three sections: The first "full period" section looks at the change in (relative) prices from one quarter before the first bid of the acquirer to one quarter after consummation of the merger; the second "announcement period" section looks at changes from one quarter before the first bid of the acquirer to one quarter after this bid; the third "completion period" section looks at changes from one quarter before consummation to one quarter after. The table is also vertically divided into two sections. The left section looks at the merging firms' (relative) price changes, while the right section looks at rivals' (relative) price changes on the routes served by the merging firms. Within each of these sections, (relative) price changes are computed separately, depending on whether one of the merging firms was financially distressed prior to the merger. Descriptions of the variables in table 3.5 are in the notes to the table.

Looking at price changes for the merging firms, we see that relative prices rose by an average of 3.25% over the full sample period in mergers involving firms that were not financially distressed. They rose substantially more (26.35%) in mergers involving a financially distressed firm. The announcement period and completion period changes are interesting as well. One might expect market power effects to be felt prior to the actual merger (as the management teams spend time together), while merger-related efficiencies would occur only after completion. For mergers involving "normal firms" we indeed see that prices rise in the announcement period and fall—although not as much—in the completion period.[54] (The patterns for mergers involving a failing firm are more puzzling.) Price changes for rival firms again follow similar patterns. Kim and Singal also examine through regression analysis the relationship between the change in relative fares and the change in the Herfindahl-Hirschman Index. Consistent with the efficiency interpretation just given, they find that for mergers involving "normal firms," the size of the price elevation during the announcement period is highly correlated with the change in concentration induced by the merger, while the fall in prices during the completion period is unrelated to this change.

Finally, Kim and Singal break the merging firms' routes into four categories depending on whether the route involves a common hub airport for the merging firms (if so, it is a "hub" route) and whether the merging firms both served the route prior to the merger (if so, it is an "overlap" market). Table 3.6 depicts their results on (relative) price changes (in percentages) for the full period. Notably for mergers involving normal firms, prices fall on "Hub only" routes (that is, nonoverlap routes involving a common hub) and they have no change on Hub/overlap routes. (Moreover, Kim and Singal show that these price reductions come entirely during the completion period.) These changes strongly suggest the presence of merger-related efficiency benefits. "Overlap only" markets show a price change like that seen in table 3.5 for the full sample. Finally, note that routes that are neither a hub route nor an overlap route also experience price increases of this magnitude. These may reveal the effect of increased multimarket contact.[55]

Peters [2003], which was largely focused on evaluating merger simulation techniques (see section 3.5), also documents the service changes and entry events that followed six of these mergers. Peters shows that flight frequency

Table 3.5
Changes in relative fares of merging and rival firms

	Merging firms			Rival firms		
Variable	All mergers	Mergers between normal firms	Mergers with a failing firm	All mergers	Mergers between normal firms	Mergers with a failing firm
Full period:						
Sample size	11,629	8,511	3,118	8,109	5,578	2,531
Relative fares, beginning	0.9602**	1.0325**	0.7626**	0.9140**	0.9745**	0.7807**
	(0.8238**)	(0.8982**)	(0.6883**)	(0.8645**)	(0.9218**)	(0.7588**)
Relative fares, ending	1.0159**	1.0529**	0.9148**	0.9831**	1.0085	0.9272**
	(0.8850**)	(0.9309**)	(0.8015**)	(0.9287**)	(0.9472**)	(0.8944**)
Relative fare changes:	9.44**	3.25**	26.35**	12.17**	5.94**	25.90**
Lfarchg (percentage)	(9.75**)	(3.76**)	(20.66**)	(11.20**)	(4.42**)	(23.71**)
Announcement period:						
Sample size	7,214	5,832	1,382	4,891	3,730	1,161
Relative fares, beginning	0.9792**	0.9855**	0.9530**	0.9444**	0.9499**	0.9268**
	(0.8575**)	(0.8636**)	(0.8376**)	(0.8945**)	(0.9093**)	(0.8487**)
Relative fares, ending	1.0270**	1.0754**	0.8228**	0.9807**	1.0345**	0.8079**
	(0.8947**)	(0.9440**)	(0.7337**)	(0.9208**)	(0.9634**)	(0.7882**)
Relative fare changes:	5.54**	11.32**	−18.85**	5.06**	12.64**	−19.28**
Lfarchg (percentage)	(3.81**)	(10.38**)	(−17.66**)	(3.77**)	(9.73**)	(−14.80**)

Completion period:						
Sample size	7,557	6,140	1,417	5,304	4,105	1,199
Relative fares, beginning	0.9874**	1.048**	0.7247**	0.9496**	1.0201**	0.7081**
	(0.8657**)	(0.9273**)	(0.6528**)	(0.8938**)	(0.9507**)	(0.7046**)
Relative fares, ending	0.9640**	0.9652**	0.9590**	0.9764**	0.9776**	0.9725**
	(0.8683**)	(0.8724**)	(0.8541**)	(0.9296**)	(0.9286**)	(0.9332**)
Relative fare changes:	0.21	−9.00**	40.11**	6.10**	−5.36**	45.34**
Lfarchg (percentage)	(3.31**)	(−6.82**)	(38.36**)	(7.13**)	(−3.72**)	(43.24**)

Source: Kim and Singal [1993].

Notes: Relative fare is the ratio of the fare on the sample route to the weighted average fare in the control group. The relative fares are measured at the start and end of each observation period. Lfarchg is the mean of the differences between the sample and control routes in the natural logs of the ratio of fares at the end to the beginning of each period. All numbers not in parentheses represent unweighted means of the variable. All numbers in parentheses are means weighted by the number of passengers on each route. For relative fares, statistical significance is tested using the t statistic with reference to a mean of 1.00, and for Lfarchg the significance is with reference to a mean of zero.

**Statistically significant at the 1-percent level (two-tailed test).

Table 3.6
Relative fare changes for four categories of routes

Period and subsample	Mean Lfarchg, percentage [sample size]			Mean Lhhichg, percentage [sample size]			Regression coefficient (t statistic)[a]			
	Merger between normal firms	Merger with a failing firm		Merger between normal firms	Merger with a failing firm		Constant	Normal × Lhhichg	Fail × Lhhichg	R^2_{adj}
Merging firms: Full period										
Hub/overlap	−0.33 [193]	48.91** [180]		36.35** [193]	20.13** [180]		0.3174 (9.00)	−0.4891 (−6.69)	0.0920 (1.00)	0.101
Hub only	−11.01** [291]	40.23** [331]		1.89 [291]	5.81** [331]		0.1604 (6.99)	−0.0461 (−0.45)	0.0837 (0.72)	−0.002
Overlap only	3.92** [1,205]	40.12** [566]		22.49** [1,205]	19.92** [566]		0.1535 (11.89)	−0.1370 (−4.56)	0.3512 (5.28)	0.044
Neither	3.84** [6,822]	18.28** [2,041]		0.84** [6,822]	4.02** [2,041]		0.0690 (16.59)	0.1945 (12.12)	0.1548 (3.38)	0.016

Source: Kim and Singal [1993].
Notes: Lfarchg is described in Table 3.5.
Lhhichg is the difference between the sample and control routes in the natural logs of the ratio of the Herfindahl-Hirschman index at the end to the beginning of each period.
[a] Lfarchg$_i = \alpha + \beta_1$Normal$_i \times$ Lhhichg$_i + \beta_2$Fail$_i \times$ Lhhichg$_i + \varepsilon_i$.
** Statistically significant at the 1-percent level (two-tailed test).

tended to decrease in markets that initially were served by both merging firms, and increase in markets that initially were served by only one of the merging firms.[56] The mergers also led to entry, although changes in the number of rivals were only statistically significant for three of the mergers.

Banking is another industry in which firms are required to provide the government with data on their operations. Prager and Hannan [1998] study the price effects of mergers in the U.S. banking industry from January 1992 through June 1994. They examine the change in deposit rates for three types of deposits, NOW accounts (interest-bearing checking accounts), MMDA accounts (personal money market deposit accounts), and 3MOCD accounts (three-month certificates of deposit).[57] Hannan and Prager separately examine the effects of "substantial horizontal mergers" in which the Herfindahl-Hirschman Index in the affected market increases by at least 200 points to a postmerger value of at least 1800, and "less substantial mergers," in which the Herfindahl-Hirschman Index increases by at least 100 points to a postmerger value of at least 1400 and which were not "substantial mergers." Their price data are monthly observations on deposit interest rates from October 1991 through August 1994, while their estimating equation takes the form

$$ratchg_{it} = \alpha + \sum_{t=2}^{T} \delta_t I_t + \sum_{n=-12}^{+12} \beta_n SM_{int} + \sum_{n=-12}^{+12} \gamma_n LSM_{int} + \varepsilon_{it},$$

where $ratchg_{it} = \ln(rate_{it}/rate_{i,t-1})$ and $rate_{it}$ is bank i's deposit rate in period t, I_t is a dummy variable taking value 1 in period t and 0 otherwise, SM_{int} is a dummy variable taking value 1 if bank i was exposed to a substantial horizontal merger in period $t+n$, and LSM_{int} is a dummy variable taking value 1 if bank i was exposed to a less substantial horizontal merger in period $t+n$.[58] The results from this estimation can be seen in table 3.7, where the merger exposure effects are presented in three aggregates: the premerger period ($n=-12$ to $n=0$), the postmerger period ($n=1$ to $n=+12$), and the total period.

The results indicate that substantial mergers reduce the rates that banks in a market offer. This effect is largest for NOW accounts (approximately a 17% reduction in rates), for which customers arguably have the strongest attachment to local banks, and least for three-month CD's (less than 2% reduction in rates, and not statistically significant). Notably, however, Prager and Hannan find that less substantial mergers increase rates paid in the market. One possible interpretation of this difference is that these mergers involve efficiencies (which allow banks, in the absence of other effects, to increase their rates), but the effects of these efficiencies on prices are more than offset by an increase in market power for substantial mergers. Unlike in Kim and Singal [1993], the direction of these effects is the same in the pre- and postmerger period. Finally, although the results in table 3.7 do not distinguish between the price changes for merging firms and their rivals, Prager and Hannan find that these two groups had similar price effects, paralleling the Borenstein [1990] and Kim and Singal [1993] findings on this point.

In a recent paper, Focarelli and Panetta [2003] study bank mergers in Italy during the years 1990–1998 and their effects on deposit rates. Like Kim and Singal [1993] and Prager and Hannan [1998], they separately look at announcement (which they call "transition") and completion periods. However, they look at a much longer time period after the

Table 3.7
Price effects of "substantial" and "less than substantial" bank mergers

	NOW			MMDA			3MOCD		
	Coeff.	t-stat	prob >|t|	Coeff.	t-stat	prob >|t|	Coeff.	t-stat	prob >|t|
Premerger effect									
Substantial mergers	−0.0865	−1.431	0.159	−0.0139	−0.429	0.670	0.0023	0.129	0.898
Lesser mergers	0.0585	2.050	0.046	−0.0081	−0.459	0.648	0.0148	0.877	0.385
Post merger effect									
Substantial mergers	−0.0882	−2.348	0.023	−0.0765	−4.349	0.000	−0.0178	−0.687	0.495
Lesser mergers	0.0368	1.326	0.191	0.0042	0.135	0.893	0.0443	1.689	0.098
Total effect									
Substantial mergers	−0.1747	−2.413	0.020	−0.0905	−2.317	0.025	−0.0155	−0.450	0.655
Lesser mergers	0.0953	2.422	0.019	−0.0038	−0.109	0.913	0.0590	1.728	0.091
Number of observations	13313			13498			12972		
Number of banks	435			443			433		
Average observations per bank	30.60			30.47			29.96		
Regression R^2	0.0896			0.1409			0.3586		

Source: Prager and Hannan [1998].

Notes: OLS with robust standard errors[2]; dependent variable: $ratchg_{it}$.

[1] Each regression includes 33 month indicators and 25 weighted merger indicators ($I[t=m]$ for $m = 2$ to 34 and I[bank i "exposed" to merger in month $t - n$], $n = -12, \ldots, 0, \ldots, 12$). Coefficients for these variables are not reported in order to conserve space.

[2] The estimation technique employed here allows for the possibility of error correlation across observations within the same state.

merger when examining the completion period (for each merger, they consider the effects until the end of their sample), arguing that a long time period may be required to realize efficiencies from merger. Like Kim and Singal they find evidence of market power effects during the announcement/transition period as deposit rates fall during this period. However, they find that in the long run these mergers increased deposit rates. Thus, in this case, the price-reducing effects of merger-related efficiencies seem to have dominated the price-increasing effects of increased market power.

Some recent studies have been done as well in other industries in which price data are available. Hosken and Taylor [2004] study the effects of a 1997 joint venture that combined the refining and retail gas station operations of the Marathon and Ashland oil companies. Specifically, they examine retail and wholesale price changes in Louisville, Kentucky, a city where this merger raised concentration significantly (the wholesale Herfindahl-Hirschman Index increased from 1477 to 2263; the retail index increased by over 250, ending up in the 1500–1600 range). They conclude that there is no evidence that the merger caused either wholesale or retail prices to increase.[59] In contrast, Hastings [2004] finds that rivals' prices did increase following ARCO's 1997 acquisition (through long-term lease) of 260 stations from Thrifty, an unbranded retailer. Vita and Sacher [2001] document large price increases arising from a 1990 merger between the only two hospitals in the city of Santa Cruz, California. The acquirer in this case was a non-profit hospital. Hospital markets, which also have data publicly available because of regulatory requirements, have also been the subject of some other work evaluating price and service effects of mergers; see Pautler [2003].[60]

There is one important caveat to the interpretations we have been giving to observed price changes in these studies: throughout, we have been assuming that the product remains unchanged. An alternative explanation for price increases or decreases instead may be that the merger led to changes in the quality of the merged firms' products. Thus, rather than market power, price increases may reflect quality improvements; and rather than cost reductions, price decreases may reflect quality degradation. That said, many of the papers we have discussed document patterns that are suggestive of some (if not all) of the interpretations these papers give to their findings. For example, the price increases during the Kim and Singal [1993] announcement period are unlikely to come from quality improvements. Likewise, Focarelli and Panetta [2003] explicitly examine and reject the hypothesis that the long-run increases in merging banks' interest rates that they document are because of quality degradation.

In summary, the literature documenting price effects of mergers has shown that mergers can lead to either price increases or decreases, in keeping with the central market power versus efficiency trade-off that we have discussed. There is also some evidence that more substantial mergers are more likely to raise prices. The use of postmerger evidence to evaluate techniques for prospective merger analysis is unfortunately much more limited.

Efficiencies

Just as with price effects, remarkably little has been done examining the effects of horizontal mergers on productive efficiency. Indeed, here the evidence is even thinner. Most of the work examining the efficiency effects of mergers has examined mergers in general, rather than focusing on horizontal mergers. In general, the effects need not be the same. On the one hand, there may be greater potential for synergies when the merging firms are in the same industry; on the other hand, since horizontal mergers may increase market power, even efficiency-decreasing horizontal mergers may be profitable for merging firms.[61]

Work examining mergers in general has typically found that there is a great deal of heterogeneity in merger outcomes. Some mergers turn out well, others very badly.[62] As well, the average effects are sensitive to both the time period examined and the particular sample of mergers studied. Perhaps the best-known study of postmerger performance is Ravenscraft and Scherer [1987], who document using the FTC's Line of Business data (collected for just three years, from 1974–1976) a dramatic decline in postmerger profitability of acquired lines of business, which generally were highly successful prior to acquisition. Ravenscraft and Scherer's sample, however, largely consisted of acquisitions from the conglomerate merger wave of the 1960s. Two different studies have examined data from the years following this conglomerate merger wave: Lichtenberg and Siegel [1987] and McGuckin and Nguyen [1995]. Lichtenberg and Siegel examine the effect of ownership changes on statistically estimated total-factor productivity at the plant level using the Census Bureau's Longitudinal Establishment Data (LED) for the years 1972–1981. (Total-factor productivity is determined in much of their work as the residual from estimation of a Cobb-Douglas production function.) As can be seen in table 3.8 (where "year t" is the year of the merger), in contrast to the Ravenscraft and Scherer findings, they find that acquired plants were less productive than industry averages prior to acquisition, but had productivity increases

Table 3.8
Differences in mean levels of productivity between plants changing ownership in year t and plants not changing ownership

Year	Level of productivity (residual)[a]
$t-7$	−2.6 (4.00)
$t-6$	−3.0 (5.06)
$t-5$	−3.4 (6.50)
$t-4$	−3.3 (6.77)
$t-3$	−3.3 (7.40)
$t-2$	−3.6 (8.71)
$t-1$	−3.7 (9.59)
t	−3.9 (9.10)
$t+1$	−2.9 (6.06)
$t+2$	−2.7 (6.00)
$t+3$	−2.5 (4.97)
$t+4$	−1.9 (3.52)
$t+5$	−1.9 (3.23)
$t+6$	−1.8 (2.57)
$t+7$	−1.2 (1.16)

Source: Lichtenberg and Siegel [1987].
Note:
[a] t-statistics to test H_0: difference equals 0 in parentheses.

that brought them almost up to the industry average after the acquisition. This may reflect the undoing of Ravenscraft and Scherer's inefficient conglomerate mergers.

The LED database, however, contains primarily large plants. McGuckin and Nguyen [1995] study the same question using instead the Census Bureau's Longitudinal Research Database (LRD) for the years 1977–1987. They restrict attention to mergers occurring between 1977 and 1982 and focus on the food manufacturing industry (SIC 20). This sample includes many more small plants than in Lichtenberg and Siegel's analysis. It also includes plants that only operated during part of the sample period (an "unbalanced panel"), while Lictenberg and Siegel used a balanced panel (a balanced panel may worsen selection biases). However, instead of a measure of total-factor productivity most of their analysis uses labor productivity (the average product of labor relative to the industry average product), which can be affected by shifts in the mix of inputs. In contrast to Lichtenberg and Siegel, McGuckin and Nguyen find that acquired plants have above-average productivity prior to acquisition, although they find that this is not true when they restrict attention to large plants like those studied by Lichtenberg and Siegel. Like Lichtenberg and Siegel, they find postmerger productivity improvements.

Unfortunately, neither of these studies deals with endogeneity or selection issues when estimating productivity, which we know can seriously bias productivity estimates (see Olley and Pakes [1996]). In addition, neither of these studies considers separately the effects of horizontal mergers. In fact, ideally we would like to know how horizontal mergers affect productivity *conditional* on their structural attributes (for example, potential for increasing market power).

One study that examines horizontal mergers explicitly is Pesendorfer [2003], which studies a horizontal merger wave in the paper industry during the mid-1980s. Rather than estimating productivity directly, Pesendorfer tries to infer pre- and postmerger productivity using the firms' capacity choices. (Much as we discussed in the first parts of sections 3.4 and 3.5, he infers marginal costs from the Cournot-like first-order conditions for capacity choice.) This is an interesting idea, but it is unfortunately not entirely convincing in his application.[63]

In summary, the evidence on the efficiency effects of horizontal mergers provides little guidance at this point. There is reason, however, to be hopeful that we will learn more soon. Recent work, most notably Olley and Pakes [1996], has greatly improved our ability to estimate productivity (see also Levinsohn and Petrin [2003]). The examination of the productivity effects of horizontal mergers seems a natural (and highly valuable) direction for this work to go.

4 Exclusionary Vertical Contracts

4.1 Introduction

In this chapter, I shift focus from horizontal agreements to vertical ones. By "vertical," I mean agreements between two parties located at different stages of the production and distribution chain. These parties might, for example, be a machinery manufacturer and his industrial customer, or a distributer and a local retailer. And, although not strictly "vertical" in this sense, similar principles can apply to two sellers of complementary goods (where the producer of one complementary good can be viewed as a "supplier" to the other).

While the aim of anticompetitive horizontal agreements is collusion (broadly interpreted), the concern arising from the vertical agreements, or contracts, that I focus on here is exclusion. Exclusionary vertical contracts have a long and controversial history in U.S. antitrust law and commentary. For much of the twentieth century, the U.S. courts expressed hostility toward practices such as exclusive contracts, vertical mergers, and tied sales, fearing in each case that they would serve to exclude rivals and thereby reduce competition. Then, beginning in the 1950s, these views came under a withering attack from authors whose arguments are traceable to the University of Chicago oral tradition associated with Aaron Director (for example, Director and Levi [1956], Posner [1976], Bork [1978]). In each case, this attack was two-pronged. First, using simple price theoretic or monopoly models, the Chicago School argued that the traditional concern was simply illogical: rational firms would not engage in the practice for anticompetitive reasons. Second, they suggested other efficiency-enhancing reasons why firms would want to write such contracts. The Chicago School's arguments were enormously influential and continue to affect markedly current courts' views of these practices. (As a matter of intellectual history, this is a good example of the power of theoretical models: the Chicago School had models; their opponents had none.)

Beginning in the mid-1980s, the infiltration of game theory into industrial organization allowed researchers to formally model oligopolistic markets. As a result, many old questions in the field were revisited, using formal models. Among those were questions concerning exclusionary vertical contracts. Using game theoretic models, researchers showed that the courts' traditional concerns might not be illogical after all; in well-specified models, rational firms would, in some circumstances, use such contracts to exclude rivals and reduce competition.

In this chapter, I provide an introduction to this topic. The chapter differs greatly in emphasis from chapters 2 and 3. In contrast to price fixing and horizontal mergers, exclusionary vertical contracts is one of the most controversial areas of antitrust. Moreover, it is an area in which there are new theoretical developments that are not yet widely understood, and in which there is not yet much convincing empirical work. As such, the main emphasis in the chapter is on those theoretical models and what they tell us.

I focus here on one particular type of exclusionary vertical contract: exclusive contracts. An exclusive contract states that one party to the contract will deal only with the other party for some set of transactions. They are, in a sense, the purest form of exclusionary vertical contract. Other types of exclusionary vertical contracts, such as vertical mergers and tied sales, share not only the same intellectual history (recounted earlier), but also many of the same underlying economic principles.[1]

Exclusive contracts, and exclusionary vertical practices more generally, are featured in many of the most prominent antitrust cases. In the recent *Microsoft* case [253 F.3d 34 (2001)], for example, Microsoft was accused of requiring computer manufacturers, internet service providers, and software producers to exclude, at least partially, Netscape's Navigator Web browser in favor of its own Internet Explorer browser.[2] It has also been an active area of late. Recent cases involving exclusive contracts include *U.S. v. Visa U.S.A.* [344 F.3d 229 (2003)] in which Visa was attacked for its agreements with banks that prohibited them from distributing rival credit cards, including American Express and Discover; *U.S. v. Dentsply* [399 F.3d 181 (2001)] in which Dentsply, the dominant maker of artificial teeth, was accused of illegally excluding rival manufacturers through exclusive agreements with dental wholesalers; and *Conwood v. United States Tobacco* [290 F.3d 768 (2002)] in which United States Tobacco, the dominant producer of moist snuff, was accused of illegally excluding rivals using exclusive contracts with retailers.[3]

U.S. courts apply the rule of reason when analyzing exclusive contracts, based on the view that they can create both anticompetitive harm and efficiency-enhancing benefits. I discuss both possibilities, focusing first on their possible anticompetitive effects.

4.2 The Traditional and Chicago Views of Exclusive Contracts

Through much of the twentieth century the U.S. courts treated exclusive dealing harshly, albeit via the rule of reason. The justification for this treatment was their concern that exclusive contracts might lead to "market foreclosure"; that is, exclusion of competitors and consequent monopolization. For example, in one well-known case, *Standard Fashion Company v. Magrane-Houston Company* [258 U.S. 346 (1922)], a leading manufacturer of dress patterns (Standard) contracted with prominent Boston retailer Magrane-Houston to sell its patterns on the condition that Magrane-Houston not sell the patterns of any other manufacturer. Fearful of the foreclosure of competitors from retail outlets, the court struck down the contract, arguing that

> The restriction of each merchant to one pattern manufacturer must in hundreds, perhaps in thousands, of small communities amount to giving such single pattern manufacturer a monopoly of the business in such community. Even in larger cities, to limit to a single pattern maker the pattern business of dealers most resorted to by customers whose purchases tend to give fashions their vogue, may tend to facilitate further combinations; so that plaintiff... will shortly have almost, if not quite, all of the pattern business.

Certainly, if a buyer signs an exclusive contract, all other sellers are foreclosed from competing for that buyer's business. The Chicago critique of exclusive contracts focuses, however, on whether exclusion through this means can be profitable for the seller.[4] Bork [1978, 306–307], commenting on *Standard Fashion*, put it this way (note both the attack on the view that exclusives can be anticompetitive and the suggestion of other efficiency-enhancing motives):

> Standard can extract in the prices that it charges all that its line is worth. It cannot charge the retailer that full amount in money and then charge it again in exclusivity that the retailer does not wish to grant. To suppose that it can is to commit the error of double counting.... Exclusivity has necessarily been purchased from it, which means that the store has balanced the inducement offered by Standard... against the disadvantage of handling only Standard's patterns.... The store's decision, made entirely in its own interest, necessarily reflects the balance of competing considerations that determine consumer welfare.... If Standard finds it worthwhile to purchase exclusivity..., the reason is not the barring of entry, but some more sensible goal, such as obtaining the special selling effort of the outlet.

To see this argument more formally, consider the following simple model of exclusive contracting: There are three parties, a buyer (B), an incumbent seller (I), and a potential entrant (E). Initially, the potential entrant is not in the market, and so the buyer can contract only with the incumbent. The buyer's demand is $D(p)$ when facing price p. The incumbent's cost is c_I per unit. The potential entrant must incur an entry cost of $f > 0$ to enter the market; if it does so, its marginal cost is then $c_E < c_I$.

The timing of the "exclusive contracting game" is as follows: First, I can offer B an exclusive contract along with a payment t in return for B signing the contract. Second, B decides whether to accept the contract. Third, after observing whether B has signed an exclusive contract, E decides whether to enter (and incur the entry cost f). Finally, whichever firms are in the market name prices to B, who then chooses from whom and how much to purchase.[5]

For simplicity, assume that should E enter, E wins B's business at a price just below c_I. Formally, this is true if $p = c_I$ solves $\max_{p \leq c_I}(p - c_E)D(p)$.[6] Finally, to focus on the interesting case, assume that E would enter in the absence of an exclusive contract. That is true if $(c_I - c_E)D(c_I) > f$. Of course, should E not enter, I will charge B the monopoly price p^m that solves $\max_p(p - c)D(p)$.

In this setting, by offering a large enough payment t, the incumbent certainly *can* induce the buyer to sign an exclusive contract and thereby achieve the monopoly outcome. But, is it *profitable* for him to do so? The Chicago School's answer is no. The reason is that B will not sign an exclusive contract, and commit to buying at a monopoly price, unless I compensates him for his lost consumer surplus. After all, B knows that if he does not sign he will get a competitive outcome (that is, a price of c_I). This loss is the amount $x^* = \int_{c_I}^{p^m} D(s)\,ds$, equal to the total shaded area in figure 4.1. But, if I offers B this amount of compensation, I incurs a loss since its monopoly profit π^m on sales to B will equal only the darkly shaded area in the figure, which is less than the required compensation x^*. The difference arises precisely because of the deadweight loss of monopoly pricing. Thus, while I can get B to sign and thereby exclude E, it is not profitable for I to do so.

We have assumed a very specific bargaining process between B and I in the first two stages of the game (I makes B a take-it-or-leave-it offer). But the conclusion is more general than this. Indeed, as long as B and I bargain under complete information, we expect them to reach an agreement

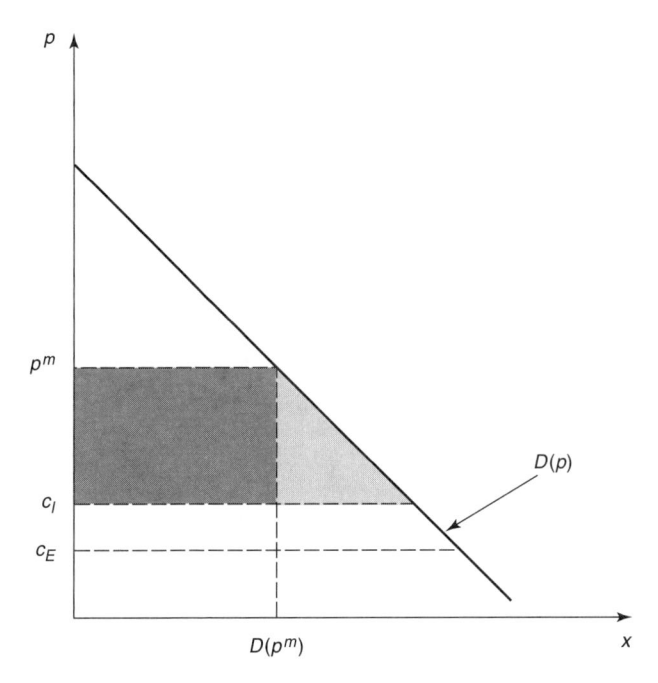

Figure 4.1
The Chicago School argument

that maximizes their joint payoff, regardless of how their respective bargaining powers and positions affect the split of this joint payoff. This reflects what I call the *bilateral contracting principle*: if two parties (i) contract in isolation, (ii) have complete information about each others' payoffs, and if (iii) lump-sum transfers are possible, then they will reach an agreement that maximizes their joint payoff. Here B and I's joint payoff is $\pi^m + \int_{c_I}^{\infty} D(s)\,ds - x^*$ if an exclusive is signed, and $\int_{c_I}^{\infty} D(s)\,ds$ if it is not. Since $\pi^m - x^* < 0$, not signing an exclusive, and thereby allowing entry, maximizes their joint payoff.

4.3 Anticompetitive Exclusive Dealing: First-mover Models

The Chicago critique, while very insightful, turns out to be rather special. In recent years, a number of authors have shown how sensible alterations to this Chicago School model can make exclusive contracts a profitable strategy for excluding rivals. These models all have the feature that some form of externality arises from an exclusive contract signed by two parties onto other individuals, and this externality makes the contract jointly optimal for the contracting parties. In this section, I describe two models of anticompetitive exclusive contracting in which, like the simple Chicago School model, the incumbent has a first-mover advantage in being able to contract with buyers prior to an entrant's arrival in the market.

Partial Exclusion through Stipulated Damages

The first such model was due to Aghion and Bolton [1987] who showed that a buyer and seller could use stipulated damage clauses to extract profits from a potential entrant. The basic idea is that a buyer and a seller can use a stipulated damage to make the buyer less willing to switch to an entrant. By doing so, they can strategically force the entrant to lower the price he offers the buyer, which increases the buyer and seller's joint profits. The damage provision typically also creates an inefficiency, because the damage clause is exclusionary, leading the buyer to buy from the entrant less frequently than is socially efficient.

To see Aghion and Bolton's point, suppose as before that there are three parties: a buyer B, an incumbent I, and a potential entrant E. Assume now that B needs at most one unit of the good and values it at v. The incumbent's and entrant's costs now satisfy $(c_I - c_E) > f$, so that E will enter once again if B and I do not sign a contract.

The important change from the Chicago School model is that now B and I can sign a contract that specifies a price p for the good and a damage payment d that B must pay to I should B instead buy from E.[7] The timing of the game is similar to the Chicago School model: First I and B can agree to a contract with price and damage terms (p, d). We will be agnostic about the precise bargaining process they follow, assuming only that it satisfies the bilateral contracting principle stated in section 4.2.[8] Second, E decides whether to enter (and pay f). Finally, if E enters he offers a price p_E to B, who decides whether to buy from I or E; if E does not enter, B buys from I (assuming $p < v$).

To see how the ability to specify price and damage terms matters, start at the end of the game, after B and I have signed a contract with terms (p, d) and E has entered and offered price p_E. In this circumstance, B will decide from whom to purchase by comparing the incumbent's price p to the total cost of buying from E, $p_E + d$. Equivalently, we can think of B comparing I's "effective price" $p - d$ (the incremental cost of buying versus not buying from I) with E's price p_E. So B will buy from E provided that $p_E \leq p - d$. This implies that E will find it profitable to make a sale to B if and only if $c_E \leq p - d$, and when he does so he will set $p_E = p - d$.[9]

It is now easy to see which contract B and I optimally will sign. Observe that the largest possible aggregate surplus in this setting is $v - c_E - f$, the aggregate surplus if E enters and makes a sale to B. Consider a contract that sets I's effective price $p - d$ equal to (or just slightly above) $c_E + f$. At this effective price, E is just barely profitable if he enters and sells to B at price $p - d$. Thus, he will do this, and earn (essentially) zero. But this means that with this contract the largest possible surplus is achieved, and that together B and I get all of it. They cannot do better than this.

The lesson is that by setting the stipulated damage appropriately (to induce the right effective price), B and I can extract all of the surplus that E brings to the market. Intuitively, by setting a low effective price, the contract puts B in a tough bargaining position when he deals with E, forcing E to lower his price offer to B (from c_I without a contract, to $c_E + f$ with a contract) if he wants to make the sale.

So far, however, there is nothing inefficient about this; it is just a pure transfer from E to B and I. However, if we change the model slightly to incorporate uncertainty over E's marginal cost c_E (as Aghion and Bolton do), then inefficiency arises as well. To see a simple example, imagine that $v = 1$, $c_I = \frac{1}{2}$, and c_E is uniformly distributed between 0 and 1. Assume also that $f = 0$. In this case, social efficiency calls for E to make the sale whenever $c_E < \frac{1}{2}$. This can be achieved either by having no contract (which results in a Bertrand pricing game between I and E) or, alternatively, by having a contract with $p - d = \frac{1}{2}$. Now consider B and I's optimal contract. Letting $\Delta \equiv p - d$ denote the effective price in the contract, this involves (by the bilateral contracting principle) choosing Δ to maximize their joint payoff:

$$\max_{\Delta} \ \Pr(c_E < \Delta)(v - \Delta) + \Pr(c_E \geq \Delta)\left(v - \frac{1}{2}\right).$$

Here, $(v - \Delta)$ is B and I's joint payoff when E makes the sale at price Δ, while $(v - \frac{1}{2})$ is their joint payoff when instead I makes the sale to B. The terms $\Pr(c_E < \Delta)$ and $\Pr(c_E \geq \Delta)$ are the probabilities of these two events given the effective price Δ. Substituting for the values of these probabilities given the uniform distribution of c_E, this problem becomes

$$\max_{\Delta} \; \Delta(v - \Delta) + (1 - \Delta)\left(v - \frac{1}{2}\right).$$

The optimum is $\Delta^* = \frac{1}{4}$, which results in less entry than is socially optimal (E enters and makes a sale only when $c_E < \frac{1}{4}$, rather than when $c_E < \frac{1}{2}$).

Intuitively, B and I together act like a monopsonist, using their contract to commit to a price (Δ) at which they are willing to buy from E. Like any monopsonist, they trade off the probability of making a purchase against the price they must pay E for the good, and end up purchasing the good too infrequently.

Two further points are worth noting about the Aghion and Bolton model. First, the result depends on B and I's ability to commit to the terms of their contract. This could be undermined if they are able to renegotiate those terms once E enters. In some cases, this can completely vitiate the value of the contract. For example, suppose that once E makes his (take-it-or-leave-it) offer, B and I are able to renegotiate their contract costlessly. By the bilateral contracting principle, they will reach an efficient agreement given E's offer, buying from E if and only if $p_E \leq c_I$.[10] But if E anticipates such renegotiation, he always will offer price $p_E = c_I$ regardless of the contract B and I have signed, and none of E's profits will be extracted (see Spier and Whinston [1995]).[11]

Second, observe that while the Aghion and Bolton model provides an important contrast to the Chicago School result, it is not a good model of the complete exclusion that occurs with exclusive contracts. The reason is that the whole point of Aghion and Bolton's stipulated damage contract is to extract some of E's profit; if E never enters, then there is no profit to extract. Thus, if we want to explain the use of exclusive contracts, we need to look elsewhere. The next model does just this.

Externalities across Buyers

To develop a model in which exclusive contracts are signed for anticompetitive motives, let us return to the Chicago School model. In that model, B's insistence on compensation for his lost surplus made inducing him to sign an exclusive contract an unprofitable proposition for I. To change this calculation, suppose instead that there is more than one buyer and that E has scale economies (possibly because of an entry cost), as in Rasmussen, Ramseyer, and Wiley [1991] and Segal and Whinston [2000a].[12] In that case, entry will occur only if a sufficient number of buyers have not signed exclusive contracts. As a result, the contract signed by any one buyer can have a negative externality on all other buyers by reducing the likelihood of entry. (The protection of competition is, in a sense, a public good.) Intuitively, in such circumstances, the incumbent may find it worthwhile to induce a particular buyer or subset of buyers to sign because by doing so he can monopolize *other* buyers without paying them anything. More subtle is the fact that, in the end, the incumbent may not need to pay compensation to any of the buyers if they each expect that enough other buyers will sign anyway.

To make these points clearer, consider a simple example with three buyers. Suppose that each buyer has demand curve $D(\cdot)$, and that as before I's unit cost is c_I while E has entry cost $f > 0$ and marginal cost $c_E < c_I$. For illustrative purposes, imagine that the monopoly profit from any single buyer is $\pi^m = 9$, and that each buyer loses $x^* = 12$ if he foregoes competition (hence, the deadweight loss from monopoly pricing is 3). To introduce externalities across buyers, suppose that the entry cost f is such that it takes two free buyers for E to be willing to enter:

$$2(c_I - c_E)D(c_I) > f > (c_I - c_E)D(c_I).$$

There are a number of possible bargaining processes one could consider here in terms of who makes offers and in what sequence, whether contracts are observable, and whether I can discriminate across buyers by offering different deals to different buyers. Here we examine three possibilities.[13]

Suppose, first, that I makes simultaneous public offers to the three buyers (that is, the offers are observable to all buyers) and cannot discriminate among them. Hence, I offers each buyer the same payment t to sign. For any strictly positive offer $t < x^*$, there are two possible equilibrium responses by the buyers. One possibility is that none sign: if a buyer expects all other buyers to reject I's offer, he will reject it as well since he anticipates E's entry and the compensation offered by I is less than his benefit from competition, x^*. The other possibility is that all sign: as long as each buyer expects all others to sign, he will reason that E will not enter regardless of his own decision. In this case, as long as I offers even a penny the buyer will surely take it. Thus, there is an equilibrium in which I gets every buyer to sign for free. (Or, certainly, for a penny each.)

While this establishes the possibility of a rational incumbent using exclusive contracts for anticompetitive ends, one might worry that the result is fragile, since it relies on buyers failing to coordinate on what is for them a Pareto superior equilibrium response (all rejecting I's offers). Once I can discriminate across buyers, however, the anticompetitive use of exclusive contracts becomes a much more robust phenomenon. To see this, suppose that I can make simultaneous but distinct public offers to the buyers. Then, in this example, I always will exclude E. In particular, if I offers $t = 12 + \varepsilon$ for any small $\varepsilon > 0$ (that is, 12 plus a "penny") to two of the three buyers, those buyers will accept regardless of what they think other buyers are doing (they are being paid strictly more than their value from losing competition). By doing so, I earns monopoly profits from three buyers, while compensating only two buyers for their lost surplus; I's net gain from exclusion is then $3(9) - 2(12) = 3 > 0$. The incumbent is able to "divide and conquer" the buyers, taking advantage of the negative externalities they impose on one another.

In fact, the incumbent's ability to do this may be even greater than that. Imagine, instead, that I approaches the buyers *sequentially*, making an offer first to buyer 1, then to buyer 2, and finally to buyer 3. Observe, first, that by the logic in the previous paragraph, if buyer 1 rejects I's offer, then I will find it worthwhile to induce buyers 2 and 3 to sign. Thus, buyer 1, recognizing that if he does not sign the other buyers will, is willing to sign for (essentially) free. Once buyer 1 has done so, buyer 2 finds himself in a similar situation: if he rejects I's offer, I will find it worthwhile to pay 12 to buyer 3 to earn the monopoly profit of 9 from each of buyers 2 and 3 (he gets the monopoly profit from buyer 1, who has already signed, in any case). So buyer 2 will also sign for free. The result is that, in this simple example, the incumbent excludes for free. More generally, the ability of the incumbent to approach buyers sequentially both reduces the cost of successful exclusion, and makes it more likely that the incumbent will find exclusion profitable.[14] In fact, as the number of symmetric buyers grows large, so that each buyer becomes a very small part of aggregate demand, the incumbent is certain to be able to exclude for free (see Segal and Whinston [2000a]).

Thus, once there are multiple buyers, rational incumbents may find exclusion through exclusive contracts to be profit maximizing.

A number of points are worth noting about this result. First, the critical factor leading to this conclusion is the presence of scale economies, which makes E's entry decision for one buyer depend on the availability of other buyers. This suggests that the presence of scale economies should be one of the central factual questions in settings in which exclusive contracts are alleged to be harming competition. However, scale economies need not be in the form of entry costs to get exclusionary effects. For example, similar effects can arise if there are instead demand-side economies of scale arising from network externalities. Also, cost-based scale economies could take a less extreme form than here. For example, E might have a more continuous investment in cost reduction whose optimal level is lower when he anticipates making fewer sales (an entry cost is just an extreme form of this, where paying f lowers marginal cost from infinity to c_E).[15]

Second, buyers are symmetric in this model. With asymmetrically sized buyers, we would expect buyers of different sizes to get different offers from the incumbent. Specifically, we would expect that large buyers, who are pivotal to whether profitable exclusion can occur, would get offered better deals than small buyers.

Third, entry is a one-time possibility in the model. In reality, it is likely to be a continuing concern. To succeed in continuing exclusion, an incumbent needs to ensure that the number of free buyers is low at every point in time. This will involve the incumbent staggering the expiration dates of his contracts if these are of limited duration. With staggered expirations, the number of free customers at any point in time is inversely related to the contracts' duration; the longer the duration, the fewer contracts are up for renewal at any time.[16]

Fourth, one might ask how this result would be affected if the buyers were not final customers, but rather were firms that compete with one another. Competition among buyers has two opposing effects on the likelihood of profitable exclusion. First, it can reduce the number of free buyers that E needs for entry to be profitable. For example, if the buyers are identical homogeneous retailers, then E need only gain access to one retailer to serve the entire market. Second, it changes the loss that a buyer anticipates from foregoing competition. Retailers, for instance, may pass through much or all of any reduction in input prices, so they may see little loss from signing contracts that prevent entry.

To see an example of these two effects, imagine that there are $N \geq 2$ identical homogeneous retailers who, for simplicity, have no marginal costs other than input acquisition costs. Let $D(\cdot)$ now be the aggregate demand function. If E does not enter, then all retailers earn zero, since I will set its input price to every retailer at its monopoly level, the price p^m that solves $\max_p (p - c_I) D(p)$. If E enters and at least two retailers are free, then E will sell to all free retailers at the input price that solves $\max_{p \leq c_I} (p - c_E) D(p)$. These retailers will make all of the sales in the market (captive retailers will be priced out of the market) but again will earn zero profit. Finally, if E enters and only one retailer is free, this retailer may make a positive profit. If E's cost advantage $(c_I - c_E)$ is small, E will set its input price equal to c_I and this retailer will earn zero. However, if E's cost advantage is large and demand is sufficiently elastic at $p = c_I$, then E will set its input price below c_I, and the free retailer will earn a strictly positive profit $\pi_R^* > 0$.

Now consider the outcome of exclusive contracting at the beginning of the game. When retailers earn zero profit no matter what, I can sign each of them for free. They simply see no gain from competition because they do not care about the gain to final consumers. In this case, competition among buyers makes exclusion easier. On the other hand, if E would set its price to a single free retailer below c_I, and if this outcome generates enough profit for E to cover its fixed entry cost f, then I needs to pay π_R^* to *every* retailer to exclude E. This will not be profitable for I if the number of retailers N is large enough. In that case, competition among buyers makes exclusion harder.[17]

Fifth, one might wonder what happens when it is possible to sign exclusive contracts containing damage terms. In this case, the incumbent faces a choice: take advantage of contracting externalities to exclude E using exclusive contracts, or allow E to enter but use damages to extract E's profit as in Aghion and Bolton [1987]. Each can emerge as the most profitable choice under some circumstances (see Segal and Whinston [2000a]).

Sixth, once we consider the possibility for contracts to specify terms of trade, one might wonder about the extent to which fixed-quantity contracts (which specify a definite future trade and a given price) can substitute for exclusive contracts as an exclusionary device. This becomes relevant, for example, if we want to know whether a firm prohibited from using exclusive contracts simply can start using quantity contracts to accomplish the same end. In fact, in the previous model, if quantity contracts were allowed, an incumbent seeking to deter entry would prefer to sign buyers to long-term quantity contracts since these would still exclude but would involve no deadweight loss from monopoly pricing. Thus, in this case, such contracts are *better* than exclusive contracts for deterring entry.

This is not always the case, however. At an intuitive level, think of your local supermarket. If a manufacturer of potato chips tries to use quantity contracts (contracts that directly buy shelf space) to keep rival potato chip makers out of the store, it will have to buy up enough of the store's shelf space so that the store's marginal value of the remaining space for selling other products is sufficiently high that rival potato chip makers are unable to buy any space profitably. This amount of shelf space is likely to be a large share of the store, and excluding rivals in this way will cost a great deal. In contrast, when an exclusive contract is possible, no additional space need be purchased. It is only necessary to compensate the store for not selling other potato chips rather than compensating both for this and for lost opportunities to sell other products.

To see a simple formal model where this difference between exclusive and quantity contracts arises starkly, suppose that instead of E's product being cheaper to produce, it is of higher quality. In particular, suppose that I and E both have marginal cost c, but that I's product is worth v to each of the N buyers in the market (who each have a desire for one unit at most) while E's product is worth $v + \Delta$, where $\Delta > 0$. If $N(\Delta - c) - f > 0$, quantity contracts will not deter E's entry, since each consumer would be willing to pay Δ for a unit of E's product even if he has already committed to buy from I. Exclusive contracts, on the other hand, would prevent buyers from doing this. We will see additional examples of this difference between exclusive contracts and quantity contracts in the next section.

Seventh, how does successful exclusion affect welfare here? In the present model, E's entry is efficient by assumption since $3(c_I - c_E) > f$. Thus, entry deterrence reduces aggregate surplus. More generally, E's profit in this model equals exactly his incremental contribution to aggregate surplus, so he makes a socially optimal entry decision. This is not a robust result, however. In oligopolistic markets with scale economies, entrants may have too large an incentive to enter because part of their profit represents "business stealing" from existing firms (see, for example, Mankiw and Whinston [1986]). This possibility makes the welfare economics of exclusion unclear in general, an uncomfortable but nevertheless important fact.[18] Indeed, the papers in this literature that have strong welfare conclusions achieve this by making strong assumptions, such as the absence of fixed costs and Bertrand postentry pricing.[19]

Finally, this model provides our first example of a model in which contracting externalities arise *among the contracting parties*. In this model, the joint payoff of I and the three buyers is maximized by having no exclusives signed (exclusion lowers their joint payoff by $3x^*$). Were they to write a single multilateral contract (as in "Coasian bargaining"), this joint profit-maximizing outcome would be the result (by reasoning similar to the bilateral contracting principle). But contracts here are *bilateral*, written between pairs of agents, and externalities arise from I's contract with one buyer onto other buyers. These externalities result in an outcome that fails to maximize the contracting parties' joint payoff. Segal [1999] provides an illuminating discussion of this type of contracting externality. They will play an important role in the next section, where we study situations in which several firms compete to sign exclusive contracts with buyers or suppliers.

4.4 Anticompetitive Exclusive Dealing: Competing for Exclusives

In the first-mover models we have just studied, only the incumbent firm is able to get buyers to sign exclusive deals. In actual markets (and many antitrust cases), however, there are often a number of competitors trying to secure exclusive deals. In this section, we look at the potential for anticompetitive exclusive contracts to arise in such settings. The discussion here is somewhat more difficult than in other sections of the chapter. Some readers may prefer to skip ahead to section 4.5.

As in the first-mover models, the presence of contracting externalities plays a central role in the discussion. In the models we study here, however, two kinds of contracting externalities are present simultaneously. First, as in the Aghion and Bolton [1987] model, there are externalities on parties who are not involved in the contracting process. Second, as in the Rasmussen, Ramseyer, and Wiley [1991] and Segal and Whinston [2000a] model, there are externalities among parties involved in the contracting process that arise from the fact that contracts are bilateral.

More specifically, these models combine a few key ideas:

1. *In these models, there are some "outside parties" who are not part of the contracting process, but who may benefit from competition among some of the parties who are involved in the contracting process.* For example, final consumers, who are not part of the contracting process between manufacturers and retailers, can benefit from enhanced retail competition. As another example, manufacturers who are negotiating with a local retailer may compete against each other in another local retail market or a market for inputs. Participants in

those other markets are better off if this competition is more intense.

2. *In these models, the joint payoff of the parties involved in the contracting process is enhanced if they can restrict the level of competition enjoyed by those outside parties. Were the contracting parties able to write a multilateral contract to maximize their joint profit, this contract would be structured to reduce that competition.* For example, the joint profit of an upstream manufacturer and his downstream retailers is enhanced by restricting downstream retail competition to increase the retail price. Likewise, the joint profit of manufacturers and a local retailer is greater if they reduce competition among the manufacturers in the other markets in which they compete.

3. *Without an ability to write a multilateral contract, contracting externalities among the parties involved in the contracting process may prevent them from achieving this joint profit-maximizing outcome using simple sales contracts. When this happens, exclusive contracts—which eliminate contracting externalities—may emerge as a second-best way to achieve this objective.* The first two points establish that the contracting parties together can have an exclusionary motive. This last point (which returns to a theme introduced in section 4.3) shows why simple quantity contracts may be insufficient to achieve this exclusionary end, so that exclusive contracts are necessary. This is the most difficult part of the argument, and I develop it in detail here. As an example, when an upstream manufacturer sells through downstream retailers, their joint incentive is to implement the monopoly retail price. The manufacturer could try to accomplish this by selling the monopoly quantity to one of the downstream retailers. In the absence of an exclusive, however,

the manufacturer may be tempted to sell to other retailers as well because he will not internalize the negative externality those sales impose on the first retailer. If he does so, the additional sales will undermine the possibility of achieving the monopoly retail price. An exclusive prevents the manufacturer from making sales to other retailers.

While all of these elements may not be completely clear at this point, they should be soon. Equally important, as we study examples of such models in this section, understanding these key elements should make clear what drives their results. It should also help those who want to construct their own models of exclusive dealing, tailored to the facts of particular industries, by making clear the "ingredients" they will need.

In the rest of this section, I discuss three settings in which contracting parties compete for exclusives that are signed to facilitate the reduction of competition that other ("outside") parties enjoy. In the first, a manufacturer commits to selling exclusively through one retailer as a means of reducing retail competition; in the second, a retailer commits to carrying exclusively the product of one manufacturer as a way to reduce competition among the manufacturers for inputs; in the third, a local retailer commits to carrying exclusively the product of one manufacturer as a means of reducing competition among the manufacturers in other local retail markets. Although the settings differ, the fundamental economic forces in these three settings are identical, and are exactly the three key ideas listed earlier. After considering these three examples, the section ends with a discussion of models in which multiple buyers and sellers are involved in the contracting process.

Exclusives to Reduce Retail Competition
I begin with a model, due to Hart and Tirole [1990] in which exclusive contracts are adopted to reduce retail competition (see also O'Brien and Shaffer [1992] and McAfee and Schwartz [1994]).[20] In this model, there is a single upstream manufacturer of a good (M), and two retailers who sell the good to consumers (R_A and R_B). The manufacturer produces output at a constant unit cost c_M, while each retailer R_j has a constant unit cost c_R (excluding the cost of purchasing the good from the manufacturer).[21]

Market Outcome without Exclusives It will be instructive, for the moment, to ignore the possibility of exclusive contracts being signed. In this case, contracting and competition work as follows: First, M makes simultaneous private offers to each retailer R_j of the form (x_j, t_j), where x_j is the quantity offered and t_j is the total payment required. By "private," I mean that each retailer observes only his own offer. Second, the retailers simultaneously announce whether they accept M's offer. A retailer that rejects it has nothing to sell and earns zero. Third, retail competition occurs. This competition takes the form of a simultaneous quantity-choice game in which each retailer puts up for sale all of the units he has purchased and prices clear the retail market. Generalizing somewhat the Hart and Tirole [1990] setup, I allow the retailers to be differentiated (perhaps because of location) so that the price received by R_j when the quantities available for sale at retail are x_A and x_B is $p_j(x_A, x_B)$. R_j then earns $\pi_j(x_A, x_B) \equiv [p_j(x_A, x_B) - c_R]x_j$ less the payment t_j, while M earns $\pi_M(x_A, x_B) \equiv t_A + t_B - c_M(x_A + x_B)$. Figure 4.2 depicts the basic contracting and competition structure. The circle around the manufacturer and two retailers represents the

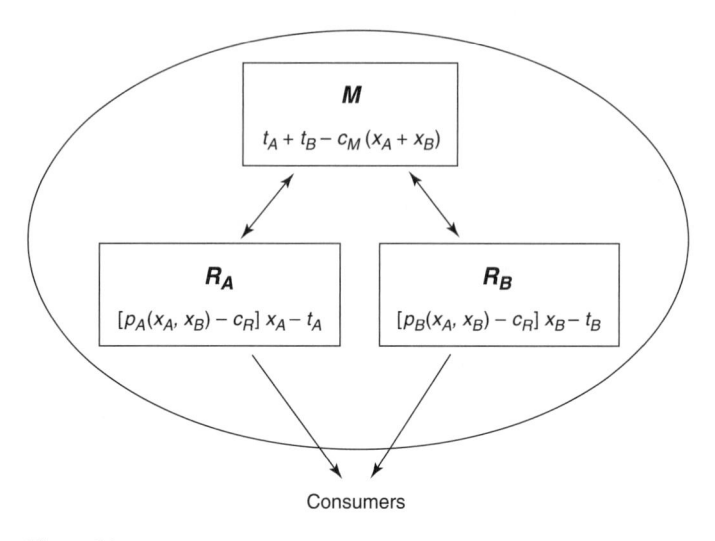

Figure 4.2
The Hart-Tirole [1990] model

fact that they are involved in the contracting process, while consumers are not.

This bargaining process, in which M makes offers to the two retailers, has less of the flavor of "competitors trying to secure exclusive deals" than if instead the retailers make offers to M. Here, because it is easier, I follow Hart and Tirole [1990] by having M make the offers to the retailers. Segal and Whinston [2003] refer to this as the *offer game*, since the single party (here, M) makes offers to the many parties on the other side of the market (here, the retailers). Bernheim and Whinston [1998] study instead the *bidding game*, in which the parties on the more numerous side of the market instead make simultaneous offers ("bids") to the single party (see also Bernheim and Whinston [1986a, 1986b]). As I discuss later, the results with this different bargaining process would be similar.

In what follows, I highlight two special cases. The first is where the two retailers sell their products in distinct local markets. In this case, each retailer R_j faces an inverse demand that is independent of the sales level of the other retailer R_{-j}, so that $p_j(x_A, x_B) \equiv P_j(x_j)$. The second, studied in Hart and Tirole [1990], is the other extreme in which the two retailers are completely undifferentiated. In this case, downstream competition takes the standard Cournot form with $p_1(x_A, x_B) = p_2(x_A, x_B) \equiv P(x_A + x_B)$, where $P(\cdot)$ is the market inverse demand function.

Before studying this contracting process, let us look at what outcome maximizes the joint profit of the manufacturer and two retailers. The sales levels (x_A^{**}, x_B^{**}) that maximize this joint profit solve the problem

$$\max_{x_A, x_B} \sum_{j=A,B} [p_j(x_A, x_B) - (c_M + c_R)] x_j. \tag{4.1}$$

This is the problem of a monopolist who sells two differentiated products, each with marginal cost $c_M + c_R$. I denote the maximized joint profit by $\Pi^{**} \equiv \sum_{j=A,B} [p_j(x_A^{**}, x_B^{**}) - (c_M + c_R)] x_j^{**}$.

In the special case in which the retailers sell in distinct markets, x_j^{**} is the monopoly quantity for a local monopolist who faces inverse demand $P_j(x_j)$ and has marginal cost $c_M + c_R$. In the special case of undifferentiated retailers, every solution to (4.1) involves selling the aggregate quantity $X = x_1 + x_2$ that maximizes $[P(X) - (c_M + c_R)]X$. I denote this joint monopoly quantity by X^{**}.

It will also be useful for what follows to define the joint profit-maximizing sales level for each product if it is the only product being sold. For product j ($j = A, B$), this is the quantity x_j^e that solves

$$\max_{x_j}[p_j(x_j,0) - (c_M + c_R)]x_j. \tag{4.2}$$

I denote the level of this maximized "exclusive" joint profit by $\Pi_j^e \equiv [p_j(x_j^e,0) - (c_M + c_R)]x_j^e$ for $j = A, B$. Observe that $\Pi_j^e \leq \Pi^{**}$, since some joint profit may be lost when only one retailer sells the product.

Now let us examine the outcome of the contracting process. Will the manufacturer and retailers achieve the joint monopoly profit Π^{**}? It may seem that since there is an upstream monopolist the answer will be yes. In fact, contracting externalities combined with private offers will lead to the opposite conclusion. The reason, roughly speaking, is that with private offers the manufacturer always can make additional sales secretly to a retailer. Moreover, when contracting externalities are present, the manufacturer will have an incentive to sell more than the monopoly level because he and the retailer he secretly sells to will ignore the negative effect those additional sales have on other retailers. Let us look at this point in more detail.

With private offers, when a retailer receives an offer he must form some conjecture about the offer that the other retailer has received to decide whether to accept M's offer. This is so because the price the retailer receives will be affected by how much the other retailer is buying. The literature has often adopted the assumption of "passive beliefs," which holds that each retailer R_j has a fixed conjecture $(\bar{x}_{-j}, \bar{t}_{-j})$ about the offer that is being received by the other retailer, R_{-j}; that is, R_j's conjecture is unaffected by the offer that R_j himself receives. Moreover, in an equilibrium, each retailer j's fixed conjecture must be correct: that is, it must coincide with the contract that retailer $-j$ is actually signing.[22,23]

Under this passive-beliefs assumption, an extension of the bilateral contracting principle holds: in any equilibrium each manufacturer-retailer pair will agree to a contract that maximizes their joint payoff, taking as given the contract being signed between M and R_{-j}. To see why, suppose that M is writing contract $(\bar{x}_{-j}, \bar{t}_{-j})$ with R_{-j}. If R_j correctly anticipates this (and holds this belief fixed), then R_j will be willing to pay all of his anticipated profit, $[p_j(x_j, \bar{x}_{-j}) - c_R]x_j$, in return for x_j units. Holding his contract with R_{-j} fixed, M will choose the quantity he offers R_j to maximize his own profit. This profit is

$$t_j + \bar{t}_{-j} - c_M(x_j + \bar{x}_{-j})$$
$$= [p_j(x_j, \bar{x}_{-j}) - c_R]x_j - c_M x_j + \bar{t}_{-j} - c_M \bar{x}_{-j}$$
$$= \{[p_j(x_j, \bar{x}_{-j}) - (c_M + c_R)]x_j\} + \{\bar{t}_{-j} - c_M \bar{x}_{-j}\}, \qquad (4.3)$$

which is exactly the joint profit of M and R_j.

This joint profit of M and R_j consists of two terms. The first term in braces is the *bilateral surplus* between M and R_j, the joint profit created because of their trade x_j holding $\bar{x}_{-j}$ fixed, while the second term in braces is M's profit from his trade with R_{-j}. Intuitively, since M can extract all of R_j's profit in return for the x_j units, he will choose x_j to maximize M and R_j's bilateral surplus. Thus, we see that in a passive beliefs equilibrium M's trades with the two retailers, x_A^* and x_B^*, must maximize the bilateral surplus of each manufacturer-retailer pair, taking M's trade with the other retailer as given. This tells us that (x_A^*, x_B^*) must satisfy:

$$x_A^* \text{ solves } \max_{x_A}[p_A(x_A, x_B^*) - (c_M + c_R)]x_A \qquad (4.4)$$

$$x_B^* \text{ solves } \max_{x_B}[p_B(x_A^*, x_B) - (c_M + c_R)]x_B. \qquad (4.5)$$

Conditions (4.4) and (4.5) are *exactly* the conditions that would hold if we were instead in a setting in which M did not exist and R_1 and R_2 competed as duopolists, each with marginal cost $c_M + c_R$. In essence, each manufacturer-retailer pair acts just like one of those duopolists. The joint profit in this outcome is $\hat{\Pi} \equiv \sum_{j=A,B}[p_j(x_A^*, x_B^*) - (c_M + c_R)]x_j^*$. Since M makes take-it-or-leave-it offers to the retailers, he receives all of this profit.

To understand the implications of this result, consider first the special case in which the retailers sell in distinct local markets. In this case, conditions (4.4) and (4.5) become

x_A^* solves $\max_{x_A}[P_A(x_A) - (c_M + c_R)]x_A$

x_B^* solves $\max_{x_B}[P_B(x_B) - (c_M + c_R)]x_B$,

so the outcome coincides with the joint monopoly outcome. This occurs because there are no contracting externalities among the parties involved in the contracting process: each retailer's profit $\pi_j(\cdot)$ is independent of M's sales to the other retailer. This reflects a general principle: *when contracting externalities are absent, bilateral contracting achieves the joint profit-maximizing outcome* (for the parties involved in the contracting process).[24]

Suppose, instead, that the retailers are undifferentiated. Now contracting externalities are present because the more R_{-j} buys from M, the lower is the market price, and the lower is R_j's profit. In this case, conditions (4.4) and (4.5) become

$$x_A^* \text{ solves } \max_{x_A}[P(x_A + x_B^*) - (c_M + c_R)]x_A \qquad (4.6)$$

x_B^* solves $\max_{x_B}[P(x_A^* + x_B) - (c_M + c_R)]x_B.$

These are exactly the conditions for the standard Cournot duopoly outcome for duopolists whose marginal costs are each $c_M + c_R$.

At first, it may seem surprising that M can do no better than the Cournot duopoly profit. He makes all the offers in this game. Why cannot M simply impose the monopoly outcome? The explanation is that M is hampered by a commitment problem arising from the combined presence of the contracting externality and private offers.

To see this point, let us try out the monopoly solution as a possible equilibrium and see where it breaks down. Suppose that to implement the monopoly outcome M offers R_A the "monopoly contract" $\hat{x}_A = X^{**}$, and $\hat{t}_A = [P(X^{**}) - c_R]X^{**}$, and offers nothing to R_B. That is, M offers to sell R_A exactly the monopoly quantity, offers R_B nothing, and requires R_A to pay all of his resulting profit. Clearly, if these are the equilibrium offers, R_A is (just) willing to accept. However, this does not survive as an equilibrium with private offers and passive beliefs. To see why, suppose that M deviates and privately offers to sell a small amount of output to R_B. Specifically, let M offer R_B the contract $\tilde{x}_B = \varepsilon$ and $\tilde{t}_B = [P(X^{**} + \varepsilon) - c_R]\varepsilon$ for a small $\varepsilon > 0$. R_B is willing to accept this offer, which requires that he pay exactly the profit he earns if R_A still purchases the monopoly quantity X^{**}. Moreover, since offers are private, R_A does not know that this deviation has occurred, and he continues to accept his contract. Does M benefit from this deviation? M's net profits from dealing with R_A do not change. M's net profits from dealing with R_B on the other hand are

$$\tilde{t}_B - c_M \varepsilon = [P(X^{**} + \varepsilon) - c_R]\varepsilon - c_M \varepsilon$$
$$= [P(X^{**} + \varepsilon) - (c_M + c_R)]\varepsilon. \qquad (4.7)$$

Since $P(X^{**}) - (c_M + c_R) > 0$ (price exceeds marginal cost at the monopoly sales level), this is necessarily positive for a small enough quantity ε. Hence, the deviation increases M's profits. In essence, because offers are private, M is tempted to sell output secretly to R_B.[25] Though this reduces the joint profits of M and the two retailers, M's profit increases because the deviation imposes a negative externality on R_A.

In this equilibrium, M gets all of the profits because of his ability to make take-it-or-leave-it offers to the retailers. With other bargaining processes this would no longer be true, but the failure to achieve joint profit maximization when contracting externalities are present would remain. Bernheim and Whinston [1985, 1986a, 1986b, 1998] and Segal and Whinston [2003, section 7], for example, study instead a bargaining process in which (in this model) the retailers make simultaneous offers to M. In this "bidding game," those offers take the form of nonlinear payment schedules $t_j(x_j)$ that denote how much each retailer j is willing to pay for various quantities. With this bargaining process, bilateral contracting again achieves a joint profit-maximizing outcome when contracting externalities are absent and fails to do so when contracting externalities are present. However, the retailers instead receive strictly positive profits.[26,27]

Market Outcome When Exclusives Are Possible Now let us introduce the possibility that M might offer an exclusive contract to a retailer. Formally, a contract now may specify (x, e, t) where $e = 1$ if the contract is exclusive and $e = 0$ if it is nonexclusive. M can choose to offer either or both retailers nonexclusive contracts, but can offer only one contract if he chooses to offer an exclusive contract.

The only other changes concern beliefs. Passive beliefs in response to an unanticipated offer from M now cannot make sense in some circumstances. For example, passive beliefs cannot make sense when M deviates and offers R_j an exclusive contract when R_j was expecting R_{-j} to be offered a contract. Likewise, passive beliefs cannot make sense when M deviates and offers R_j a contract when R_j was expecting M to offer R_{-j} an exclusive contract. In what follows, I alter the assumption of passive beliefs in two ways. First, I assume that when a retailer is offered an exclusive contract he knows that the other retailer has not received any offer. Second, I assume that whenever R_j is offered the equilibrium nonexclusive quantity x_j^* he believes that M has also offered R_{-j} his equilibrium nonexclusive quantity x_{-j}^*.[28]

Observe, first, that when exclusives are possible, if M offers R_j the exclusive contract in which $x_j = x_j^e$ and $t_j = [p_j(x_j^e, 0) - c_R]x_j^e$, R_j will accept this contract since it gives him a payoff of exactly zero (he pays M exactly his profits). By doing this, M can earn the maximal exclusive joint profit of Π_j^e. Next, note that if there is an equilibrium in which an exclusive is not signed, each M/R_j pair must be maximizing its bilateral surplus and so this must involve the quantities (x_A^*, x_B^*) and give M a profit of $\hat{\Pi}$, just as before. Together, these facts immediately imply that the equilibrium involves an exclusive contract with R_j (with trade x_j^e) whenever $\Pi_j^e > \max\{\Pi_{-j}^e, \hat{\Pi}\}$.

Suppose instead that $\hat{\Pi} > \max\{\Pi_A^e, \Pi_B^e\}$, so that the equilibrium joint profit in the absence of exclusives exceeds the joint profit in any exclusive contract. In this case, the equilibrium contracts must be nonexclusive. To see this, observe that under our assumptions on beliefs, we cannot have an exclusive contract being signed since M can earn $\hat{\Pi}$ (which exceeds Π_A^e and Π_B^e) by deviating and offering nonexclusive contracts with trades x_A^* and x_B^* to the two retailers.

Finally, if $\hat{\Pi} = \max\{\Pi_A^e, \Pi_B^e\}$ then both exclusive and nonexclusive contracts can arise in equilibrium. To summarize:

With private offers (and our assumptions about beliefs) the equilibrium contracts are:

- If $\Pi_j^e > \max\{\Pi_{-j}^e, \hat{\Pi}\}$: An exclusive contract with R_j with trade x_j^e;
- If $\hat{\Pi} > \max\{\Pi_A^e, \Pi_B^e\}$: Nonexclusive contracts with both retailers and trades of (x_A^*, x_B^*).
- If $\hat{\Pi} = \Pi_j^e = \max\{\Pi_A^e, \Pi_B^e\}$: Both an exclusive contract (with trade x_j^e) and nonexclusive contracts (with trades x_A^* and x_B^*) can arise in equilibrium.

Thus, the equilibrium contracting outcome, whether exclusive or nonexclusive, maximizes the joint profit of the contracting parties, but taking into account any inefficiency (from a joint-profit standpoint) of nonexclusive contracting. Intuitively, this involves a trade-off between the benefit of selling M's product at both retailers and the costs arising from contracting externalities when both retailers are active. Indeed, note that when $(x_A^{**}, x_B^{**}) \gg 0$ contracting externalities are *necessary* to get an exclusive contracting outcome, since without contracting externalities, $\hat{\Pi} = \Pi^{**} > \max\{\Pi_A^e, \Pi_B^e\}$.

To see the implications of this conclusion more concretely, consider first the case in which the retailers sell in distinct local markets. In this case, $\hat{\Pi} = \Pi_A^e + \Pi_B^e = \Pi^{**} > \max\{\Pi_A^e, \Pi_B^e\}$, and so we *never* will see exclusives. Intuitively, in this case nonexclusives involve no contracting externality, and so an exclusive outcome merely sacrifices the profit from selling in one of the markets.

At the other (Hart and Tirole) extreme in which the retailers are undifferentiated, $\Pi_A^e = \Pi_B^e = \Pi^{**} > \hat{\Pi}$, and so M *always* will sign an exclusive with one of the retailers. Intuitively, there is no loss from selling through a single retailer in this case, and contracting externalities are eliminated with exclusive representation. This exclusive outcome results in lower output and a higher price than when exclusives are banned (the monopoly output rather than the Cournot duopoly output). Indeed, both consumer surplus and aggregate surplus are necessarily lower.

For cases between the two extremes of distinct local markets and undifferentiated retailers we may see either exclusive or nonexclusive outcomes; which one arises depends on the relative benefits of avoiding contracting externalities and selling through two versus only one retailer.

It should be noted, however, that the strong welfare conclusion with undifferentiated retailers depends on the absence of fixed costs for the retailers. For example, suppose that each retailer also incurs fixed costs of $f > 0$ if active. It is still the case that the joint profit-maximizing outcome involves exclusion of one retailer, since we still have $\Pi_j^e = \Pi^{**}$ for $j = A, B$. But two other conclusions may change. First, exclusion sometimes will be sustainable using a quantity contract, without any need for an explicit exclusivity provision. For example, the small deviation from the joint monopoly outcome that we considered previously is no longer profitable once there are fixed costs because the benefit of selling a small amount to R_B is outweighed by the fixed cost f. Any profitable deviation to R_B must involve a nontrivial quantity, and such a profitable deviation may not exist. Thus, a quantity contract now may be a perfect substitute for an exclusive contract. (In contrast, when $f = 0$ the model provides another example in which exclusive contracts are more effective for exclusion than are quantity contracts.) In this case, a ban on exclusives would have no effect on the market outcome.

A second difference concerns the welfare effect of banning exclusives when the outcome without exclusives still has M selling to both retailers. In this case, a ban on exclusive contracts still raises consumer surplus, but may lower aggregate surplus. The reason (again) is that with Cournot retail competition, entry into the retail sector may be excessive from a social perspective because of business stealing.[29]

Recall that here we have focused on the case in which M makes offers to the retailers. In fact, we would get exactly the same general characterization of when exclusives arise, involving the same comparison between $\hat{\Pi}$ and $\max\{\Pi_A^e, \Pi_B^e\}$, using the Bernheim and Whinston [1986a, 1998] bidding-game bargaining process in which the retailers make offers. The only difference is that the exact extent of the loss from contracting externalities (that is, the exact value of $\hat{\Pi}$) can differ from the case in which M makes the offers.

Finally, observe that in this type of model, exclusionary contracts need not have long durations to have an anticompetitive effect, in contrast to our conclusion when looking at first-mover models. Indeed, we even could imagine these contracts being renewed each morning. Since the economic motives are the same each day, the equilibrium outcome will be as well. The same will be true of the model of exclusives to reduce competition in input markets that is discussed next. This issue is of some importance in many exclusive-dealing cases. Often, it is argued that short-term exclusive contracts pose no risk of exclusion, and so must have been adopted for procompetitive reasons (which we discuss in section 4.5). In its recent *Dentsply* decision [399 F.

3d 181 (2005)], however, the Third Circuit Court of Appeals ruled in favor of the government in a case alleging that Dentsply, a maker of dentures, had used exclusive contracts with dental wholesalers to exclude rival manufacturers. Dentsply's exclusive agreements with wholesalers were "at will"; a wholesaler could end its relationship with Dentsply at any time, albeit at the cost of no longer carrying Dentsply's products.[30]

Exclusives to Reduce Competition in Input Markets

I now develop a model, based on Bernheim and Whinston [1998], in which exclusives are adopted as a means of reducing competition in input markets. Here, the vertical structure is reversed from that in the previous subsection, so that there is a single retailer (R) serving a local market, and two manufacturers (M_A and M_B) competing to make sales to that retailer. It will be useful, for the moment, to focus only on this market (later I introduce input market competition). I assume that in selling quantities x_A and x_B of the two products, the retailer faces inverse demands $p_A(x_A, x_B)$ and $p_B(x_A, x_B)$. The retailer's constant unit cost is c_R. The manufacturers, on the other hand, each have constant unit cost c_M. Figure 4.3 depicts this setting. As before, the circle indicates that consumers do not take part in the contracting process.

Bernheim and Whinston assume that bargaining over contracts has M_A and M_B making simultaneous offers to R, who then chooses which contracts, if any, to accept. For expositional continuity, here I assume instead that the contract formation stage involves R making simultaneous private offers (x_j, t_j) to M_A and M_B. That is, I stay with the same "offer game" bargaining process that we analyzed in the model of exclusives to reduce retailer competition, in

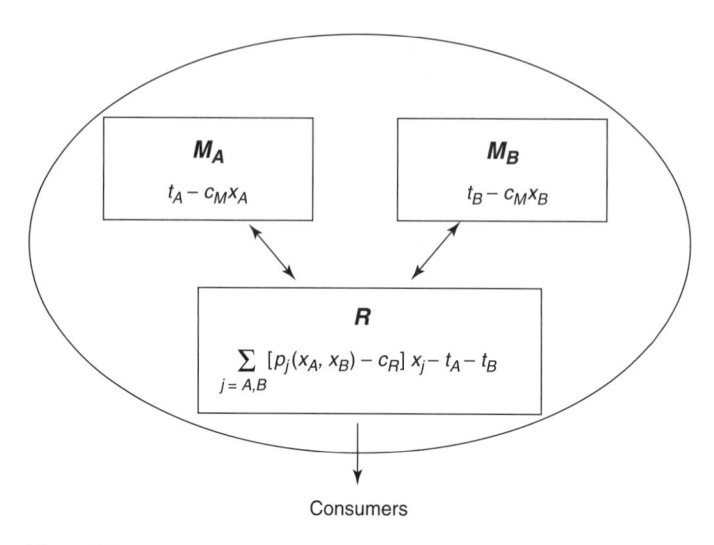

Figure 4.3
The Bernheim-Whinston [1998] model

which the vertical level with a single party makes offers to the vertical level with more than one party. As noted earlier, the basic conclusions from these two bargaining processes are similar.

Before introducing input market competition, let us look at the outcome of contracting in its absence.[31] Here, the joint profit-maximizing outcome for the retailer and two manufacturers has sales levels (x_A^{**}, x_B^{**}) that solve

$$\max_{(x_A, x_B)} \sum_{j=A,B} [p_j(x_A, x_B) - (c_M + c_R)]x_j. \tag{4.8}$$

Thus, we have $\Pi^{**} = \sum_{j=A,B}[p_j(x_A^{**}, x_B^{**}) - (c_M + c_R)]x_j^{**}$.

Looking again at figure 4.3, there are no contracting externalities here: given its contractual trade with R, M_j's profit

$t_j - c_M x_j$ is *unaffected* by changes in R's trade with M_{-j}.[32] Thus, our previous analysis tells us that bilateral contracting maximizes the joint profit of the three parties, so that $\hat{\Pi} = \Pi^{**}$. Moreover, as long as $(x_A^{**}, x_B^{**}) \gg 0$, we have $\Pi_j^e < \Pi^{**}$ for $j = A, B$. Hence, in this case, even if exclusives are possible, they will not arise. If, instead, $x_j^{**} = 0$ for some j, then $\Pi_{-j}^e = \hat{\Pi}$. In that case, while the joint profit-maximizing outcome can be sustained with an exclusive contract, it can also be sustained with a nonexclusive quantity contract that simply has M_{-j} selling x_{-j}^{**} to R.[33,34]

Note that we also would reach exactly the same conclusion if each manufacturer had a fixed cost $f > 0$. Fixed costs make it more likely that only one manufacturer is active in the joint profit-maximizing outcome. But, since contracting externalities are absent, even when this is so the joint profit-maximizing outcome can be sustained without exclusive contracts.

One can view this conclusion as providing a second setting in which Bork's view (quoted earlier) of the *Standard Fashion* case is correct: if Magrane-Houston is a local monopolist (and if the manufacturers' competition elsewhere is unrelated to their competition in Boston), then Magrane-Houston exactly balances "the inducement offered by Standard...against the disadvantage of handling only Standard's patterns" and makes the choice that maximizes the joint profits of the vertical structure.[35]

This result offers an interesting contrast to our findings in the model of exclusives to reduce retail competition. There we saw that bilateral contracting failed to achieve efficiency when there was competition among some of the contracting parties (there, the retailers) in dealing with outside parties (there, the consumers). Here, we see that it does achieve efficiency when there is a single contracting party who deals with the outsiders.[36] Only in the former case does the desire to extract rents from dealings with outsiders lead to exclusives being signed. Intuititively, because only one contracting party interacts with the outsiders here, they already are able to "monopolize" outsiders; there is no concern that competition will limit this ability, and so there is no need to use exclusives to maintain it.

Suppose now that the two manufacturers compete in buying inputs. For simplicity, let us model this by supposing that the costs of these inputs depend on M_A and M_B's total output, so that their unit costs are now given by the strictly increasing function $c_M(x_A + x_B)$. Figure 4.4 depicts this new environment. The important change is that contracting externalities now are present. As a result, bilateral contracting in the absence of exclusives no longer will result

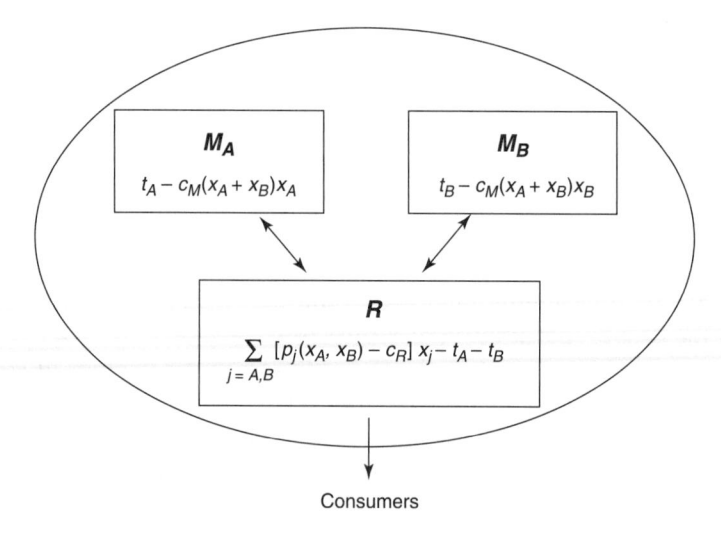

Figure 4.4
The Bernheim-Whinston [1998] model with input market competition

in joint profit maximization for R and the two M's, and so we will have $\hat{\Pi} < \Pi^{**}$. This can lead to an exclusive contract being signed between R and one of the M's.

Indeed, suppose we look at the case in which the manufacturers are undifferentiated and downstream consumers all have the same valuation p for each unit of their products. In this case, $p_A(x_A, x_B) = p_B(x_A, x_B) = p$ for all (x_A, x_B), and the model becomes isomorphic to the Hart and Tirole [1990] model of undifferentiated retailers [it is just flipped vertically: formally, the retail revenue per unit p replaces the previous upstream unit cost c_M, and the input cost $c_M(x_A + x_B)$ replaces the previous retail gross margin, $P(x_A + x_B) - c_R$]. Hence, in this case, we *always* would see an exclusive being signed whose motivation is to reduce the manufacturers' competition for inputs. Aggregate welfare, as well as the welfare of consumers and input suppliers, also declines.

Exclusives to Reduce Competition in Another Retail Market

I now consider a third model whose analysis fits into this same framework. This is the model in Bernheim and Whinston [1998] in which the manufacturers compete in another retail market. As in the model of exclusives to limit competition in input markets, we begin with an existing retail market with a monopoly retailer and two manufacturers, M_A and M_B. The general model has the following structure: There are two periods. At the start of period 1, the retailer in the existing market (now labeled R_1) and the two M's write long-term bilateral contracts for supply in period 2 (they also agree to supplies in period 1, but this is immaterial for our conclusions about exclusives, and so I suppress it). Between periods, M_B may make an investment i_B in cost

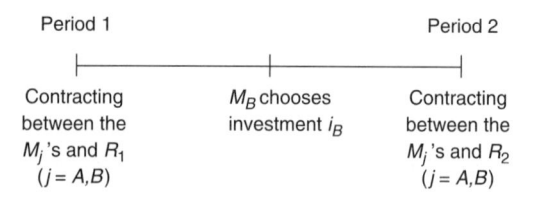

```
Period 1                           Period 2
├──────────────────┼──────────────────────────┤
Contracting        M_B chooses      Contracting
between the        investment i_B   between the
M_j's and R_1                       M_j's and R_2
(j = A,B)                           (j = A,B)
```

Figure 4.5
Timing in the Bernheim and Whinston [1998] model of exclusives to reduce competition in another retail market

reduction at cost $f(i_B)$. Finally, in period 2, a second retail market with monopoly retailer R_2 emerges and the two M's compete in making sales to R_2. The timing is depicted in figure 4.5.

Let us first see at a general level how the presence of R_2 changes the model. Here, the profits (including f) of the two manufacturers in this second market, say π_2^A and π_2^B, depend on M_B's level of investment in cost reduction. In turn, M_B's desired investment in cost reduction will depend on the outcome of contracting with R_1 (cost reduction is more attractive for M_B the higher is his sales level with R_1). Thus, at the time of contracting with R_1, we can think of the profits π_2^A and π_2^B as functions of M_A and M_B's contractual commitments (x_{1A}, x_{1B}) with R_1: $\pi_2^A(x_{1A}, x_{1B})$ and $\pi_2^B(x_{1A}, x_{1B})$. Moreover, because of the possibility of monopolizing R_2, the joint profit of R_1 and the two manufacturers may be highest if x_{1B} is low enough so that M_B chooses not to invest. Now consider the contracting process with R_1. This has the same structure as in figure 4.3, but now each M_j's profit function includes the future profits from market 2: $t_j - c_M x_j + \pi_2^j(x_{1A}, x_{1B})$. With these future profits included, contracting externalities are present, which can lead to exclusives being signed.

An Example To see more concretely how this works, let us consider a simple example. The example also will allow us to look at what happens if exclusives are banned. Suppose that the manufacturers produce an undifferentiated product. R_1's value for the product is v_1 per unit, for up to two units. R_2, on the other hand, wants at most one unit of the product and has value v_2 for it. Each manufacturer can produce at most one unit in a given retail market. The manufacturers' costs differ. M_A's unit cost is c_A. M_B's costs depend on his level of investment. We will suppose that M_B's investment decision is an extreme one: if M_B invests $f > 0$, his unit cost is $c_B < c_A$; otherwise, his unit cost is infinite. To keep it simple, assume that $\min\{v_1, v_2\} > c_A > c_B$. This condition implies that once M_B has invested, he is the low-cost producer. Also, if M_B does not invest, it is efficient for M_A to make sales to both retailers. Finally, assume that M_A and M_B engage in Bertrand bidding for the business of R_2 in period 2.[37]

Let us ask first when it is socially efficient for M_B to invest and be active. This is the case if the net surplus from M_B's presence is positive; that is, if

$$(v_1 - c_B) + (c_A - c_B) > f. \qquad (4.9)$$

The first term on the left-hand side is the social value of M_B supplying R_1 with a second unit, and the second term is the social gain from cheaper production of R_2's single unit; these are compared with the cost of M_B's investment.

In contrast, M_B will choose not to invest if he is excluded from R_1's business if by investing and competing for R_2's business he would earn a negative profit. This happens if

$$(c_A - c_B) < f. \qquad (4.10)$$

In what follows, I assume that this condition holds to focus on the interesting case. (If this condition did not hold, exclusion would be impossible.)

Next, given that (4.10) holds, what sales levels to R_1 maximize the joint profit of R_1 and the two manufacturers? The joint profit-maximizing outcome is one of two possibilities: Either (i) R_1 contracts for one unit from M_A and none from M_B, M_B does not invest, and M_A monopolizes R_2, selling him one unit at price v_2, or (ii) R_1 buys one unit from each manufacturer, M_B invests, and M_B sells one unit to R_2 at price c_A after competing with M_A for R_A's business. The first outcome, which involves exclusion of M_B, generates a larger joint profit than the second if

$$(v_1 - c_B) + [(c_A - c_B) - (v_2 - c_A)] < f. \tag{4.11}$$

The first term on the left-hand side is the same as in (4.9). The second term is the difference between the manufacturers' joint profits in selling to R_2 when they compete, $(c_A - c_B)$, and when M_A monopolizes R_2, $(v_2 - c_A)$. Condition (4.11) will be satisfied when the profit from M_A monopolizing R_2 is large. When (4.11) holds, we have $\Pi_A^e = \Pi^{**} = (v_1 - c_A) + (v_2 - c_A)$.

Finally, when joint profits are maximized by excluding M_B, can a joint profit of Π_A^e be achieved without an exclusive? To do so, R_1 would have to buy only one unit from M_A and none from M_B. But R_1 then may have an incentive to deviate by also buying a unit from M_B. R_1 will do so if the bilateral surplus from trading with M_B (given his one-unit trade with M_A) is positive. This is the case if $(v_1 - c_B) + (c_A - c_B) > f$, which is exactly the same condition as (4.9). (The first term on the left-hand side of this inequality is again the surplus from R_1 receiving a second unit from M_B, while the second term is M_B's profit from selling to R_2.) Thus, when (4.9) and (4.11) hold we have $\max\{\hat{\Pi}, \Pi_B^e\} < \Pi_A^e = \Pi^{**}$, so R_1 will sign an exclusive with M_A whose purpose is the reduction of competition in selling to R_2.

In this setting, a ban on exclusive contracting would prevent M_B's exclusion and raise aggregate welfare. More generally, however, banning exclusives in this type of setting does not necessarily prevent exclusion and raise aggregate welfare. Bernheim and Whinston [1998], for example, show that in some cases such a ban simply may lead to exclusion of M_B through quantity contracts, and this may be even less efficient than exclusion by means of an exclusive contract. To see the idea, suppose instead that R_1's valuations are $\bar{v}_1$ and $\underline{v}_1 < \bar{v}_1$ for the first and second units, respectively. Suppose also that the manufacturers can supply any number of units in each retail market. Finally, suppose that $\bar{v}_1 > c_A > \underline{v}_1 > c_B$. Thus, efficiency calls for M_B to supply R_1 with two units if he is active, and for M_A to supply R_1 with only one unit if M_B is not active. In this setting, if R_1 and M_A sign an exclusive contract, then R_1 will buy only one unit from M_A. However, if exclusives are banned and $(\underline{v}_1 - c_B) + (c_A - c_B) > f$, selling one unit to R_1 will not exclude M_B because R_1 and M_B would find it worthwhile to trade a unit. In that case, R_1 and M_A may end up excluding M_B by signing a quantity contract for two units.[38] This outcome is even less efficient than is exclusion through an exclusive contract.[39]

Multiseller/Multibuyer Models

In all of the models we have studied in this section, simultaneous contracting always took place between one buyer and several sellers, or between one seller and several buyers (these were "triangular" market structures). The reason is that little is known theoretically about how to handle contracting with several parties on both sides of the market when contracts can have general forms. Indeed, the theory literature on "contacting with externalities" has been almost exclusively limited to triangular market structures.[40]

Of course, in most actual markets there is more than one participant on both sides of the market. Thus, developing models that reflect this reality is a high priority. Although only a conjecture, combining the insights of the Bernheim and Whinston [1998] model with the Rasmussen, Ramseyer, and Wiley [1991]/Segal and Whinston [2000a] model (section 4.3) strongly suggests that we should see similar results arising from such models. For example, in the Bernheim and Whinston [1998] model, R_2 does not participate in the initial contracting with M_A and M_B. But the Rasmussen, Ramseyer, and Wiley [1991]/Segal and Whinston [2000a] model suggests that even if R_2 was part of this initial contracting process, externalities across the retailers could lead to an exclusionary outcome.

The leading multiseller/multibuyer model is Besanko and Perry [1994].[41] In their model, two symmetric manufacturers of differentiated products sell to retailers. There is free entry into the retail sector, and active retailers are spaced evenly along a circular product space. Each manufacturer first decides whether to use exclusive or nonexclusive contracts. If either manufacturer chooses exclusivity, then each manufacturer is able to sell to half of the retailers (the manufacturers alternate retailers along the circle). If, instead, both choose nonexclusive representation, then each can sell to every retailer. Note that, by assumption, exclusives cannot be used to exclude a rival manufacturer from the market, only from half the stores, and only by a manufacturer excluding himself from the other half. Moreover, there are no manufacturer investment decisions that might be reduced if store access is limited.

After the exclusivity choices are made, retailers make their entry decisions. Besanko and Perry allow for a retailer's fixed cost to be lower under exclusivity (since only one brand need be carried). Next, the manufacturers name simple linear wholesale prices (they cannot discriminate in their offers across retailers nor use nonlinear pricing schemes). Thus, the set of allowed contracts is highly restricted. Active retailers then decide on their retail prices. Demand for each consumer on the circle takes a logit form, with no outside good (so welfare distortions arise only from changes in consumer brand choices, transportation costs, and retailer fixed costs).

In the Besanko and Perry model, exclusives do several things. First, they make consumers travel further (around the circle) to make purchases. Second, they increase product differentiation at the retail level by intermingling retailer and brand differentiation. This leads to larger retail and wholesale markups for any given number of retailers. This effect, plus the possibly lower fixed costs, leads to more entry of retailers under exclusivity. This additional entry ameliorates the pricing and extra travel effects at the cost of greater fixed costs. In the end, Besanko and Perry show that manufacturer profits are higher with exclusive dealing. Computational results suggest that consumer welfare generally falls, profits increase, and aggregate surplus falls unless the fixed-cost reduction from exclusivity is large.

Further study of multiseller/multibuyer models should be a high priority. Aside from their greater realism, those models would allow us to address some important questions. For example, defendants in exclusive dealing investigations often point to evidence that other (smaller) competitors are using similar contracts as evidence that exclusives are not anticompetitive, but rather promote efficiency. To what extent is this a valid argument? As another example, for what seller market structures is the anticompetitive use of exclusive contracts likely to arise? Given that the literature on anticompetitive exclusive dealing largely has focused on producing "possibility results" in simple market settings (for example, two retailers, or two manufacturers) to counter Chicago School arguments, gaining an understanding of the likelihood of anticompetitive effects in richer market structures is of critical importance. Answers to these types of questions require models with competing sellers and (for realism) more than one buyer.

4.5 Procompetitive Justifications for Exclusive Contracts

Up to this point we have focused entirely on the use of exclusive contracts for anticompetitive purposes. But, as the Chicago School emphasized, exclusive contracts may serve to enhance economic efficiency, rather than detract from it. Moreover, the U.S. courts have recognized these arguments, and treat exclusive dealing cases through a rule-of-reason standard. In this section, I examine procompetitive motives for exclusive contracts. I begin with the most commonly discussed rationale, the ability of exclusive contracts to protect relationship-specific investments, including those that are subject to free riding.

Exclusive Contracts and Protection of Investments

The exclusive-dealing literature contains a number of informal arguments that suggest that exclusive contracts may encourage parties to make noncontractible investments that enhance the value of their trading relationship. The most well-known of those arguments is due to Marvel [1982], who argued that an exclusive contract may promote efficiency when investments are subject to expropriation through free riding. (The argument is related to Telser's [1960] theory of exclusive territories and resale price maintenance.) To take a concrete example, when a manufacturer advertises and brings customers into a retail store, the retailer may be able to switch those customers to other products that offer him a higher margin. If so, the manufacturer's incentives to advertise will be attenuated. An exclusive contract eliminates the retailer's ability to do this, thereby encouraging the manufacturer to advertise.

Others have suggested related but distinct motivations. Klein [1988], for example, argues that GM and Fisher's 1919 exclusive contract, in which GM agreed to buy only Fisher autobodies, was designed to protect Fisher's investments in specialized equipment. Masten and Snyder [1993] discuss United Shoe Machinery Corporation's contracts with shoe manufacturers, which required them to use only United's machines. [These contracts were the focus of the famous *United Shoe Machinery* case; 258 U.S. 451 (1922).] They argue that United needed to protect its investments in training shoe manufacturers how to efficiently organize their production processes. In the absence of an exclusive, they argue, a shoe manufacturer could use this knowledge with other firms' shoe machines, which would reduce United's incentives to make efficient investments in training. (This is actually a version of Marvel's free-rider story.) Bork [1978], in the passage I quoted earlier, suggested that exclusives may help encourage retailer loyalty (see also Areeda and Kaplow [1997]).

Segal and Whinston [2000b] evaluate these arguments by studying a formal model of exclusive contracting in the

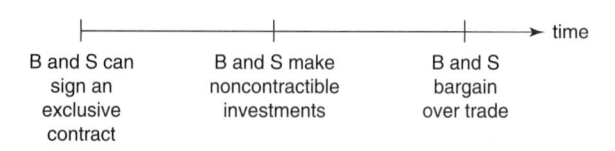

Figure 4.6
Timing in the Segal-Whinston [2000b] model of exclusives and noncontractible investments

presence of noncontractible investments. The model is a version of a "hold up" model, in which a buyer (B) and seller (S) may initially contract prior to making noncontractible investments. In addition, there is an external source (E) for the product, from whom B might procure the good instead.

The timing of the model is shown in figure 4.6. B and S can first agree to a contract. This initial contracting is incomplete: the *only* thing the contract can specify is exclusivity (as in the Chicago School model from section 4.2).[42] Next, B and S make noncontractible investments that determine B's value from trade with both S and E, as well as S's cost. These values and cost are observable by all parties. Then B and S bargain over trade. I assume here that this takes the form of Nash bargaining where B and S reach an efficient agreement and split evenly the surplus their agreement generates over their disagreement payoffs (which correspond to their outside trade options). In the event that they do not reach an agreement, B can buy from E provided that B is not bound to S by an exclusive contract.

An Irrelevance Result To begin, let us look at a simple case designed to formalize Klein's story. Suppose that B needs at most one unit of the product. His values are v for S's product and v_E for E's product. After contracting, S may make a relationship-specific investment $i_S \geq 0$ (measured in terms of its cost). If S invests i_S, then his marginal cost of producing a unit is $c(i_S)$ where $c'(i_S) < 0$. For example, S may construct some specialized machinery that lowers his cost of producing the product that B needs. Suppose that the external source E is competitive and has unit cost c_E (one can imagine that there are many possible external suppliers). For simplicity, assume also that $v > c_E > c(i_S)$ for all i_S, so that efficiency calls for B to always buy from S. The efficient investment i_S^{**} then solves the problem

$$\max_{i_S}[v - c(i_S)] - i_S,$$

and satisfies (if interior) the first-order condition $c'(i_S^{**}) = -1$.

Now let us consider the effect of an exclusive contract. Let e denote the level of contractual exclusivity, with $e = 1$ denoting an exclusive contract and $e = 0$ indicating no exclusivity. (We also can allow intermediate levels of exclusivity by taking e to be the probability that exclusivity is enforced.) Since trade between B and S always is efficient, bargaining always results in B and S agreeing to trade. S's payoff from this bargaining given exclusivity level e and investment level i_S, and ignoring his investment cost i_S, is equal to his disagreement payoff plus half of the surplus from their trade, which is

$$u_S(i_S|e) \equiv d_S(i_S|e) + \frac{1}{2}\{[v - c(i_S)] - d_B(i_S|e) - d_S(i_S|e)\}$$

$$= \frac{1}{2}[v - c(i_S)] + \frac{1}{2}d_S(i_S|e) - \frac{1}{2}d_B(i_S|e), \tag{4.12}$$

where $d_B(i_S|e)$ and $d_S(i_S|e)$ are B and S's disagreement payoffs. Here the disagreement payoffs take the form

$$d_S(i_S|e) = 0 \tag{4.13}$$

$$d_B(i_S|e) = \left\{ \begin{array}{l} (v_E - c_E) \text{ if } e = 0 \\ 0 \text{ if } e = 1 \end{array} \right\}, \tag{4.14}$$

because S has no other trading options and B is free to trade with E only if $e = 0$.

Examining (4.12)–(4.14), confirms that an exclusive contract worsens B's bargaining position by removing his option of buying from E. This raises S's payoff. But does it increase S's incentive to invest? The answer is no. To see why, observe first that to increase S's investment incentive, exclusivity must raise S's *marginal return to investment*. From (4.12), we see that the level of exclusivity e affects S's payoff only through its effect on B's disagreement payoff d_B (recall that $d_S = 0$). But, as (4.14) shows, S's investment i_S has no effect on B's disagreement payoff d_B regardless of whether there is exclusivity. Thus, while exclusivity changes S's payoff, it has no effect on S's marginal returns to investment. In short, exclusivity is *irrelevant* for both investment and efficiency.[43]

What drives this irrelevance result? The answer is that S's investment is purely *internal* in this example; that is, it affects only the value of B and S's trade, and has no effect on disagreement payoffs. Since exclusivity only alters disagreement payoffs, in that case it can have no effect on investment. For exclusivity to matter, noncontractible investments must have an *external* component, affecting B's value of trade with E, and therefore disagreement payoffs.

Effects of Exclusivity In the Klein [1988] story of the GM-Fisher relationship, investment is purely internal. In contrast, in the arguments for exclusivity by Marvel [1982], Masten and Snyder [1993], Bork [1978], and Areeda and

Kaplow [1997], investments do affect external value. For example, the advertising and training investments that Marvel [1982] and Masten and Snyder [1993] discuss increase not only the value of trade between B and S, but also the value of trade between B and E (this is the free-riding issue). Likewise, one can interpret the "loyalty" argument of Bork [1978] and Areeda and Kaplow [1997] as saying that the retailer (the buyer in our model) can make investments that raise his value of trade with B at the expense of lowering his value of trade with E (for example, he can design his store to more effectively highlight S's products or focus his time on learning about S's products). Notice, though, that these various arguments differ in two dimensions: (i) who is making the investment (B or S), and (ii) whether an investment that raises internal value raises or lowers external value. It turns out that the effects of exclusivity on investments and efficiency critically depend on these two characteristics of the investments.

Seller Investments Consider, first, the case of an investment by S that raises not only the value of internal trade but also B's value of trade with E, as in Marvel [1982] and Masten and Snyder [1988]. Segal and Whinston [2000b] call this a situation in which S's investments in internal and external value are *complements*. Specifically, let $v(i_S)$ and $v_E(i_S)$ denote B's values of trade with S and E and assume that $[v'(i_S), v'_E(i_S)] \gg 0$ (complementary investment effects). Then S's payoff (again, excluding the investment cost) is

$$u_S(i_S|e) = \frac{1}{2}[v(i_S) - c(i_S)] - \frac{1}{2}\left\{ \begin{array}{l} v_E(i_S) - c_E \text{ if } e = 0 \\ 0 \text{ if } e = 1 \end{array} \right\}.$$

When $e = 0$, S will limit his investment because it increases B's disagreement payoff (the term in braces). An exclusive eliminates this concern, and therefore raises S's marginal return to investment, just as Marvel [1982] and Masten and Snyder [1993] suggest. In contrast, an exclusive would reduce the incentives for an investment by S that lowers B's value of trade with E $[v'_E(i_S) < 0]$; that is, when the investments by S in internal and external value are *substitutes*.

Buyer Investments Suppose, instead, that B is the one to invest. The investment raises his value of trade with S, $v(\cdot)$, and also affects his value of trade with E, which I now write as $v_E(i_B)$. In the Bork [1978] and Areeda and Kaplow [1997] retailer loyalty story, we have $v'_E(i_B) < 0$, since more investment by B in raising his value of trade with S lowers his value of trade with E. That is, B's investments in internal and external values are substitutes. We can also think of investments by B for which investments in internal and external values are complements. For example, if GM makes investments in its dealer network or in advertising its cars to consumers, those investments raise the value of producing a car whether GM buys its car bodies from Fisher or someone else.

To see how an exclusive affects B's investment incentives, let us look at B's bargaining payoff (again, ignoring B's investment cost). This is

$$u_B(i_B|e) = \frac{1}{2}[v(i_B) - c(i_B)] + \frac{1}{2}\left\{\begin{array}{l} v_E(i_B) - c_E \text{ if } e = 0 \\ 0 \text{ if } e = 1 \end{array}\right\}.$$

An exclusive lowers the level of B's investment when investment in internal and external values are complements, because it eliminates the positive effect of B's investment on his disagreement payoff (the term in braces). In contrast, exclusivity raises the level of B's investment when they are substitutes. Thus, in the case of retailer loyalty, exclusiv-

	Investment by:	
	S	B
Complementary investment effects	Investment ↑	Investment ↓
Substitutable investment effects	Investment ↓	Investment ↑

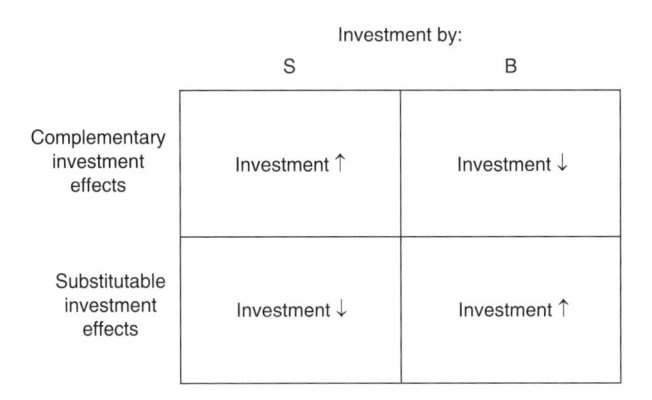

Figure 4.7
Effects of exclusivity on investment that raises internal value

ity increases the retailer's investments toward S's product, exactly as Bork [1978] and Areeda and Kaplow [1997] suggest. Figure 4.7 summarizes these effects of exclusivity on investments.

Welfare Effects We also can ask whether these effects of exclusivity on investments raise or lower welfare. When E is competitive, as we have assumed here, this simply amounts to asking whether B and S's joint payoff is higher or lower under an exclusive contract.[44] In general, an exclusive that increases investment will increase (decrease) welfare when the investment would be underprovided (overprovided) without the exclusive. Figure 4.8 summarizes the welfare effects. Exclusivity necessarily increases welfare if either S invests and investment in internal and external value are complements, or if B invests and they are substitutes. When B invests and they are complements, a more partial result holds. Exclusivity lowers welfare whenever $v'(\cdot) - c'(\cdot) >$

	Investment by:	
	S	B
Complementary investment effects	Welfare ↑	Welfare ↓*+
Substitutable investment effects	Welfare ↓*+	Welfare ↑

* When $e \approx 1$.
\+ When $v'(\cdot) - c'(\cdot) > v'_E(\cdot)$ if B invests or when $v'(\cdot) - c'(\cdot) > -v'_E(\cdot)$ if S invests.

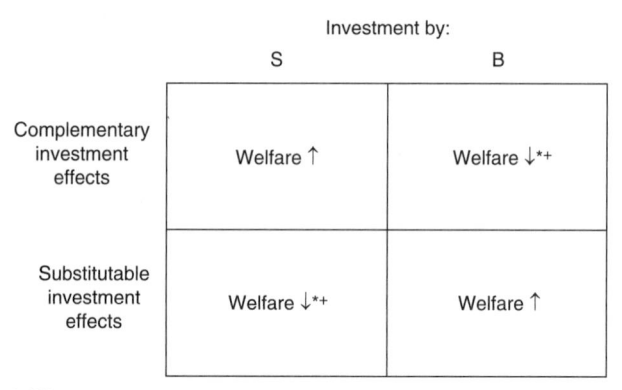

Figure 4.8
Effects of exclusivity on welfare

$v'_E(\cdot)$, so that the internal marginal return to investment exceeds the external one. This condition implies that there is underinvestment in the absence of the exclusive, which the exclusive worsens. It is also true that starting near full exclusivity (e near 1), a small increase in exclusivity is bad. Again, this is so because near full exclusivity there is underinvestment. Finally, a similar result is true when S makes a substitutable investment: near full exclusivity or when $v'(\cdot) - c'(\cdot) > -v'_E(\cdot)$ there is underinvestment, so an increase in exclusivity (which lowers S's investment) is bad.[45]

The results in figure 4.8, combined with the irrelevance result, can be very useful in evaluating firms' procompetitive justifications in antitrust investigations. By asking who is making noncontractible investments and what those investments do, one can ask whether the parties really would have an incentive to sign an exclusive contract for the purpose of protecting noncontractible investments. For example, in a DOJ investigation into contracting practices in the computerized ticketing industry, the leading ticketer, Ticketmaster, had exclusive contracts with concert venues having 80–95% of the available seating capacity in many cities. Ticketmaster argued that those exclusives were not designed to exclude rivals, but rather to protect Ticketmaster's relationship-specific investments both in training a venue's personnel in the use of its system and in tailoring its software to the specific needs of a venue. However, because of the proprietary nature of Ticketmaster's system, the investments could not be used by a venue in conjunction with other systems, so they were internal in our terminology. The irrelevance result therefore casts doubt on the claimed efficiency motivation for Ticketmaster's exclusive contracts.

Of course, in markets with multiple buyer-seller pairs, what is good for one pair need not be good for buyers and sellers collectively. Besanko and Perry [1993] study a model of exclusivity with multiple manufacturers and multiple retailers. The model has three manufacturers (who set linear wholesale prices) and a competitive retail sector. Demand comes from a representative consumer with symmetric linear demand functions. A manufacturer's investment lowers a retailer's marginal cost of selling his product, but also is subject to Marvel-style free riding because it lowers the retailer's marginal costs of selling other manufacturers' products. In this strategic setting, exclusive dealing encourages a manufacturer to invest, but this is bad for other manufacturers' profits. Hence, if all manufacturers adopt exclusive dealing, all may be worse off. In Besanko and Perry's model either no manufacturers may adopt exclusive dealing, only some may do so, or all manufacturers may do so. Consumer and aggregate welfare, however, are both highest in their model when all manufacturers adopt exclusive dealing.

Other Justifications

Exclusives can serve procompetitive purposes other than protecting noncontractible relationship-specific investments. Bernheim and Whinston [1998] show that exclusives may arise in response to inefficient incentive provision in settings of "common agency" (see also Bernheim and Whinston [1986b]). For example, each of several manufacturers may attempt to provide incentives for a common retailer to favor their product. This leads to a situation of contracting with externalities. The result is that a risk-averse retailer may face too much risk. In terms of the notation in section 4.4, this means that $\hat{\Pi} < \Pi^{**}$, and—as there—exclusive dealing may be adopted as a way to avoid these inefficiencies. A similar point is made by Martimort [1996] in a model in which a retailer knows more about his costs or demand than do the manufacturers.[46]

A second procompetitive motive for exclusive contracts is as a means to prevent inefficient entry. Recalling the Chicago School model in section 4.2, observe that in that model entry always generated a positive externality on the incumbent and buyer jointly (equal to the deadweight loss x^*). This was because of the Bertrand form of postentry competition. If, instead, postentry competition took a Cournot form, then entry may lower aggregate surplus. Whenever this is so, entry must generate a negative externality on B and I jointly. In that case, B and I can write an exclusive contract to prevent E from entering, raising both their payoff and aggregate surplus.

Inefficient entry also may arise if B can sponsor an entrant, as noted by Innes and Sexton [1994]. For example, it

Exclusionary Vertical Contracts

can be worthwhile for B to subsidize E's entry even when E is less efficient than I. Here, too, B and I can sign an exclusive contract to prevent this inefficient behavior. For example, a coal mine and a railroad may sign an exclusive contract to prevent the coal mine from inefficiently attempting to bypass the railroad once the railroad has laid its track to the mine.

4.6 Empirical Evidence

Empirical evidence on the motives and effects of exclusive contracting is remarkably limited. Much of the existing literature consists of informal case-study style discussions, often of well-known antitrust cases. Formal statistical studies of market data are rare.

Marvel [1982] is the best-known informal discussion of exclusive dealing. He discusses two examples. The first is the *Standard Fashion* case. Standard had exclusive contracts with approximately 40% of the 52,000 pattern outlets in the United States. Marvel argues that these contracts were unlikely to have an anticompetitive effect. As evidence he cites their two-year duration, the fact that their expirations were staggered across retailers, the fact that competitors also used exclusive contracts, and the fact that manufacturers appeared to compete for desirable retailers.[47] Our discussion earlier suggests that none of these facts is necessarily inconsistent with exclusionary motives for these contracts. Marvel also cites the postdecision changes in the industry, noting that by 1959 the largest pattern manufacturer had a 50% share, an even larger share than Standard had at the time of the case. Yet, equally notable is the fact that this leading share was held by Simplicity Pattern Company, a new entrant in 1927. Second in share with 35% was

McCall's, a competitor who developed a new pattern manufacturing process in 1920, in the wake of the district court's decision (in 1918) against Standard.[48]

Marvel also argues that Standard used these exclusives to prevent free riding on manufacturer investments. The problem facing Standard, he asserts, was that Standard invested in finding good patterns, which could be copied by rivals once found to be successful. Note that exclusives would prevent this type of free riding only if consumers could not readily buy copied patterns from other retailers in the market. Thus, if Marvel is right about style copying being a problem, then protection of Standard's fashion investments in fact may have required exclusion of rivals from the market.

Marvel's main evidence for the importance of Standard's investments in fashion is the fact that Standard's wholesale pattern prices were significantly above cost when exclusives were allowed, but fell and were replaced by up-front charges when exclusives were prohibited. He interprets this as evidence that wholesale prices were originally the means to charge for design investments, but that in the absence of exclusivity these charges had to come in the form of fixed fees. However, this kind of pricing change also is consistent with the "common agency" incentive provision models discussed in section 4.5. In those models, firms lower their marginal charges to attract retailer business in the absence of exclusivity. Marvel also argues that the rise of Simplicity (which produced simple dress patterns) is evidence that design investments were reduced following the decision. Whether this is true, or has another explanation (for example, is just part of a change in demand or the development of cheap mass-production techniques), is unclear.

Marvel also provides an interesting discussion of the structure of the insurance industry, focusing on the difference between direct-writing companies and those who use independent agents. Direct-writing companies sell insurance directly to customers, and so employ their own sales force that handles only the company's insurance. Independent agents, on the other hand, sell insurance from several companies. Strictly speaking, this is an example of vertical integration, not exclusive dealing. Nonetheless, there are close parallels.[49] Marvel argues that direct writing is adopted to avoid free riding in insurance lines in which manufacturers are likely to engage in marketing investments. He cites evidence that direct writing occurs in insurance lines with a diffuse clientele (where manufacturer investment in identifying prospects is more important) and in lines where manufacturer advertising is greater.

Grossman and Hart [1986] also discuss the distinction between direct writing and sales through independent agents. They argue that the key distinction is in who owns the list of customers, and therefore in who has the right to continue the customer relationship should the relationship between the insurance company and the agent end. With direct writing it is the insurance company; with independent agents it is the agent. They argue that when the agent needs to put in great effort to keep the customer happy and therefore to renew, the agent owns the list. (An example would be helping with a claim in property-casualty insurance.) In contrast, when the agent's investments are not so important for encouraging renewal (as with life insurance), the company—which must make investments in developing new insurance products—tends to own the list. They cite evidence that 65% of premiums in property-casualty insurance are generated by independent agents, while this figure is only 12% in life insurance.

In fact, the Marvel and Grossman-Hart arguments are closely related. Both are about noncontractible investments. They differ, however, in the nature of investments. Thinking in terms of the Segal and Whinston [2000b] categories of investments, Marvel focuses on investments by the company that have complementary effects on internal and external values. Grossman and Hart, on the other hand, imagine that both the company and the agent are making investments. The company's investments in developing new products have complementary effects on internal and external value, and so are similar in nature to Marvel's investments. The agent's investments in giving good claim service, on the other hand, are also likely to be complementary, and so they discourage the use of exclusives.

Quite different in nature is Heide, Dutta, and Bergen [1998]. They conducted a survey of distribution managers of industrial machinery and electronic/electric equipment. Of the 147 who responded (460 were contacted), 47 used exclusive contracts. Heide, Dutta, and Bergen conclude that exclusives are more likely when there is a concern about free riding and when an exclusive does not impose high costs on final customers. They find that the use of exclusives is unrelated to whether "entry into this product category by new competitors is likely," which they interpret as evidence against the anticompetitive use of exclusives. Of course, one might worry that exclusives could cause a low likelihood of entry. More generally, one also might question whether managers in surveys are likely to report behavior that can be viewed as anticompetitive.

Two published papers use event-study methods (like the Mullin, Mullin, and Mullin [1995] paper discussed in chapter 3) to shed light on the effects of exclusive contracts. Marin and Sicotte [2003] look at the stock price effects of a number of events that changed the probability that (legal) ocean shipping cartels would be allowed to employ exclusive ("dual rate") contracts with customers. These contracts offered discounts of roughly 20% to customers who shipped exclusively with a company. Many observers felt that the sole purpose of these contracts was to prevent entry of noncartel shipping firms. In 1956 a federal appeals court ruled that such contracts were illegal, a decision that was affirmed by the U.S. Supreme Court in 1958. In response, Congress wrote and then passed new legislation exempting these contracts from antitrust scrutiny. This legislation was eventually signed into law by President Kennedy in 1961.

Marin and Sicotte find that events that seemed to increase the likelihood of exclusives being legal increased shipping companies' values. More interesting, with only one exception they had the opposite effect on the values of companies in industries that were net exporters and used shipping extensively, suggesting that customers were indeed harmed by these contracts.[50]

Mullin and Mullin [1997] look at stock price reactions to the announcement in 1906 of U.S. Steel's long-term lease of the iron ore properties of the Great Northern Railway. The transaction gave U.S. Steel the exclusive right to mine those properties for an indefinite duration until the ore resources were exhausted. The ore resources involved were substantial: the contract anticipated production that was equal to 44 percent of U.S. Steel's Lake Superior ore production in 1905. Moreover, contemporary observers emphasized the potential foreclosure effects of U.S. Steel's control of ore resources. Mullin and Mullin show that the railroads, significant customers of U.S. Steel, experienced positive stock-price responses to the announcement of the lease.

All of the published papers I am aware of that look directly at the effects of exclusivity on market outcomes involve the beer industry. The beer market is characterized by two kinds of exclusive arrangements. First, beer manufacturers frequently grant their distributors (wholesalers, who in turn sell to retailers) exclusive rights to sell within their territory. Over time, and in different states, these rights have been significantly affected by federal and state laws. For example, between the Supreme Court's 1967 *Schwinn* decision (388 U.S. 365) and its 1977 *Sylvania* decision (433 U.S. 36), exclusive territories were per se illegal (this did not eliminate territorial exclusivity entirely since the brewers could terminate dealers for selling out of their territories). Likewise, one state—Indiana—bans such arrangements. On the other hand, many other states, such as Illinois, mandate that brewers assign exclusive territories. Second, the two largest brewers, Anheuser Busch and Miller, have contracts with some of their distributors requiring that they not distribute other brands of beer. (Anheuser Busch at one time called its program to expand its number of exclusive distributors its "100% Share of Mind" program.)

Regarding exclusive territories, papers by Culbertson and Bradford [1991] and Sass and Sauerman [1993, 1996] document that exclusive territories result in higher retail prices. At the same time, the Sass and Sauerman papers also show that the amount of beer consumed is, if anything, larger in states that allow exclusive territories. They interpret this as evidence that exclusives do in fact encourage distributor effort. The Sass and Sauerman [1993] paper, for example, uses panel data on beer sales and prices by state from 1982–1987 to estimate demand and supply functions for beer (using two-stage least squares). They find that exclusive territories increase the demand for beer at any given price (reflecting, in their view, increased distributor efforts), but reduce the supply at any given price (reflecting the reduction in competition). The net effect, according to their reduced form price and quantity estimates, is that exclusive territories increase price (states that mandate exclusives have prices that are roughly 7 percent higher), but result in no decrease in quantity.

Sass [2005] studies the determinants and effects of exclusive contracts limiting distributors to selling a single brewer's beer. His data comes from a 1996–1997 survey of beer wholesalers conducted for the National Beer Wholesalers Association. (The sample included 391 responses and had a 21% response rate.) Sass finds that a distributor is more likely to be exclusive when its territory is more populous, when its largest brewer has a higher market share in its state, and when the state allows billboard beer advertisements. The first two results are consistent with the idea that a brewer can induce a distributor to carry it exclusively only when it generates enough profit on its own. The second also is possibly consistent with foreclosure of rival brewers from low-cost distribution. The third finding is consistent with Marvel's hypothesis that important manufacturer promotional efforts encourage exclusive dealing. Sass also looks at the effects of exclusives on prices and per capita sales. He finds that prices are somewhat higher with exclusives (about 4 percent) while sales are much higher (roughly 30 percent). Whether the latter effect is because exclusives are more likely for a popular brand, because exclusive dealers put in more effort as a result of the exclusive, or because distributors that are signed up to be exclusive dealers are inherently more effective is not clear. Finally, Sass looks at prices and sales of rival brewers and distributors when Anheuser Busch has an exclusive distributor in their territory. He finds no statistically significant effects on them, suggesting an absence of foreclosure.

Two recent working papers by Asker [2004a, 2004b] also look at the effects of exclusive contracts with beer distributors, but take a much more structural approach. Asker also focuses on a particular market, Chicago in 1994, so he is able to have a fairly complete picture of the competitive structure facing brewers and distributors. His data includes information on distributor territories and brands, and the wholesale price paid and retail prices charged by a large supermarket chain in the city. Asker first estimates a demand model for beer, along the lines of the random coefficient discrete choice models discussed in chapter 3. As there, he uses these estimates to infer marginal costs, although he needs to take account of the vertical hierarchy of pricing decisions to do so. He does this by treating the brewer as choosing the retail price to the chain, taking into account its own and its distributor's marginal costs. In solving this problem, the brewer takes into account how the supermarket will adjust its retail prices for the various beers it sells in response to the brewer's price change. This leads to a first-order condition that he uses to infer marginal costs.[51]

Asker then looks at three issues. First, he shows that demand is higher when a beer is sold through an exclusive distributor. Second, he documents that marginal costs are lower when a beer is sold through an exclusive distibutor. (As in Sass [2005], whether the exclusive causes these two differences is not entirely clear.) Third, he shows that smaller rival brewers' marginal costs are not higher when Anheuser Busch and Miller both have exclusive distributors in an area. Like Sass [2005], he concludes that these exclusive contracts seem to enhance efficiency and do not lead to foreclosure of smaller brewers. These papers are still in an early stage. Overall, they represent the most sophisticated attempt to look at the effects of exclusives and seem likely to spur further work of this type.

Notes

Chapter 1

1. Two excellent antitrust casebooks that offer excerpts from major U.S. Supreme Court precedents, interesting discussions, and provocative questions are Areeda and Kaplow [1997] and Posner and Easterbrook [1981]. For an encyclopedic discussion of antitrust law, see Areeda and Hovenkamp [2004].

2. A new and updated version of Posner's book is also now available [2001].

3. Readers familiar with the antitrust laws can safely skip ahead to chapter 2. For those who want to read more, see Areeda and Kaplow [1997, ch. 1] and Posner and Easterbrook [1981, ch. 1]. (The latter reference predates changes in the criminal penalties that I discuss later.)

4. Bork creates some confusion by actually referring to this as the "consumer welfare" standard, having in mind that both consumers of the product and shareholders of the firm are, ultimately, consumers (see, for example, Bork [1978, 110–111]).

5. For example, should a merger of competitors that creates a perfectly discriminating monopolist and leads to a small increase in productive efficiency be allowed? While such a merger necessarily raises aggregate surplus it will also make consumers who are not shareholders worse off.

6. In contrast, Canada's Competition Act appeared until recently to adopt explicitly an aggregate surplus test for horizontal mergers, and the Canadian Competition Bureau's Merger Enforcement Guidelines adopted this stance as well. More recently, however, the Canadian Federal Court of

Appeal has held in the *Superior Propane* case (2001 FCA 104) that the Act should be interpreted as allowing for different weights on consumer and producer surplus.

7. For example, several cases in the late 1970s that sought to broaden the application of the antitrust statutes in the collusion area (such as the ready-to-eat breakfast cereal case accusing the cereal oligopoly of jointly stifling competition through product proliferation, and the case against the makers of lead-based antiknock additives for certain price preannouncements and best-price provisions in their contracts) were brought by the FTC rather than the DOJ.

8. Note that the DOJ must provide evidence about the size of the convicted firms' gains or victims' losses to impose such a fine, in contrast to the current $10 million maximum fine, which requires only evidence that a violation has taken place.

9. Often settlement negotiations in government cases result instead in a *consent decree* prior to a court decision in the case. One feature of such decrees is that they cannot be used by later plaintiffs as evidence of the accused firm's guilt. Thus, private plaintiffs hoping to recover damages are disadvantaged significantly when the government agrees to a consent decree with an accused firm instead of successfully litigating the case. Under the *Tunney Act*, some judicial oversight occurs to help assure that consent decrees are in the public interest, but for a variety of reasons this oversight is very limited in scope.

10. The Court ruled in the *Hanover Shoe* case [392 U.S. 481 (1968)] that a defendant cannot escape damages by showing that a plaintiff passed the overcharge on (for example, in a competitive industry with constant marginal cost, the overcharge would be fully passed on and the immediate buyers would have no change in their profits), and went further in the *Illinois Brick* case [431 U.S. 720 (1977)] by ruling that only an immediate buyer can sue. Although these rulings may appear to be a strange way to assign damages, one possible justification is that since immediate buyers are the most likely parties to detect a conspiracy, they should be the ones who are incented to do so.

11. Baker [1988] instead models the probability of detection ϕ as a function of the aggregate output x, which is equivalent to having ϕ depend on p^* rather than p. In this case, as long as $[1 - \phi(p^m, t)t] > 0$, it is always possible to generate an effective price equal to the monopoly price p^m by setting $p = (p^m - \phi(p^m, t)tc)/(1 - \phi(p^m, t)t)$. More generally, one might expect both p and x to matter (or equivalently, p and p^*), since the aggregate damages to be paid will be $(p - c)x$.

12. For example, if c is random (with full support), both c and whether collusion is taking place are unobservable to consumers, and if the probability of collusion is small, then a consumer's belief that collusion is taking place will be small regardless of the price charged by the cartel. Thus, there will be a minimal effect from an increase in the damage multiple on a buyer's willingness to pay.

Chapter 2

1. Price fixing therefore includes market division and bid-rigging schemes, which can both be viewed as a form of price or output agreement. It can also include related types of agreements, such as a limitation on hours of operation (say, for retail stores). Also, although for simplicity I will refer to sellers colluding throughout most of the chapter, price-fixing law also applies to buyer cartels.

2. The clearest enunciation of the per se rule probably is found in Justice Douglas' opinion in *Socony-Vacuum Oil* [310 U.S. 150 (1940)]: "Price-fixing combinations are illegal per se; they are not evaluated in terms of their purpose, aim, or effects in the elimination of competitive evils."

3. Matters become more complicated, however, once product differentiation is introduced, since consumers may benefit directly from the introduction of additional products. Fershtman and Pakes [2000] provide a related result in a computational analysis of a dynamic model. There, allowing more effective price collusion leads to greater product variety (that is, more entry) and greater quality (because of a greater incentive to invest to capture market share), which in their simulations offsets any negative effect on consumer welfare from higher prices.

4. For one exception, see Beckner and Salop [1999]. As one application of optimal statistical decision making, for example, we would expect optimal antitrust policies in countries with less-developed legal systems (that is, higher costs of judicial administration) to involve greater use of per se rules. As another application, we would expect that as economists become better at providing evidence of particular price-fixing conspiracies' effects, optimal policy would shift toward less reliance on a per se rule.

5. A particularly amusing example of the extremes to which a purely semantic approach can take the Court can be found in Justice Blackmun's concurrence in the *Topco* case [405 U.S. 596 (1972)] involving a cooperative of small to medium-sized groceries' development of a private label. Blackmun laments, "Today's ruling will tend to stultify competition. The per se

rule, however, now appears to be so firmly established by the Court that, at this late date, I could not oppose it. Relief, if any is to be forthcoming, apparently must be by way of legislation."

6. For example, in *Broadcast Music* [441 U.S. 1 (1979)], the Supreme Court, asked to rule on whether a blanket license issued by a copyright cooperative is "price fixing," noted that "easy labels do not always supply ready answers": the blanket license involves price fixing in the literal sense, but "[a]s generally used in the antitrust field, 'price fixing' is a short-hand way of describing certain categories of business behavior to which the *per se* rule has been held applicable."

7. This is, in fact, somewhat inaccurate, since the U.S. courts typically did not enforce naked price-fixing agreements even before passage of the Sherman Act. (This is why, for example, the Joint Executive Committee cartel described in Porter [1983] had to revert to price wars rather than courts to enforce their agreement.)

8. The Sherman Act also prohibits other activities that may aid firms in colluding such as the exchange of side payments and certain types of information.

9. For an introduction to this literature, see Farrell and Rabin [1996]. The literature on cheap talk originated with Crawford and Sobel [1982].

10. A further complication in predicting the effect of communication about intended play on repeated oligopoly outcomes is that the ability to coordinate on desirable outcomes may actually *undercut* a cartel's ability to maintain high prices by reducing the likelihood of punishments following a deviation (see McCutcheon [1997]). Interestingly, Genesove and Mullin [2001] note that episodes of cheating in the Sugar Institute cartel of 1927–1936 (which engaged in extensive communication) were rarely met with retaliation unless they were gross violations of the cartel's agreement.

11. Kuhn [2001, 16–17] and Neven [2001, 71–76] also discuss some of this work.

12. Athey and Bagwell still assume away the coordination problem by focusing on the cartel's most profitable equilibrium. Regarding the incentive problem, it was clear in the previous static mechanism-design papers that for large enough discount factors, firms could be prevented from deviating from their assigned prices or outputs. What is new in Athey and Bagwell [2001] is the characterization of how the cartel adapts for lower discount factors and the use of future play as a transfer.

13. In this regard, it is interesting to note Genesove and Mullin's [2001] description of the extensive communication among members of the Sugar Institute cartel aimed at adjudicating claimed defections and proposing appropriate punishments.

14. Sproul attempts to choose the related prices to have a close correlation to the price of the product in question prior to the indictment yet to be relatively unaffected by the indictment or other factors affecting the market in which the indictment occurred.

15. In constructing these figures, the underlying series are aligned again so that the event in question occurs in the same numbered month in each case; Sproul chooses this month based on the average number of months between the indictment and the relevant event (for example, on average, seven months elapsed between the indictment and the imposition of government penalties, thus government penalities were imposed in "month 107"). Also indicated in each figure is the number of cases used to construct the index in question; missing information means that this number is less than twenty-five in each figure.

16. Note, however, that the percentage effect on consumer surplus may be substantially larger than the percentage effect on price. If, for example, demand takes the constant elasticity form $x(p) = p^{-\varepsilon}$, for $\varepsilon > 1$, then when price increases from p to αp (where $\alpha > 1$) the percentage reduction in consumer surplus is given by

$$\frac{CS(\alpha p) - CS(p)}{CS(p)} = \alpha^{1-\varepsilon} - 1.$$

Thus, when $\varepsilon = 2$, a 4.6% increase in price leads to a 4.6% decrease in consumer surplus. However, if $\varepsilon = 4$, it would lead instead to a 12.6% reduction in consumer surplus.

17. Newmark [1988] argues that even BNS's small effect is the result of some data problems in their study.

18. Daughety and Forsythe [1987], for example, show an effect of communication on cooperative behavior in experimental repeated Cournot games even after communication has been stopped.

19. Three of the thirteen defendants were located in southwestern Ohio, the rest were from eastern Ohio.

20. To get his estimate of the item's value, Kwoka adjusts the knock-out auction winning bid to account for the fact that a loser in the knock-out auction received a share of the winning bid.

21. In addition to the studies noted, Taylor [2002] provides some evidence using aggregate output data that the National Industrial Recovery Act of 1933, which organized cartels in various industies and provided for a time some element of governmental enforcement, had the effect of reducing output. Baldwin, Marshall, and Richard [1997] examine bidding behavior in U.S. forest timber sales. In their case, they do not have any direct evidence that collusion occurred. Rather, they fit structural models of noncooperative and cooperative bidding behavior, test which fits the data better (they find that the cooperative model does), and measure the difference in prices that would be expected to obtain were the firms to follow the noncooperative model instead of the cooperative one. They find that the forest service earns roughly 7.9% less revenue under the collusive mode of behavior. It should be noted, however, that the noncooperative behavior that Baldwin, Marshall, and Richard document may have been the result of tacit coordination rather than price fixing.

22. Note that the elasticity of demand could also affect the incentives to cheat on any given agreed-upon price (in a simple repeated Bertrand pricing game, however, it does not).

23. The experimental literature does offer some support for Hay and Kelley's implicit assumption, at least in certain circumstances. That literature provides some evidence that coordination in repeated oligopoly settings is difficult in the absence of communication once the number of players is larger than two or three (see, for example, Holt [1993]).

24. Added to this list is, of course, anything else that the antitrust authorities use as signals to launch investigations.

25. These are cases won at trial or settled with a plea of *nolo contendre*. Hay and Kelley restrict their attention to price-fixing agreements among competitors (for example, resale price-maintenance cases brought under section 1 of the Sherman Act are excluded).

26. For some cases in which the four-firm concentration ratio is unavailable, Hay and Kelley calculate market concentration by dividing 100 by the total number of firms in the market and multiplying by 4. Thus, these concentration figures represent a lower bound on the four-firm concentration ratio, assuming of course that Hay and Kelley (and the DOJ Fact Memoranda that they rely on) have not defined the market too narrowly.

27. Note, however, that four-digit industries may differ marketly from the "markets" identified by the DOJ (and, therefore, by Hay and Kelley) in these antitrust investigations. For example, the four-digit Ready-Mix Con-

crete Industry (#3273) had a 1982 four-firm concentration ratio of 6%, but it is a highly localized industry with significantly higher concentration in local markets.

28. The most likely effect working in the other direction is the antitrust agencies' possible tendency to look for price fixing in concentrated markets. Nonetheless, the diversity of ways in which these conspiracies were detected suggests that this probably does not undercut the conclusion that concentrated markets are more likely to engage in price fixing.

Some more recent papers have looked at factors explaining cartel formation in settings in which cartels were legal (although their agreements still were not enforced by courts). Symeonidis [2003] examines British cartels in the 1950s before passage of the 1956 Restrictive Trade Practices Act. Dick [1996a] looks at export cartels formed under the Webb-Pomerene Export Trade Act of 1918. While these papers avoid the problem of the DOJ's investigation strategy, the determinants of cartel formation could be different in this different legal environment. (In general, there should be a connection in equilibrium between the DOJ's investigation process and the cartel-formation process.) Also related are papers looking at the duration of legal cartels, such as Suslow [1988], Marquez [1994], and Dick [1996b].

29. One possible exception to this conclusion arises in settings in which firms possess independent private information. In this case, we might infer that communication is taking place if we see a firm's behavior varying with private information that should only be known to other firms (or, equivalently, correlated with other firms' behavior, conditional on observables). The difficulty in making such an inference, however, arises from the possibility that firms may obtain some imperfect signals of each others' information even without communication.

30. As previously noted, there is some experimental evidence that successful coordination in repeated oligopoly games is unlikely in the absence of explicit communication once the number of players exceeds two or three. If this were true in actual markets, evidence of cooperative behavior in such circumstances should lead to an inference that price fixing is likely. Given its importance for inferences of price fixing from behavioral evidence, it would be good to see more work addressing this issue.

31. For a useful discussion of these cases, see Areeda and Kaplow [1997, 264–286].

32. See, for example, Posner's recent judicial opinion in the high-fructose corn syrup case (2002 U.S. App. LEXIS 11940) and Carlton, Gertner, and Rosenfield [1997].

Chapter 3

1. Indeed, concern over the fate of small (and often inefficient) businesses frequently led the courts to use merger-related efficiencies as evidence *against* a proposed merger during this period.

2. We assume here that these costs represent true social costs. Reductions in the marginal cost of production because of increased monopsony power resulting from the merger would not count as a social gain. Likewise, if input markets are not perfectly competitive, then reductions in cost attributable to the merger must be calculated at the true social marginal cost of the inputs rather than at their distorted market prices.

3. Specifically, the welfare loss caused by a small reduction in output is equal to the price-cost margin.

4. On this point, see also the discussion in Baker [1999a].

5. Besanko and Spulber [1993] provide an interesting argument for why it may be better to commit an antitrust authority (the agencies and courts) to a consumer surplus standard even though the true welfare objective is aggregate surplus maximization. In their model, the antitrust authority cannot observe the cost improvement generated by a merger, although the firms proposing the merger can observe this. The model has firms first decide whether to propose a merger (at a fixed cost), and then the authority decides whether to block the merger if proposed. In their equilibrium, which is necessarily in mixed strategies, the authority is indifferent about blocking a merger. This implies that proposed mergers necessarily reduce aggregate surplus net of the fixed cost if the authority uses an aggregate surplus criterion. By committing to a consumer surplus criterion, the set of consummated mergers in equilibrium instead raises aggregate surplus.

6. Formally, (A1) and (A2) have the following implications:

(i) Each firm i's profit-maximization problem, given the joint output of its rivals X_{-i}, is strictly concave and therefore has a unique solution. Moreover, letting $b_i(X_{-i})$ denote firm i's best-response function, $b_i(\cdot)$ is nonincreasing and $b_i'(X_{-i}) \in (-1, 0)$ at all X_{-i} such that $b_i(X_{-i}) > 0$.

(ii) The equilibrium aggregate output is unique. To see this, define each firm i's *aggregate output best-response function* as $\lambda_i(X) = \{x_i : x_i = b_i(X - x_i)\}$. For a given level of aggregate output X, this function gives the output level for firm i that is consistent with X if firm i is playing a best response to its rivals' aggregate output. By observation (i), this output level is unique, is nonincreasing in X, and is strictly decreasing in X wherever

$\lambda_i(X) > 0$. The equilibrium aggregate output is then the unique solution to $\sum_i \lambda_i(X) = X$.

(iii) For any set of firms I, define its *equilibrium best-response function*

$$b_I^e(X_{-I}) \equiv \left\{ \sum_{i \in I} x_i : x_i = b_i(X_{I/\{i\}} + X_{-I}) \text{ for all } i \in I \right\}.$$

This gives, conditional on X_{-I}, the (unique) aggregate output for firms in set I that results if all of the firms in set I are playing best responses. It is the solution to $\sum_{i \in I} \lambda_i(X_I + X_{-I}) = X_I$. From this, one can see that $b_I^e(\cdot)$ is nonincreasing and $b_I^{e\prime}(X_{-I}) \in (-1, 0)$ whenever $b_I^e(X_{-I}) > 0$, just like the individual best-response functions.

(iv) The premerger equilibrium joint outputs of the merging and non-merging firms $(\hat{X}_{12}, \hat{X}_{-12})$ are the unique solution to

$b_{12}^e(\hat{X}_{-12}) = \hat{X}_{12}$

$b_{-12}^e(\hat{X}_{12}) = \hat{X}_{-12}.$

The postmerger equilibrium joint outputs $(\bar{X}_{12}, \bar{X}_{-12})$ are the unique solution to

$b_M(\bar{X}_{-12}) = \bar{X}_{12}$

$b_{-12}^e(\bar{X}_{12}) = \bar{X}_{-12},$

where $b_M(\cdot)$ is the best-response function of the merged firm. Given the properties of these best-response functions noted in observation (iii), aggregate output increases after the merger if and only if $b_M(\hat{X}_{-12}) > b_{12}^e(\hat{X}_{-12})$.

7. A proof of this result goes as follows: Given the premerger aggregate output of firm 1 and firm 2's rivals, $\hat{X}_{-12}$, let $(\bar{x}_1, \bar{x}_2)$ denote the merged firm's best response. Also, let $b_i(\cdot)$ be the premerger best-response function of firm i for $i = 1, 2$. Observe, first, that after the merger we must have $\bar{x}_1 \leq b_1(\bar{x}_2 + \hat{X}_{-12})$ and $\bar{x}_2 \leq b_2(\bar{x}_1 + \hat{X}_{-12})$. (Formally, this can be established using a simple revealed preference argument; intuitively, the merged firm reduces both of its plants' outputs below their unmerged best responses since it internalizes the externality that each plant's output has on its other plant.) Now suppose, contrary to our hypothesis, that $\bar{x}_1 + \bar{x}_2 > \hat{x}_1 + \hat{x}_2$. Clearly $\bar{x}_i > \hat{x}_i$ for either $i = 1$ or $i = 2$; without loss of generality, suppose that $\bar{x}_2 > \hat{x}_2$. Then

$\bar{x}_1 \leq b_1(\bar{x}_2 + \hat{X}_{-12}) < b_1(\hat{x}_2 + \hat{X}_{-12}) = \hat{x}_1.$

But, $\bar{x}_1 < \hat{x}_1$ implies that

$\bar{x}_1 + \bar{x}_2 \leq \bar{x}_1 + b_2(\bar{x}_1 + \hat{X}_{-12}) < \hat{x}_1 + b_2(\hat{x}_1 + \hat{X}_{-12}) = \hat{x}_1 + \hat{x}_2,$

which is a contradiction.

Spector [2003] shows that if one adds the assumption that the merger is profitable (as we do below when considering effects on aggregate surplus), then price cannot fall after a merger that involves no synergies even if entry occurs after the merger.

8. Note that in the Cournot model a merger need not increase the profits of the merging firms because of rivals' resulting output expansion (Salant, Switzer, and Reynolds [1983]; see also Perry and Porter [1985]).

9. $\frac{dx_i}{dX}$ is equal to $\lambda_i'(\hat{X})$, the derivative of firm i's aggregate output best-response function (see note 6). We get $\frac{dx_i}{dX}$ from implicitly differentiating the expression $P'(X)x_i + P(X) - c_i'(x_i) = 0$. Note that $\frac{dx_i}{dX} = \left(\frac{dx_i}{dX_{-i}}\right) \Big/ \left(1 + \frac{dx_i}{dX_{-i}}\right)$, where $dX_{-i} \equiv \sum_{j \neq i} dx_j$ and $\frac{dx_i}{dX_{-i}}$ is the slope of firm i's best-response function $b_i'(X_{-i})$.

10. In particular, this is so if $[P''(\cdot), P'''(\cdot), c_i''(\cdot), -c_i'''(\cdot)] \geq 0$.

11. If the inverse demand function is linear, then dE is also negative whenever $s_I > \frac{1}{2}$.

12. Note that when a merger will instead *lower* price, dE is positive when the reverse of condition (3.13) holds. In that case, a merger is more likely to have a positive external effect when the merging firms are large and the nonmerging firms are small (and hence, not very efficient). In fact, Levin [1990] shows that (in an environment with constant returns to scale) if the most efficient nonmerged firm is less efficient than the merged firm and price falls following the merger, then the merger necessarily increases aggregate surplus.

13. Although they bear some superficial resemblance to the concentration tests that appear in the DOJ/FTC *Horizontal Merger Guidelines* (see section 3), they differ from the *Guidelines'* tests in some significant ways, such as the fact that increases in the concentration of nonmerging firms can make the merger more desirable socially.

14. In this regard, it appears from event study evidence that, on average, mergers increase the joint value of the merging firms, although there is a large variance in outcomes across mergers (Andrade, Mitchell, and Stafford [2001], Jensen and Ruback [1983]). One might take the view, in any case, that antitrust policy should not concern itself with stopping mergers based on unresolved agency problems within the merging firms.

15. One exception is Gowrisankaran [1999] who allows for a merger-specific "synergy" (effectively, a reduction in fixed costs) in his computational model of endogenous mergers.

16. In particular, efficiency in this sense *decreased* as the industry went from monopoly to a more competitive market structure. However, overall industry productivity increased over time as capital was reallocated toward more efficient firms.

17. In contrast, Gerstle and Waldman [2004] show that when used goods are of lower quality than new ones and consumers differ in their willingness to pay for high quality, a newly-formed monopolist will be able to raise price right away and welfare losses are larger than in the setting studied by Carlton and Gertner.

18. This point is also related to the literature on contracting with externalities (for example, Segal [1999]) discussed in chapter 4.

19. A copy of the *Guidelines* can be found at http://www.usdoj.gov/atr/public/guidelines/horiz_book/hmg1.html and http://www.ftc.gov/bc/docs/horizmer.htm.

20. The *Guidelines* state that

The Agency will not challenge a merger if cognizable efficiencies are of a character and magnitude such that the merger is not likely to be anticompetitive in any relevant market. To make the requisite determination, the Agency considers whether cognizable efficiencies likely would be sufficient to reverse the merger's potential to harm consumers in the relevant market, e.g., by preventing price increases in that market.

Note, however, that this test is stated as a sufficient condition for approving a merger, not as a necessary one. This ambiguity may seem a bit odd, but is probably deliberate. The agencies have some prosecutorial discretion, and can approve mergers that the courts might block. While the courts' standard is not totally clear either, it surely leans more toward a consumer surplus standard than is the preference of the economists at the agencies. In addition, there appears to be some difference in the standards applied by the DOJ and the FTC, with the FTC more inclined toward a consumer surplus standard than the DOJ. (Since the agencies tend to specialize in reviewing mergers in different industries, this has the effect of applying somewhat different standards in different industries.) On this issue, see also Werden [1997].

21. More generally, such an equation could be estimated on a panel data set of many markets observed over time.

22. This correlation would not be present, for example, if the firms have constant marginal costs and engage in Bertrand pricing prior to the merger.

23. The discussion in the text takes the price of substitutes q as exogenous. However, this price may also be correlated with ε and may need to be instrumented.

24. Berry, Levinsohn, and Pakes build on previous work by Bresnahan [1987], as well as a large literature on discrete choice and product characteristics (see, for example, McFadden [1981] and the references therein). For further reading on these methods, see Ackerberg et al. [forth.].

25. If individual-level demographic and purchase data are available, then the parameters in (3.20) can be estimated at an individual level; otherwise, the population distribution of demographic variables can be used with aggregate data, as in Nevo [2001].

26. To see this, recall that in the logit model, the demand for good k given price vector p and M consumers is

$$x_i(p) = M \frac{e^{a_k \cdot \beta - \alpha p_k}}{\sum_j e^{a_j \cdot \beta - \alpha p_j}},$$

so the ratio of the demands for any two goods j and k is independent of the prices of all other goods.

27. The fact that two products with the same market shares have the same cross-elasticity of demand with any third product in fact follows from the additive independent and identically distributed error structure of the logit model [which implies that they must have the same value of $(a_j \cdot \beta - \alpha p_j)$], not the extreme value assumption. The extreme value assumption implies, however, the stronger IIA property mentioned in the text.

28. See Olley and Pakes [1996] and Griliches and Mairesse [1995] for discussions of these issues.

29. The same type of inference can be made with multiproduct firms using a somewhat more complicated equation. See Nevo [2001].

30. Alternatively, given a behavioral assumption, one can try to econometrically infer costs by jointly estimating demand and the firms' supply relations as discussed in Bresnahan [1989].

31. More formal consumer-survey methods can also be used; see, for example, the discussion in Baker and Rubinfeld [1999].

32. The use of price in structure-conduct-performance studies was most forcefully advocated by Weiss [1990].

33. For an interesting discussion of the use of econometric evidence in the case, see Baker [1999b].

34. The data were actually a panel of stores over time, rather than just a single cross section or time series as in equation (3.25).

35. The case was presented before the Surface Transportation Board, which has jurisdiction over railroad mergers.

36. Often some of the other right-hand side variables are endogenous as well. For example, in studies of airline pricing, it is common to include the load factor on a route—the share of available seats that are sold—as a right-hand side variable affecting costs.

37. See Peters [2003] for one look at this question.

38. Alternatively, one could simply compare the actual premerger prices with those predicted under various behavioral assumptions, as in Nevo [2000b].

39. See Peters [2003] for a discussion of how different assumptions about the demand structure affect these conclusions.

40. It should be noted, however, that Peters looks only at the year following consummation of the merger. These changes may be more significant over a longer period.

41. A similar derivation can be done to derive instead a residual ordinary (rather than inverse) demand function.

42. That is, the function $\bar{B}_{-1}(\cdot)$ is the sum of the quantities in the vector function $B_{-1}(\cdot)$.

43. In the special case in which the merged firm will act as a Stackleberg leader, we can however use the estimates of (3.22) and (3.23) to derive the postmerger prices by solving $\max_{x_1, x_2} \sum_{i=1,2} [R_i(x_1, x_2, z, w_3) - c_i] x_i$ for the merged firm's optimal quantities (x_1^*, x_2^*) and then computing $p_1^* = R_1(x_1^*, x_2^*, z, w_3)$ and $p_2^* = R_2(x_1^*, x_2^*, z, w_3)$.

44. In principal, we can try to distinguish between anticompetitive and precedent effects by looking for differential stock-price responses among rivals: competitive effects should be felt more strongly by rivals that compete more closely with the merging firms. In this way, Prager [1992] finds evidence of precedent effects in her study of the 1901 merger between Great Northern Railway and the Northern Pacific Railway. One caveat, however, is that in some cases the precedent effect also may be more relevant for these same firms.

45. The set of steel rivals excludes the Great Northern Railway which had a complicated relationship with USS because of USS's lease of the Great

Northern Railway's iron ore holdings. Mullin, Mullin, and Mullin examine the effects of the events on the Great Northern Railway separately, which are not reported here.

46. The railroads were both customers and suppliers to USS since a great deal of steel was shipped by rail. Mullin, Mullin, and Mullin argue that the effects on both suppliers and customers should be similar because they would both depend on only the change in the output of steel.

47. Street rail stock prices were available only toward the end of the sample period. Note also that table 5 in the paper, from which the results in table 3.3 are drawn, also reports the effect of these events on the Great Northern Railway.

48. The studies in Kaplan [2000], for example, illustrate how the stock market's initial reaction to a merger is often a poor forecast of the merger's ultimate profitability.

49. Pautler [2003] surveys some articles that are not discussed here, including studies looking at profitability, stock price reactions, and other effects.

50. To the extent that the limited amount of work is because of a lack of data, one way to enhance our knowledge (or at least that of the DOJ and FTC) may be for the enforcement agencies to require parties to approved (or partially approved) mergers to provide the agencies with information for some period of time after their merger.

51. NW and RC accounted for 42% and 37% respectively of enplanements at Minneapolis; TW and OZ accounted for 57% and 25% of enplanements at St. Louis.

52. Note that this average price change is therefore not equal to the change in the average relative prices reported in the relative-price columns.

53. Werden, Joskow, and Johnson [1991] also look at these two mergers. Using somewhat different techniques from Borenstein, they also find that the NW-RC merger increased prices substantially, while the TW-OZ merger had smaller (but, in their case, still positive) price effects on routes for which the merging firms were active competitors. Peters [2003] also reports price changes for these same mergers in his study of six mergers during this period. His data show instead that prices increased 7.2% and 16% in the NW-RC and TW-OZ mergers, respectively, in markets that were initally served by both merging firms. Peters reports that they increased 11% and 19.5%, respectively, in markets where these firms faced no premerger competition.

54. It is perhaps a little surprising, however, that substantial efficiencies would be realized so soon after completion. Moreover, there is some evidence (Kole and Lehn [2000]) that these mergers may have led to increases rather than decreases in marginal costs.

55. Evans and Kessides [1994] perform a structure-conduct-performance-style study of the relationship between airline prices and both concentration and multimarket contact during this period and find positive and economically significant price effects from both factors. Their findings also provide indirect evidence on the effects of the airline mergers during this period because most of the changes in concentration and multimarket contact in their sample were attributable to mergers.

56. Borenstein [1990] and Werden, Joskow, and Johnson [1991] report similar changes in service following the NW-RC and TW-OZ mergers.

57. MMDA accounts have restricted check-writing privileges.

58. In fact, matters are somewhat more complicated than this, because the pricing data are at the bank level, not the market (SMSA) level. Hence, the merger exposure variables are actually weighted averages (by deposits) of the exposures that a given bank i has in the various markets in which it operates.

59. Wholesale prices did increase significantly fifteen months after the merger, but the authors argue that this was because of an unrelated supply shock.

60. In an older study, Barton and Sherman [1984] document the price changes that occurred following the 1976 and 1979 acquisitions of two competitors by a manufacturer of two types of duplicating microfilm. They provide evidence consistent with price increases following the merger. The data they use comes as a result of a 1981 FTC antitrust suit seeking to reverse the acquisitions.

61. One reason for greater synergies simply may be that the managers of the acquiring firm are more likely to understand the business of the acquired firm; see, for example, Kaplan, Mitchell, and Wruck [2000].

62. This is also consistent with the event-study analysis of stock price returns, which finds wide variation in how the market evaluates announced mergers. At the same time, as the case studies in Kaplan [2000] document, a merger's performance may end up being very different from the market's initial forecast.

63. This is true for several reasons. First, the investment first-order conditions he uses are entirely static, while investment choices are likely to be affected by dynamic considerations. Second, his procedure relies on an assumed investment-cost function (this might not be necessary if one instead has panel data). Finally, one cannot distinguish whether the changes in marginal cost he derives reflect shifts of the plant's marginal-cost function or movements along an unchanging function.

Chapter 4

1. Rey and Tirole [forth.] also provide an excellent introduction to this area. Two of the original contributions on vertical mergers and tying, respectively, not discussed here, are Ordover, Saloner, and Salop [1990] and Whinston [1990]. For a discussion more focused on jurisprudence, see Krattenmaker and Salop [1986].

2. One difference between the *Microsoft* case and the models explored here is that the source of Microsoft's market power came not from its position in browsers, but rather from its Windows operating system. Thus, the case involved issues of leveraging market power from one product to another. The other major issue in the case was related to Microsoft's bundling of Internet Explorer with Windows. For more detail on the use of exclusive contracts and bundling (or "tying") in the case, see Whinston [2001].

3. For a summary of federal exclusive-dealing cases that reached at least the appellate level before 1990, see Frasco [1991].

4. Although I will typically suppose that it is a buyer who is subject to an exclusivity provision, similar ideas apply when a seller is so bound.

5. Two implicit assumptions are embedded in this structure. First, when B and I initially contract, B cannot contract with E instead at that time. For example, the identity of E may not be known, or E may not be a credible supplier at that time. Second, while B and I contract on exclusivity, they do not contract directly on future trade of the good. For example, the exact specifications of the good that B will want may be unclear at that point (see, for example, Grossman and Hart [1986]).

6. When the entrant's monopoly profit $(p - c_E)D(p)$ is concave in p, this is true when its monopoly price is above c_I.

7. The contract is, in essence, an option contract, giving B the choice of whether to buy at price p, or not to buy and make payment d.

8. In the original Aghion and Bolton paper, I makes a take-it-or-leave-it offer to B.

9. In fact, the only thing that matters here for E and B's behavior is the effective price $p - d$. Thus, provided lump-sum, up-front transfers are possible at the time they sign their contract (as we have assumed), B and I could just as well not specify a stipulated damage (that is, set $d = 0$) and set only a price p in their contract.

10. A similar conclusion holds if when B breaches the contract the court requires him to pay only damages that reimburse I for his lost profits, $p - c_I$. In this case, B will always make an efficient breach decision.

11. In many standard multiparty bargaining solutions, such as the Shapley Value, the existence of the contract between B and I would reduce E's payoff and raise the joint payoff of B and I. In these bargaining processes, there is (implicitly at least) the possibility that B and I are unable to renegotiate their contract. Another reason why renegotiation of the contract may be imperfect is that asymmetric infomation may exist between B and I after E enters. In particular, I may not be able to observe the offer that E makes to B. In this case, I may be suspicious when B suggests a renegotiation that, say, lowers d, since B will have an incentive to suggest this even when he receives an offer from E that is less than $p - d$. (For a discussion of contract renegotiation under asymmetric information see Dewatripont [1988].)

12. Aghion and Bolton [1987] also consider a model of multiple buyers and note the presence of externalities across buyers. In contrast to Rasmussen, Ramseyer, and Wiley [1991] and Segal and Whinston [2000a], they assume that I can make contingent offers to buyers whose terms depend directly on whether other buyers have signed contracts with I.

13. These are three specific models of multilateral contracting with externalities (see, for example, Segal [1999] and Segal and Whinston [2003]). In each of these models, contracts are publicly observed, as assumed in the Rasmussen, Ramseyer, and Wiley [1991] and Segal and Whinston [2000a] papers. One could also imagine settings in which contracts are privately observed, as in the models discussed in section 4.4.

14. For example, if $\pi^m = 7$ and $x^* = 12$ (and I still needs to sign two buyers to exclude E) then I cannot exclude profitably with simultaneous offers, but can exclude at a cost of 12 with sequential offers (I offers buyer 1 a payment of 12 to sign him, and then can sign buyers 2 and 3 for free).

15. See, for example, Stefanadis [1997].

16. The continuing success of this strategy also depends on E not being able to contract with buyers for future sales prior to entry.

17. Fumagalli and Motta [2003] discuss the effect of competition on the number of buyers needed for exclusion, while Simpson and Wickelgren [2004] discuss the pass-through effect. Stefanadis [1998] also studies a model with competing buyers, but he assumes that I's contracts can specify a linear wholesale price at which the buyer can make purchases, but cannot include any lump-sum payment.

18. This is true not only for exclusionary vertical contracts, but also for unilateral exclusionary behavior such as predatory pricing.

19. For example, returning to the Aghion and Bolton model with uncertain entrant costs, our strong welfare conclusion there came from the assumption of Bertrand postentry pricing.

20. The main focus of Hart and Tirole [1990] was actually vertical integration, but their model can be applied directly to the study of exclusive contracts, as done here.

21. The assumptions of constant returns to scale and identical costs for the two retailers are inessential for the conclusions below, but do simplify the exposition. The assumption of constant returns to scale for the manufacturer, on the other hand, is relevant for the attractiveness of the restrictions on beliefs I impose below. See note 23 for more on this.

22. Formally, we are looking at weak perfect Bayesian equilibria with additional restrictions on off-equilibrium path beliefs (see, for example, Mas-Colell, Whinston, and Green [1995]).

23. Passive beliefs need not always make sense. For example, if M did not have constant returns to scale, then the amount he wants to trade with R_{-j} would be affected by the amount he trades with R_j. Segal and Whinston [2003] characterize equilibrium contracting outcomes without assuming passive beliefs. By expanding the set of allowable contracts to include option contracts from which M can choose, they establish conditions under which the joint profit-maximizing outcome can be ruled out for *any* beliefs when contracting externalities are present.

24. In fact, this is true for *any* beliefs that the retailers might hold, not just passive beliefs. This is because, in the absence of contracting externalities, the amount a retailer is willing to pay is independent of his beliefs.

25. As this suggests, in the present model if M's offers were instead public (as in the multibuyer model of section 4.3), then the joint profit-maximizing

outcome would be sustainable. For a discussion of the general conditions under which joint profit maximization fails to arise with both public and private offers, see Segal [1999].

26. In the Bernheim and Whinston bidding-game approach, the joint profit-maximizing outcome is sustained when contracting externalities are absent using "sell-out" contracts. In these contracts, each retailer j offers the manufacturer a nonlinear total-payment schedule of the form $t_j(x_j) = F_j + P_j(x_j)$, from which the manufacturer can choose how much to sell. Given schedules of this form, the manufacturer chooses the sales levels (x_A^{**}, x_B^{**}). The fixed transfer F_j is set at the level that makes the manufacturer indifferent about accepting j's contract, which gives each retailer j a profit exactly equal to his incremental contribution to the joint profit of the three parties.

This bargaining process frequently has multiple equilibria. Bernheim and Whinston focus on the equilibrium that is best for the retailers (who move first, making the offers). As a general matter, both bargaining processes have multiple equilibria. In the offer game these arise because of freedom in specifying off-equilibrium path beliefs; in the bidding game these arise because of freedom in specifying unchosen offers.

27. Bernheim and Whinston [1998, section (IVC)] and Segal and Whinston [2003, section 7] characterize equilibria in bidding game models with contracting externalities.

28. It is the second of these that is perhaps a strong assumption. Without this assumption there would always be an exclusive equilibrium (perhaps in addition to a nonexclusive one) since, for any offer that M makes to R_j, R_j could believe that M is selling a large enough quantity to R_{-j} that he should reject M's offer. This parallels the finding in Bernheim and Whinston [1998] that there is always an exclusive equilibrium in their bidding-game model (in the absence of their equilibrium refinement). In a bidding game this arises because if R_{-j} makes only an exclusive offer to M, then it is a best response for R_j to do so as well. Thus, an equilibrium always exists in which only exclusive offers are made.

29. To take a simple example, imagine that there are three consumers who each want at most one unit of a divisible good. Two consumers have a valuation of 8, while the third has a valuation of 2. Production is costless and the entry cost is $f = 1$. In this case, when exclusives are allowed, two units are sold by a single retailer, but when exclusives are banned, two units are again sold, but by two retailers. Hence, aggregate surplus is lower when exclusives are banned.

30. The Third Circuit came to a similar conclusion regarding contractual duration in the recent *LePage's v. 3M* case [324 F.3d 141 (2003)]. In this case,

3M was accused of offering a rebate program in which it offered discounts on its transparent adhesive tape that were tied to a customer's purchases of other 3M products. Although that case was formally about tied sales, such sales have much in common with exclusive-dealing agreements.

31. O'Brien and Shaffer [1997] also study this case.

32. This conclusion does not depend on our assumption of constant returns to scale; it is true as long as each M_j's costs depend only on his own output level x_j.

33. In the Bernheim and Whinston [1998] bidding-game approach, the outcome (x_A^{**}, x_B^{**}) is again sustained using "sell-out" contracts.

34. The ability of firms to offer lump-sum payments is important for this conclusion. For example, exclusive contracts might arise if contracts can specify only a simple linear price (see Mathewson and Winter [1987]).

35. The only difference from Bork is that this outcome need not maximize either consumer or aggregate surplus. (It does maximize aggregate surplus if the retailer can price discriminate perfectly.)

36. We will see in section 4.5 that this conclusion must be qualified when moral hazard problems are present.

37. It might seem strange that R_1 makes offers to the manufacturers, but the manufacturers make offers to R_2. The reason for the latter assumption is to ensure that M_A earns a positive profit from selling to R_2 when M_B is excluded. In the original Bernheim and Whinston [1998] paper, the M's make offers to both retailers. I have R_1 making offers here only to simplify the exposition by maintaining the same bargaining model as in the earlier models of this section.

38. This can increase the joint profit of R_1 and the two manufacturers if $(\underline{v}_1 - c_B) + (c_A - c_B) + [(c_A - c_B) - (v_2 - c_A)] < f$.

39. Bernheim and Whinston [1998] show this using their bidding-game bargaining process. To analyze this example instead with an offer game one needs to move away from passive beliefs, even when exclusives are not possible, since whenever R_1 offers to buy two units from M_j, M_j should realize that R_1 has not offered a contract to M_{-j}. Moreover, the outcome in which R_1 and M_A exclude M_B using a nonexclusionary contract for two units is sustainable as an equilibrium in an offer game only if either M_A does not hold passive beliefs or we introduce option contracts of the type considered by Segal and Whinston [2003] (otherwise R_1 would deviate and instead offer M_A a nonexclusive contract for purchase of just one unit).

40. One recent exception is Prat and Rustichini [2003]. A second exception is the Hart and Tirole [1990] model in which there is a second upstream firm with higher marginal cost than M. Although I do not discuss that model here, introducing a second less-efficient manufacturer into the model of exclusives to reduce retail competition with undifferentiated retailers would still lead to exclusive dealing in some cases, but not in all. See also Rey and Verge [2004] and Spector [2004].

41. Stefanadis [1997] also studies a multiseller/multibuyer model. In his model, each seller can contract with only one of the buyers.

42. Segal and Whinston [2000b] briefly discuss the case in which B and S can also specify trade terms in their initial contract.

43. With or without exclusivity, S's equilibrium investment level, i_S^*, satisfies the first-order condition $\frac{1}{2}c'(i_S^*) = -1$ (if it is strictly positive).

44. Segal and Whinston [2000b] also consider cases in which E is not competitive. In this case, there is a difference between what is good for B and S jointly and what is socially optimal, since B and S will have incentives to extract some of E's surplus, much as in Aghion and Bolton [1987].

45. For a discussion of welfare results when internal trade is not always efficient, see Segal and Whinston [2000b].

46. These papers provide alternatives to the Segal and Whinston [2000b] model for formalizing the Bork [1978] retailer-loyalty argument.

47. Marvel draws the first three facts from evidence in pre-Clayton Act cases concerning the industry, and so it is not clear whether they still applied by 1918 when the district court ruled in the *Standard Fashion* case.

48. Ornstein [1989] also argues that the postdecision experiences following five well-known cases in which exclusive contracts were deemed illegal illustrate that these contracts were not anticompetitive. One of these is the *Standard Fashion* case, where he repeats Marvel's arguments. In two of the other four cases (the *United Shoe Machinery* and *Beltone* cases) the leading firm did in fact lose substantial share following the decision. Ornstein argues that this was for reasons unrelated to the decisions and that the level of market concentration did not change.

49. Indeed, if one views the key difference as ownership of the list of customers (with vertical integration, the company owns the list), as argued in the Grossman and Hart [1986] paper that we discuss next, and if access to the list is essential for an agent continuing to sell to a customer, then vertical integration is equivalent to exclusive dealing. See Segal and Whinston [2000b] for more on this.

50. Marin and Sicotte also look separately at net-importing industries. The results here are less strong than for net-exporting industries. This may be because domestic producers in net-importing industries can either be distributors of foreign-made products (who would be hurt by price increases in shipping) or competitors with foreign producers who sell in the United States (who would be helped by price increases in shipping). No similar ambiguity arises for net-exporting industries.

51. Similar methods were used by Villas-Boas [2003] in her study of vertical pricing in the yogurt market.

References

Ackerberg, D., L. Benkard, S. Berry, and A. Pakes. Forthcoming. Econometric tools for analyzing market outcomes. In *Handbook of Econometrics*, ed. J. J. Heckman. Amsterdam, the Netherlands: Elsevier.

Aghion, P., and P. Bolton. 1987. Contracts as a barrier to entry. *American Economic Review* 77 (June): 388–401.

Andrade, G., M. Mitchell, and E. Stafford. 2001. New evidence and perspectives on mergers. *Journal of Economic Perspectives* 15: 103–120.

Areeda, P., and H. Hovenkamp. 2004. *Antitrust law: An analysis of antitrust principles and their application.* New York: Aspen Law & Business.

Areeda, P., and L. Kaplow. 1997. *Antitrust analysis: Problems, text, cases.* 5th ed. New York: Aspen Law & Business.

Asker, J. 2004a. Measuring advantages from exclusive dealing. Mimeo.

Asker, J. 2004b. Diagnosing foreclosure due to exclusive dealing. Mimeo.

Athey, S., and K. Bagwell. 2001. Optimal collusion with private information. *RAND Journal of Economics* 32: 428–465.

Athey, S., K. Bagwell, and C. Sanchirico. 2004. Collusion and price rigidity. *Review of Economic Studies* 71 (April): 317–349.

Ausubel, L. M., and R. J. Deneckere. 1987. One is almost enough for monopoly. *RAND Journal of Economics* 18: 255–274.

Baker, J. B. 1988. Private information and the deterrent effect of antitrust damage remedies. *Journal of Law, Economics, and Organization* 4 (Fall): 385–408.

Baker, J. B. 1999a. Developments in antitrust economics. *Journal of Economic Perspectives* 13: 181–194.

Baker, J. B. 1999b. Econometric analysis in *FTC v. Staples*. *Journal of Public Policy & Marketing* 18: 11–21.

Baker, J. B., and T. F. Bresnahan. 1985. The gains to merger or collusion in product-differentiated industries. *Journal of Industrial Economics* 33: 427–444.

Baker, J. B., and T. F. Bresnahan. 1988. Estimating the residual demand curve facing a single firm. *International Journal of Industrial Organization* 6: 283–300.

Baker, J. B., and D. L. Rubinfeld. 1999. Empirical methods used in antitrust litigation: Review and critique. *American Law and Economics Review* 1: 386–435.

Baldwin, L. H., R. C. Marshall, and J.-F. Richard. 1997. Bidder collusion at forect service timber sales. *Journal of Political Economy* 105: 657–699.

Barton, D. M., and R. Sherman. 1984. The price and profit effects of horizontal merger: A case study. *Journal of Industrial Economics* 33: 165–177.

Beckner, C. F. III, and S. C. Salop. 1999. Decision theory and antitrust rules. *Antitrust Law Journal* 67: 41–76.

Benoit, J.-P. 1984. Financially constrained entry in a game with incomplete information. *RAND Journal of Economics* 4: 490–499.

Bernheim, B. D., and M. D. Whinston. 1985. Common marketing agency as a device for facilitating collusion. *RAND Journal of Economics* 16: 269–281.

Bernheim, B. D., and M. D. Whinston. 1986a. Menu auctions, resource allocation, and economic influence. *Quarterly Journal of Economics* 101 (February): 1–31.

Bernheim, B. D., and M. D. Whinston. 1986b. Common agency. *Econometrica* 54 (July): 923–942.

Bernheim, B. D., and M. D. Whinston. 1990. Multimarket contact and collusive behavior. *RAND Journal of Economics* 21: 1–26.

Bernheim, B. D., and M. D. Whinston. 1998. Exclusive dealing. *Journal of Political Economy* 106 (February): 64–103.

Berry, S. T. 1994. Estimating discrete choice models of product differentiation. *RAND Journal of Economics* 25: 242–262.

Berry, S. T., J. Levinsohn, and A. Pakes. 1995. Automobile prices in market equilibrium. *Econometrica* 63: 841–890.

Berry, S. T., and A. Pakes. 1993. Some applications and limitations of recent advances in empirical industrial organization: Merger analysis. *American Economic Review Papers and Proceedings* 83: 247–252.

Besanko, D., and M. Perry. 1993. Equilibrium incentives for exclusive dealing in a differentiated products oligopoly. *RAND Journal of Economics* 24 (Winter): 646–667.

Besanko, D., and M. Perry. 1994. Exclusive dealing in a spatial model of retail competition. *International Journal of Industrial Organization* 12 (September): 297–329.

Besanko, D., and D. F. Spulber. 1993. Contested mergers and equilibrium antitrust policy. *Journal of Law, Economics, and Organization* 9: 1–29.

Bloch, F. 1996. Sequential formation of coalitions in games with externalities and fixed payoff division. *Games and Economic Behavior* 14: 90–123.

Block, K. B., F. C. Nold, and J. G. Sidak. 1981. The deterrent effect of antitrust enforcement. *Journal of Political Economy* 89: 429–445.

Bolton, P., and D. Scharfstein. 1990. A theory of predation based on agency problems in financial contracting. *American Economic Review* 80: 93–106.

Borenstein, S. 1990. Airline mergers, airport dominance, and market power. *American Economic Review* 80: 400–404.

Bork, R. H. 1978. *The antitrust paradox: A policy at war with itself*. New York: Basic Books.

Bresnahan, T. F. 1987. Competition and collusion in the american automobile industry: The 1955 price war. *Journal of Industrial Economics* 35: 457–482.

Bresnahan, T. F. 1989. Empirical methods in industries with market power. In *Handbook of Industrial Organization* vol. II, eds. R. Schmalensee and R. Willig. Amsterdam, the Netherlands: Elsevier.

Brock, W., and J. Scheinkman. 1985. Price-setting supergames with capacity constraints. *Review of Economic Studies* 52: 371–382.

Carlton, D. W., and R. H. Gertner. 1989. Market power and mergers in durable goods industries. *Journal of Law and Economics* 32: 203–226.

Carlton, D. W., R. H. Gertner, and A. Rosenfield. 1997. Communication among competitors: Game theory and antitrust. *George Mason Law Review* 5: 423–440.

Choi, D., and G. C. Philippatos. 1983. Financial consequences of antitrust enforcement. *Review of Economics and Statistics* 65: 501–506.

Coase, R. H. 1972. Durability and monopoly. *Journal of Law and Economics* 15: 143–149.

Compte, O. 1998. Communication in repeated games with imperfect private monitoring. *Econometrica* 66: 597–626.

Compte, O., F. Jenny, and P. Rey. 2002. Capacity constraints, mergers, and collusion. *European Economic Review* 46: 1–29.

Connor, J. M. 2001a. *Global price fixing: Our customers are the enemies*. Boston: Kluwer Academic Publishers.

Connor, J. M. 2001b. "Our customers are our enemies": The lysine cartel of 1992–1995. *Review of Industrial Organization* 18: 5–21.

Cramton, P., and T. Palfrey. 1990. Cartel enforcement with uncertainty about costs. *International Economic Review* 31: 17–47.

Crawford, V. 1998. A survey of experiments on communication via cheap talk. *Journal of Economic Theory* 78 (February): 286–298.

Crawford, V., and J. Sobel. 1982. Strategic information transmission. *Econometrica* 50: 1431–1451.

Culbertson, W. P., and D. Bradford. 1991. The price of beer: Some evidence from interstate comparisons. *International Journal of Industrial Organization* 9: 275–289.

Daughety, A. F., and R. Forsythe. 1987. Industry-wide regulation and the formation of reputations: A laboratory analysis. In *Public regulation: New perspectives on institutions and policies*. ed. E. Bailey. Cambridge, MA: MIT Press, 347–398.

Davidson, C., and R. Deneckere. 1984. Horizontal mergers and collusive behavior. *International Journal of Industrial Organization* 2: 117–132.

Deneckere, R., and C. Davidson. 1985. Incentives to form coalitions with bertrand competition. *RAND Journal of Economics* 16: 473–486.

Dewatripont, M. 1988. Commitment through renegotiation-proof contracts with third parties. *Review of Economic Studies* 55 (July): 377–389.

Dick, A. R. 1996a. Identifying contracts, combinations and conspiracies in restraint of trade. *Managerial and Decision Economics* 17: 203–216.

Dick, A. R. 1996b. When are cartels stable contracts? *Journal of Law and Economics* 39: 241–283.

Director, A., and E. Levi. 1956. Law and the future: Trade regulation. *Northwestern University Law Review* 51: 281–296.

Eckbo, B. E. 1983. Horizontal mergers, collusion, and stockholder wealth. *Journal of Financial Economics* 11: 241–273.

Evans, W. N., and I. N. Kessides. 1994. Living by the "golden rule": Multimarket contact in the U.S. airline industry. *Quarterly Journal of Economics* 109: 341–366.

Farrell, J., and M. Rabin. 1996. Cheap talk. *Journal of Economic Perspectives* 10: 103–118.

Farrell, J., and C. Shapiro. 1990. Horizontal mergers: An equilibrium analysis. *American Economic Review* 80: 107–126.

Feinberg, R. M. 1980. Antitrust enforcement and subsequent price behavior. *Review of Economics and Statistics* 62: 609–612.

Fershtman, C., and A. Pakes. 2000. A dynamic game with collusion and price wars. *RAND Journal of Economics* 31: 207–236.

Focarelli, D., and F. Panetta. 2003. Are mergers beneficial to consumers?: Evidence from the market for bank deposits. *American Economic Review* 93: 1152–1172.

Frasco, G. 1991. *Exclusive dealing: A comprehensive case study*. New York: University Press of America.

Froeb, L. M., R. A. Koyak, and G. J. Werden. 1993. What is the effect of bid-rigging on prices? *Economics Letters* 42: 419–423.

Fumagalli, C., and M. Motta. 2003. Exclusive dealing and entry when buyers compete. Mimeo.

Genesove, D., and W. P. Mullin. 2001. Rules, communication, and collusion: Narrative evidence from the sugar institute case. *American Economic Review* 91: 379–398.

Gerstle, A. D., and M. Waldman. 2004. Mergers in durable-goods industries: A re-examination of market power and welfare effects. Mimeo.

Gowrisankaran, G. 1999. A dynamic model of endogenous horizontal mergers. *RAND Journal of Economics* 30: 56–83.

Gowrisankaran, G., and T. J. Holmes. 2004. Mergers and the evolution of industry concentration: Results from the dominant-firm model. *RAND Journal of Economics* 35: 561–582.

Green, E. J., and R. H. Porter. 1984. Noncooperative collusion under imperfect price information. *Econometrica* 52: 87–100.

Griffin, J. M. 2001. An inside view of a cartel at work: Common characteristics of international cartels. In *Fighting cartels—Why and how?* Stockholm, Sweden: Konkurrensverket, Swedish Competition Authority.

Griliches, Z., and J. Mairesse. 1995. Production functions: The search for identification. NBER working paper No. 5067.

Grossman, S. J., and O. D. Hart. 1986. The costs and benefits of ownership: A theory of vertical and lateral integration. *Journal of Political Economy* 94 (August): 691–719.

Gul, F. 1987. Noncooperative collusion in durable goods oligopoly. *RAND Journal of Economics* 18: 248–254.

Hart, O. D., and J. Tirole. 1990. Vertical integration and market foreclosure. *Brookings Papers on Economic Activity, Microeconomics*, 205–286.

Hastings, J. 2004. Vertical relationships and competition in retail gasoline markets: Empirical evidence from contract changes in southern california. *American Economic Review* 94: 317–328.

Hausman, J. A. 1996. Valuation of new goods under perfect and imperfect competition. In *The economics of new goods*, eds. T. Bresnahan and R. Gordon. Studies in Income and Wealth (58), Chicago, IL: National Bureau of Economic Research.

Hausman, J. A., G. Leonard, and J. D. Zona. 1994. Competitive analysis with differentiated products. *Annales D'Economie et de Statistique* 34: 159–180.

Hay, G. A., and D. Kelley. 1974. An empirical survey of price-fixing conspiracies. *Journal of Law and Economics* 17 (April): 13–38.

Heide, J. B., S. Dutta, and M. Bergen. 1998. Exclusive dealing and business efficiency: Evidence from industry practice. *Journal of Law and Economics* 41: 387–407.

Holt, C. 1993. Industrial organization: A survey of laboratory research. In *Handbook of Experimental Economics*, eds. J. Kagel and A. Roth. Princeton, NJ: Princeton University Press.

Hosken, D. S., and C. T. Taylor. 2004. The economic effects of the Marathon-Ashland joint venture. Mimeo.

Howard, J. H., and D. Kaserman. 1989. Proof of damages in construction industry bid rigging cases. *The Antitrust Bulletin* 34: 359–393.

Innes, R., and R. J. Sexton. 1994. Strategic buyers and exclusionary contracts. *American Economic Review* 84 (June): 566–584.

Jensen, M. C., and R. S. Ruback. 1983. The market for corporate control: The scientific evidence. *Journal of Financial Economics* 11: 5–50.

Kamien, M. I., and I. Zang. 1990. The limits of monopolization through acquisition. *Quarterly Journal of Economics* 105: 465–500.

Kandori, M., and H. Matsushima. 1998. Private observation, communication, and collusion. *Econometrica* 66: 627–652.

Kaplan, S. N., ed. 2000. *Mergers and productivity*, Chicago: University of Chicago Press.

Kaplan, S. N., M. L. Mitchell, and K. H. Wruck. 2000. A clinical exploration of value creation and destruction in acquisitions: Organizational design, incentives, and internal capital markets. In *Mergers and productivity*, ed. S. N. Kaplan. Chicago: University of Chicago Press.

Kihlstrom, R., and X. Vives. 1992. Collusion by asymmetrically informed firms. *Journal of Economics and Management Strategy* 1: 371–396.

Kim, E. H., and V. Singal. 1993. Mergers and market power: Evidence from the airline industry. *American Economic Review* 83: 549–569.

Klein, B. 1988. Vertical integration as organizational ownership: The Fisher Body–General Motors relationship revisited. *Journal of Law, Economics and Organization* 4: 199–213.

Kole, S., and K. Lehn. 2000. Workforce integration and the dissipation of value in mergers: The case of USAir's acquisition of piedmont aviation. In *Mergers and Productivity*, ed. S. N. Kaplan. Chicago: University of Chicago Press.

Krattenmaker, T. G., and S. C. Salop. 1986. Anticompetitive exclusion: Raising rivals' costs to achieve power over price. *Yale Law Journal* 209: 209–293.

Kuhn, K.-U. 2001. Fighting collusion by regulating communication between firms. *Economic Policy: A European Forum* 32: 167–197.

Kwoka, J. E., Jr. 1997. The price effects of bidding conspiricacies: Evidence from real estate auction "Knockouts." The Antitrust Bulletin 42: 503–516.

Levin, D. 1990. Horizontal mergers: The 50-percent benchmark. *American Economic Review* 80: 1238–1245.

Levinsohn, J., and A. Petrin. 2003. Estimating production functions using intermediate inputs to control for unobservables. *Review of Economic Studies* 70: 317–341.

Lichtenberg, F. R., and D. Siegel. 1987. Productivity and changes in ownership of manufacturing plants. *Brooking Papers on Economic Activity: Special Issue on Microeconomics*, Washington, D.C.: The Brookings Institution.

Mackay, R. J. 1984. Mergers for monopoly: Problems of expectations and commitment. Mimeo.

Mankiw, N. G., and M. D. Whinston. 1986. Free entry and social inefficiency. *RAND Journal of Economics* 17: 48–58.

Marin, P. L., and R. Sicotte. 2003. Exclusive contracts and market power: Evidence from ocean shipping. *Journal of Industrial Economics* 51: 193–213.

Marquez, J. 1994. Life expectancy of international cartels: An empirical analysis. *Review of Industrial Organization* 9: 331–341.

Martimort, D. 1996. Exclusive dealing, common agency, and multiprincipals incentive theory. *RAND Journal of Economics* 27 (Spring): 1–31.

Marvel, H. P. 1982. Exclusive dealing. *Journal of Law and Economics* 25 (Spring): 1–25.

Mas-Colell, A., M. D. Whinston, and J. R. Green. 1995. *Microeconomic theory*. New York: Oxford University Press.

Masten, S. E., and E. A. Snyder. 1993. United States versus United Shoe machinery: On the merits. *Journal of Law and Economics* 36: 33–70.

Mathewson, G. F., and R. A. Winter. 1987. The competitive effects of vertical agreements. *American Economic Review* 77 (December): 1057–1062.

McAfee, R. P., and J. McMillan. 1992. Bidding rings. *Amercian Economic Review* 82: 579–599.

References

McAfee, R. P., and M. Schwartz. 1994. Opportunism in multilateral vertical contracting: Nondiscrimination, exclusivity, and uniformity. *American Economic Review* 84 (March): 210–230.

McAfee, R. P., and M. A. Williams. 1988. Can event studies detect anticompetitive mergers? *Economics Letters* 28: 199–203.

McAfee, R. P., and M. A. Williams. 1992. Horizontal mergers and antitrust policy. *Journal of Industrial Economics* 40: 181–186.

McCutcheon, B. 1997. Do meetings in smoke-filled rooms facilitate collusion? *Journal of Political Economy* 105: 330–350.

McFadden, D. 1981. Econometric models of probabilistic choice. In *Structural analysis of discrete data*, eds. C. Manski and D. McFadden. Cambridge, MA: MIT Press, 198–272.

McGuckin, R. H., and S. V. Nguyen. 1995. On productivity and plant ownership change: New evidence from the longitudinal research database. *RAND Journal of Economics* 26: 257–276.

Mullin, J. C., and W. P. Mullin. 1997. United States Steel's acquisition of the Great Northern ore properties: Vertical foreclosure or efficient contractual governance? *Journal of Law, Economics, and Organization* 13: 74–100.

Mullin, G. L., J. C. Mullin, and W. P. Mullin. 1995. The competitive effects of mergers: Stock market evidence from the U.S. steel dissolution suit. *RAND Journal of Economics* 26: 314–330.

Neal Report. White House Task Force on Antitrust Policy. 1968. In Small business and the Robinson-Patman Act: Hearings before the special subcommittee on small business and the Robinson-Patman Act of the White House select committee on small business. 1969. 91st Cong., 1st sess., vol. 1.

Neven, D. 2001. "Collusion" under article 81 and the merger regulation. In *Fighting cartels—Why and how?* Stockholm, Sweden: Konkurrensverket, Swedish Competition Authority, 56–77.

Nevo, A. 1997. Demand for ready-to-eat cereal and its implications for price competition, merger analysis, and valuation of new goods, PhD diss., Harvard University.

Nevo, A. 2000a. A practitioner's guide to estimation of random coefficients logit models of demand. *Journal of Economics and Management Strategy* 9: 513–548.

Nevo, A. 2000b. Mergers with differentiated products: The case of the ready-to-eat cereal industry. *RAND Journal of Economics* 31: 395–421.

Nevo, A. 2001. Measuring market power in the ready-to-eat cereal industry. *Econometrica* 69: 307–342.

Newmark, C. M. 1988. Is antitrust enforcement effective? *Journal of Political Economy* 96: 1315–1328.

O'Brien, D. P., and G. Shaffer. 1992. Vertical control with bilateral contracts. *RAND Journal of Economics* 23 (Autumn): 299–308.

O'Brien, D. P., and G. Shaffer. 1997. Nonlinear supply contracts, exclusive dealing, and equilibrium market foreclosure. *Journal of Economics and Management Strategy* 6 (Winter): 755–785.

Olley, G. S., and A. Pakes. 1996. The dynamics of productivity in the telecommunications equipment industry. *Econometrica* 64: 1263–1298.

Ordover, J. A., G. Saloner, and S. C. Salop. 1990. Equilibrium vertical foreclosure. *American Economic Review* 80: 127–142.

Ornstein, S. 1989. Exclusive dealing and antitrust. *Antitrust Bulletin* 34 (Spring): 65–98.

Pautler, P. A. 2003. Evidence on mergers and acquisitions. *Antitrust Bulletin* 48: 119–221.

Perry, M. K., and R. Porter. 1985. Oligopoly and the incentive for horizontal merger. *American Economic Review* 75: 219–227.

Pesendorfer, M. 2003. Horizontal mergers in the paper industry. *RAND Journal of Economics* 34: 495–515.

Peters, C. 2003. Evaluating the performance of merger simulation: Evidence from the U.S. airline industry. Working Paper 32, Northwestern University, Center for the Study of Industrial Organization.

Phillips, O., and C. Mason. 1992. Mutual forebearance in experimental conglomerate markets. *RAND Journal of Economics* 23: 395–414.

Porter, R. H. 1983. A study of cartel stability: The joint executive committee, 1880–1886. *Bell Journal of Economics* 14: 301–314.

Porter, R. H., and J. D. Zona. 1993. Detection of bid rigging in procurement auctions. *Journal of Political Economy* 101: 518–538.

Porter, R. H., and J. D. Zona. 1999. Ohio school milk markets: An analysis of bidding. *RAND Journal of Economics* 30: 263–288.

Posner, R. A. 1976. *Antitrust law: An economic perspective*, Chicago: University of Chicago Press.

Posner, R. A. 2001. *Antitrust law*, 2nd edition. Chicago: University of Chicago Press.

Posner, R. A., and F. H. Easterbrook. 1981. *Antitrust: Cases, economic notes, and other materials*. 2nd ed. St. Paul, MN: West Publishing Co.

Prager, R. A. 1992. The effects of horizontal mergers on competition: The case of the northern securities company. *RAND Journal of Economics* 23: 123–133.

Prager, R. A., and T. H. Hannan. 1998. Do substantial horizontal mergers generate significant price effects? Evidence from the banking industry. *Journal of Industrial Economics* 46: 433–452.

Prat, A., and A. Rustichini. 2003. Games played through agents. *Econometrica* 71: 989–1026.

Rasmusen, E. B., J. M. Ramseyer, and J. S. Wiley. 1991. Naked exclusion. *American Economic Review* 81 (December): 1137–1145.

Ravenscraft, D. J., and F. M. Scherer. 1987. *Mergers, sell-offs, and economic efficiency*, Washington, D.C.: Brookings Institution.

Rey, P., and J. Tirole. [forth.] A primer on foreclosure. In *Handbook of industrial organization*, Vol. III, eds. M. Armstrong and R. H. Porter. Amsterdam, the Netherlands: North-Holland.

Rey, P., and T. Verge. 2004. Resale price maintenance and horizontal cartel. Mimeo.

Roberts, K. 1985. Cartel behaviour and adverse selection. *Journal of Industrial Economics* 33: 401–413.

Salant, S. W. 1987. Treble damage awards in private lawsuits for price fixing. *Journal of Political Economy* 95 (December): 1326–1336.

Salant, S. W., S. Switzer, and R. J. Reynolds. 1983. Losses from horizontal mergers: The effect of an exogenous change in industry structure on cournot-equilibrium. *Quarterly Journal of Economics* 98: 185–199.

Sass, T. R. 2005. The competitive effects of exclusive dealing: Evidence from the U.S. beer industry. *International Journal of Industrial Organization* 23: 203–225.

Sass, T. R., and D. S. Sauerman. 1993. Mandated exclusive territories and economic efficiency: An empirical analysis of the malt-beverage industry. *Journal of Law and Economics* 36: 153–177.

Sass, T. R., and D. S. Sauerman. 1996. Efficiency effects of exclusive territories: Evidence from the Indiana beer market. *Economic Inquiry* 34: 597–615.

Scherer, F. M., and D. Ross. 1990. *Industrial market structure and economic performance*. 3rd ed. Boston: Houghton Mifflin Company.

Segal, I. 1999. Contracting with externalities. *Quarterly Journal of Economics* 114: 337–388.

Segal, I., and M. D. Whinston. 2000a. Naked exclusion: Comment. *American Economic Review* 90 (March): 296–309.

Segal, I., and M. D. Whinston. 2000b. Exclusive contracts and protection of investments. *RAND Journal of Economics* 31 (Winter): 603–633.

Segal, I., and M. D. Whinston. 2003. Robust predictions for bilateral contracting with externalities. *Econometrica* 71 (May): 757–791.

Shleifer, A., and L. H. Summers. 1988. Breach of trust in hostile takeovers. In *Corporate takeovers: Causes and consequences*, ed. A. Auerbach. Chicago: University of Chicago Press, 33–56.

Simpson, J., and A. L. Wickelgren. 2004. Naked exclusion, efficient breach, and downstream competition. Mimeo.

Spector, D. 2003. Horizontal mergers, entry, and efficiency defenses. *International Journal of Industrial Organization* 21: 1591–1600.

Spector, D. 2004. Are exclusive contracts anticompetitive? Mimeo.

Spier, K., and M. D. Whinston. 1995. On the efficiency of privately stipulated damages for breach of contract: Entry barriers, reliance, and renegotiation. *RAND Journal of Economics* 26 (Summer): 180–202.

Sproul, M. F. 1993. Antitrust and prices. *Journal of Political Economy* 101: 741–754.

Stefanadis, C. 1997. Downstream vertical foreclosure and upstream innovation. *Journal of Industrial Economics* 45 (December): 445–456.

Stefanadis, C. 1998. Selective contracts, foreclosure, and the Chicago School view. *Journal of Law and Economics* 41 (October): 429–450.

Stigler, G. J. 1952. The case against big business. *Fortune Magazine*, May.

Stigler, G. J. 1964. A theory of oligopoly. *Journal of Political Economy* 72: 44–61.

Stigler, G. J., and J. K. Kindahl. 1970. *The behavior of industrial prices*. New York: Columbia University Press.

Stillman, R. 1983. Examining antitrust policy towards horizontal mergers. *Journal of Financial Economics* 11: 225–240.

Suslow, V. Y. 1988. Stability in international cartels: An empirical survey. Working Paper E-88-7, Hoover Institution Domestic Studies Program.

Symeonidis, G. 2003. In which industries is collusion more likely? Evidence from the U.K. *Journal of Industrial Economics* 51: 45–74.

Taylor, J. E. 2002. The output effects of government sponsored cartels during the new deal. *Journal of Industrial Economics* 50: 1–10.

Telser, L. G. 1960. Why should manufacturers want fair trade? *Journal of Law and Economics* 3: 86–105.

Tirole, J. 1988. *The theory of industrial organization*, Cambridge, MA: MIT Press.

Turner, D. F. 1962. The definition of agreement under the Sherman Act: Conscious parallelism and refusals to deal. *Harvard Law Review* 75 (February): 655–706.

Turner, D. F. 1969. The scope of antitrust and other economic regulatory policies. *Harvard Law Review* 82: 1207–1231.

Villas-Boas, S. B. 2003. Vertical contracts between manufacturers and retailers: An empirical analysis. Mimeo.

Vita, M. G., and S. Sacher. 2001. The competitive effects of not-for-profit hospital mergers: A case study. *Journal of Industrial Economics* 49: 63–84.

Weiss, L. W., ed. 1990. *Concentration and price*, Cambridge, MA: MIT Press.

Werden, G. 1990. Antitrust policy toward horizontal mergers: A comment on Farrell and Shapiro. Department of Justice Economic Analysis Group Discussion Paper 90-4.

Werden, G. 1997. An economic perspective on the analysis of merger efficiencies. *Antitrust*, 12–16.

Werden, G., and L. Froeb. 1994. The effects of mergers in differnetiated products industries: Logit demand and merger policy. *Journal of Law, Economics, and Organization* 10: 407–426.

Werden, G., and L. Froeb. 1998. The entry-inducing effects of horizontal mergers: An exploratory analysis. *Journal of Industrial Economics* 46: 525–543.

Werden, G. J., A. S. Joskow, and R. L. Johnson. 1991. The effects of mergers on prices and output: Two cases from the airline industry. *Managerial and Decision Economics* 12: 341–352.

Whinston, M. D. 1990. Tying, foreclosure, and exclusion. *American Economic Review* 80: 837–859.

Whinston, M. D. 2001. Exclusivity and tying in U.S. v. Microsoft: What we know, and don't know. *Journal of Economic Perpsectives* 15: 63–80.

White, L. J. 2001. Lysine and price fixing: How long? How severe? *Review of Industrial Organization* 18: 23–31.

Williamson, O. E. 1968. Economies as an antitrust defense: The welfare tradeoffs. *American Economic Review* 58: 407–426.

Yi, S.-S. 1997. Stable coalition structures with externalities. *Games and Economic Behavior* 20: 201–237.

Index

100% Share of Mind program, 194

Administration costs, 18
Administrative law judge, 10
Aggregation, 207n7
  concentration levels and, 98–99
  consumer surplus and, 101
  exclusive contracts and, 175 (*see also* Exclusive contracts)
  external effect and, 66–71
  first-mover models and, 140–151
  horizontal mergers and, 62–71, 74
  merger simulation and, 100–105
  precompetitive justifications and, 83–84
  welfare and, 185–188
Aghion, P., 140–144, 152
Agreements, 20–21
Airline industry
  Continental, 104–105
  horizontal mergers and, 76–77, 104–105, 115–123
  Northwest, 115–118
  Ozark, 115–118
  Transworld, 115–118
American Express, 135
Anheuser Busch, 194, 196–197
Antitrust law, 199n1
  administrative law judge and, 10

agreements and, 20–21
broad application and, 1–2
business scandals and, 4
cheap talk and, 21–24
Clayton Act and, 5, 7–10
communication and, 21–22
Conwood v. United States Tobacco case, 135
coordination problem and, 21–24
criminal penalties and, 8–9
decrees and, 9, 200n9
efficiencies and, 83–84
equitable relief and, 8–10
exclusive contracts and, 133–134 (*see also* Exclusive contracts)
farmers and, 4
Federal Trade Commission (FTC) Act and, 5, 7–10
formulation of, 3–4
Hart-Scott-Rodino Act and, 8
incentive problem and, 21
information revelation problem and, 24–26
Microsoft case, 135, 214n2
monetary damages and, 8–10
per se rule and, 15–19
rule of reason and, 7, 16, 136
sanctions and, 8–13, 25
Schwinn decisions and, 194

Antitrust law (cont.)
  Sherman Act and, 4–6, 9
  Standard Fashion Company v. Magrane-Houston Company case, 136–137, 169, 189–190
  Sylvania decision and, 194
  Third Court of Appeals and, 167, 217n30
  Trans-Missouri case, 16–18
  United Shoe Machinery case, 179
  United States and, 4–13
  U.S. v. Dentsply case, 135, 166–167
  U.S. v. Visa U.S.A. case, 135
Antitrust policy
  administration costs and, 18
  Clayton Act and, 5, 7–10
  collusion and, 52–55 (*see also* Collusion)
  Federal Trade Commission (FTC) Act and, 5, 7–10
  price fixing and, 15–55 (*see also* Price fixing)
  Sherman Act and, 4–10, 16, 20–24, 26, 32, 52–53, 57
Archer-Daniels Midland (ADM), 9, 37–38
ARCO, 126
Areeda, P., 182–183, 185
Ashland oil, 126
Asker, J., 196–197
AT&T, 71
Athey, S., 25–26, 202n12
Ausubel, L. M., 73
Automobile industry, 87–89
Automobiles, 53

Bagwell, K., 25–26, 202n12
Baker, J. B., 10, 105–106, 109–110
Baldwin, L. H., 204n21
Banking, 123–126
Bargaining process, 215n11
  bidding game and, 156, 166, 217n26
  competition reduction and, 167–175
  exclusive contracts and, 152–153, 156–162, 167–175
  offer game and, 156, 167–168
  outside parties and, 152–153, 170
Beckner, C. F., III, 201n4
Beer manufacturers, 194–197
Benoit, J.-P., 111
Bergen, M., 192
Bernheim, B. D., 218n39
  exclusive contracts and, 156, 162, 166–167, 176, 188
  horizontal mergers and, 76
Berry, S. T., 76, 87–88, 90
Bertrand model, 72, 102
Besanko, D., 176–177, 187, 206n5
Bidding game, 156, 166, 217n26
Bid rigging schemes, 49–51, 201n1
Bilateral contracting, 139, 160
Bloch, F., 75
Block, K. B., 28, 30
BMW, 89
Bolton, P., 111, 140–144, 152
Borenstein, S., 117, 212n53
Bork, R. H., 4, 6, 134, 137, 169, 182–183
Bradford, D., 194
Bread industry, 30
Bresnahan, T. F., 96, 102, 105–106, 109–110
Brock, W., 40
Burlington Northern Railroad, 95

Canada's Competition Act, 83–84, 199n6
Carlton, D. W., 73
Cartels, 11. *See also* Price fixing
  detection of, 38–45
  firm behavior and, 45–52
  lysine, 36–38
  ocean shipping, 193

phantom bidders and, 49–51
procurement auctions and, 35–38
Certificates of deposit (CDs), 124
Cheap talk, 21–24
Chicago School, 136–139
  Aghion-Bolton model and, 140–144
  Director and, 134
  externalities across buyers and, 144–151
  first-mover models and, 140–151
  precompetitive justifications and, 178, 180, 188
Choi, D., 31
Clayton Act, 5, 7–10
Coase, R. H., 72
Collusion, 2–3, 200n7. *See also* Price fixing
  capacity limitations and, 82
  cartel's expected profit, 11
  cheap talk and, 21–24
  cheating incentives and, 40
  coordination problem and, 21–24
  D.C. real estate case and, 36
  ease of sustaining, 81–82
  enforcement actions and, 31–32
  horizontal mergers and, 81–82
  information revelation problem and, 24–26
  lysine cartel and, 36–38
  merger simulation and, 102
  multimarket contact and, 76–77
  procurement auctions and, 33–38
  sanctions and, 9–13
  sewer construction case and, 36
  structural factors affecting, 81–82
  sustaining of, 81–82
  tacit, 21, 52–55, 76–77
Common agency, 188, 190
Communication, 202n10
  cheap talk and, 21–24
  coordination problem and, 21–24
  detection of, 38–39
  enforcement risk and, 28–32
  firm behavior and, 45–52
  future play mechanisms and, 25
  information revelation problem and, 24–26
  phantom bidders and, 49–51
  price fixing and, 21–26, 38–39
Competition, 1
  bargaining process and, 156–162
  buyer externalities and, 144–151
  Canada's Competition Act and, 83–84, 199n6
  coordination problem and, 21–24
  Cournot, 52, 54, 63, 69, 71, 74, 161, 165–166
  duopoly profit and, 161, 165–166
  durable goods and, 72
  event-study approach and, 110–114
  exclusive contracts and, 136–139 (*see also* Exclusive contracts)
  firm behavior and, 45–52
  information revelation problem and, 24–26
  oligopolistic, 17, 21–38 (*see also* Oligopolistic competition)
  per se rule and, 15–19
  precompetitive justifications and, 83–84
  price fixing and, 15–55 (*see also* Price fixing)
  railroads and, 16
  reducing retail, 155–167
  rule of reason and, 136
  Sherman Act and, 6
  Third Court of Appeals and, 167, 217n30
  Trans-Missouri case and, 16–17
  Williamson trade-off and, 58–62
Compte, O., 25–26, 40, 71–72
Concentration levels
  calculation of, 79–81
  changes in, 79–81

Concentration levels (cont.)
  Cournot equilibrium and, 96–97
  Horizontal Merger Guidelines and, 79–81
  price effects and, 93–99
Connor, J. M., 36, 38
Consent decree, 200n9
Consumer surplus, 17
Continental Airlines, 104–105
Conwood v. United States Tobacco, 135
Coordination problem, 21–24
Cournot competition
  duopoly profit and, 161, 165–166
  entry and, 74
  horizontal mergers and, 63, 69, 71
  price fixing and, 52, 54
Cournot equilibrium, 96–97, 102, 131
Cramton, P., 24
Crawford, V., 23
Credit cards, 135
Criminal penalties, 8–9
Culbertson, W. P., 194
Customer lists, 191–192

Davidson, C., 70–71
Decrees, 9, 200n9
Demand elasticity, 86, 210n26
  automobile industry and, 87–89
  Independence of Irrelevant Alternatives (IIA) and, 88–89
  production costs and, 87–93
  residual estimation and, 105–110
  selection issues and, 90–91
  substitution patterns and, 90–91
Deneckere, R. J., 70–71, 73
Dentsply, 135, 166–167
Director, Aaron, 134
Discover, 135
Dual rate contracts, 193
Duopoly profit, 17, 161, 165–166

Durable goods, 72–73
Dutta, S., 192

Eckbo, B. E., 110
Efficiency
  Cournot equilibrium and, 131
  entry and, 188–189
  exclusive contracts and, 134, 167–175, 188–189
  horizontal mergers and, 127–131
  precompetitive justifications and, 83–84
  production costs and, 86–88
  total-factor productivity and, 128, 130
Endogenous mergers, 75–76
Entry, 73–74, 83, 188–189
Equations
  Block-Nold-Sidak, 28, 30
  cartel's expected profit, 11
  concentration levels, 80, 94
  consumer surplus, 203n16
  Cournot competition, 63
  Cournot equilibrium, 96
  demand elasticity, 86
  equilibrium best-response function, 206n6
  exclusive contracts, 157–161, 168, 173–174, 181–182
  horizontal mergers, 63–68, 85–88, 91–96, 106–107, 109
  market definition, 85–88, 91–93
  merger simulation, 101
  price fixing likelihood, 39
  residual demand estimation, 106–107, 109
  retail competition, 157–161, 173
Equilibrium, 206n6, 217n28
  babbling, 21–22
  bargaining process and, 156–162
  cheap talk and, 21–24
  Cournot, 96–97, 102, 131
  demand elasticity and, 87–93

Index

exclusive contracts and, 155–167, 176–177 (*see also* Exclusive contracts)
horizontal mergers and, 66–71
incentive problem and, 21
merger simulation and, 102–105
Nash, 21, 40, 91, 102–105
price endogeneity and, 85–86
price fixing and, 40
retail competition and, 155–167
symmetry and, 97–99, 176–177
Equitable relief, 8–10
Evans, W. N., 76, 213n55
Event-study approach
exclusive contracts and, 192–194
horizontal mergers and, 110–114
Exclusionary vertical contracts, 3, 133–135
Exclusive contracts
Aghion-Bolton model and, 140–144, 152
bargaining process and, 152–153, 156–162, 167–175
Besanko-Perry model and, 176–177
bidding game and, 156, 166, 217n26
bilateral contracting and, 139, 160
Chicago School and, 134, 136–151, 178, 180, 188
Clayton Act and, 8
common agency and, 188, 190
competing for, 152–178
competition reduction and, 167–175
complementary effects and, 192
customer lists and, 191–192
dual rate contracts and, 193
duopoly profit and, 161, 165–166
effective price and, 141
efficiency and, 134
empirical evidence for, 189–197
event-study methods and, 192–194
externalities and, 144–167, 182–183
first-mover models and, 140–151
free riding and, 192
game theory and, 134
hostility for, 133–134
input market competition and, 167–171
investment protection and, 178–188
joint payoff and, 153, 168–169
loyalty and, 183–185
market outcome and, 155–167
Microsoft and, 135
multilateral contracts and, 153–154, 215nn11,13
multiseller/multibuyer models and, 175–178
noncontractible investments and, 180
offer game and, 156, 167–168
outside parties and, 152–153, 170
partial exclusion through stipulated damages and, 140–144
precompetitive justifications and, 178–189
retail competition and, 155–167, 171–175
seller profitability and, 137
Sherman Act and, 6
symmetry and, 176–177, 187
territorial, 194–197
Third Court of Appeals and, 167, 217n30
traditional view of, 136–139
Visa and, 135
welfare effects and, 185–188
Externalities
buyer investments and, 184–185
complementary, 183
empirical evidence for, 188–197
exclusive contracts and, 144–167, 182–183

Externalities (cont.)
  retail competition and, 155–167
  seller investments and, 183–184
  substitutes and, 184
  welfare effects and, 66–71, 185–188

Farmers, 4
Farrell, J.
  durable goods and, 72–73
  endogenous mergers and, 75–76
  entry effects and, 73–74
  horizontal mergers and, 62, 65–76
Federal Bureau of Investigation (FBI), 38
Federal Trade Commission (FTC), 7, 53
  collusion and, 81–82 (see also Collusion)
  concentration levels and, 79–81
  defining relevant market and, 84–93
  endogenous mergers and, 75–76
  entry effects and, 74
  firm behavior and, 47
  Horizontal Merger Guidelines and, 77–84
  market definition and, 77–79
  market factors and, 79–83
  precompetitive justifications and, 83–84
Federal Trade Commission (FTC) Act, 5, 7–10
Feinberg, R. M., 31
Fershtman, C., 201n3
Firm behavior. *See also* Industry
  exclusive contracts and, 134 (see also Exclusive contracts)
  merger simulation and, 100–105
  price fixing and, 45–55
  residual demand estimation and, 105–110
  tacit collusion and, 53–55

First-mover models
  Aghion-Bolton, 140–144
  externalities across buyers and, 144–151
  partial exclusion and, 140–144
Fisher autobodies, 179, 182, 184
Focarelli, D., 124, 126–127
Food manufacturing industry, 130
Free riding, 192
Froeb, L. M., 35–36, 73, 101
Frozen perch case, 35–36
Fumagalli, C., 216n17
Future play mechanisms, 25

Game theory
  babbling equilibrium and, 21–22
  cheap talk and, 21–24
  coordination problem and, 21–24
  exclusive contracts and, 134
  price fixing and, 40
General Motors, 179, 182, 184
Gertner, R. H., 73
Gowisankaran, G., 75
Great Northern Railway, 193–194, 211nn44,45
Green, E. J., 40, 74
Griffin, J. M., 36
Grossman, S. J., 191–192
Gul, F., 73

Hannan, T. H., 123–124
Hart, O. D., 155–157, 165, 171, 191–192, 218n40
Hart-Scott-Rodino Act, 8
Hastings, J., 126
Hausman, J. A., 89, 101
Hay, G. A., 39, 41–45
Heide, J. B., 192
Herfindahl-Hirschman Index
  banking mergers and, 123
  horizontal mergers and, 68, 80–81, 96, 99

oil industry and, 126
price fixing and, 33
Hold-out problem, 75
Holmes, T. J., 75
Holt, C., 23
Horizontal Merger Guidelines, 7, 61, 209n20
  capacity limitation and, 82
  concentration levels and, 79–81, 93–99
  demand elasticity and, 85–86
  ease of entry and, 83
  econometric approaches to, 84–99
  efficiencies and, 83–84
  market definition and, 77–79, 84–93, 99–114
  performance evaluation and, 82
  precompetitive justifications and, 83–84
  SSNIP test and, 78
  structural factors and, 81–82
  substitution patterns and, 82
  sustaining collusion and, 81–82
Horizontal mergers
  actual results examination and, 114–131
  aggregation and, 62–71, 74
  airline industry and, 76–77, 104–105, 115–123
  banking industry and, 123–126
  Bertrand model and, 72, 102
  capacity limitations and, 82
  Clayton Act and, 8
  collusion and, 81–82
  concentration levels and, 79–81, 93–99
  defining relevant market and, 84–93
  demand elasticity and, 85–93
  Department of Justice/Federal Trade Commission guidelines and, 77–84
  durable goods and, 72–73
  ease of entry and, 83
  efficiency and, 83–84, 127–131
  endogenous mergers and, 75–76
  entry and, 73–74, 83
  equations for, 63–68, 85–88, 91–96, 106–107, 109
  event-study approach and, 110–114
  examining actual results of, 114–131
  exclusive contracts and, 133–134 (*see also* Exclusive contracts)
  external effect and, 66–71
  Herfindahl-Hirschman Index and, 68, 80, 96
  hold-out problem and, 75
  Independence of Irrelevant Alternatives (IIA) and, 88–89
  inverse demand function and, 67–68
  market definition and, 77–79, 87–93, 99–114
  multimarket contact and, 76–77
  new product development and, 76
  precompetitive justifications and, 83–84
  price effects and, 62–71, 115–127
  product changes and, 127
  production costs and, 86–88
  purchase delays and, 72–73
  railroads and, 95, 112
  repeated interaction and, 71–72
  residual demand estimation and, 105–110
  scale technologies and, 74
  Sherman Act and, 6, 57
  simulation and, 100–105
  substitution patterns and, 82, 90–91
  sufficient conditions for, 62–71
  telecommunications industry and, 70–71
  U.S. court hostility and, 57–58

Horizontal mergers (cont.)
  welfare effects and, 62–74
  Williamson trade-off and, 58–62, 70
Hosken, D. S., 126
Hospitals, 126
Howard, J. H., 36

Incentive problem, 21
Independence of Irrelevant Alternatives (IIA), 88–89
Indiana, 194
Industry
  aggregate effects and, 62–71
  agreement and, 20
  airline, 76–77, 104–105, 115–118
  automobile, 87–89, 179, 182–184
  banking, 123–126
  cheap talk and, 21–24
  communication and, 17, 20–26
  coordination problem and, 21–24
  demand function and, 17
  exclusive contracts and, 152–178
    (see also Exclusive contracts)
  firm behavior and, 45–52
  food manufacturing, 130
  future play mechanisms and, 25
  health care, 126
  information revelation problem and, 24–26
  insurance, 191–192
  inverse demand function and, 63
  iron, 193–194
  National Industrial Recovery Act and, 204n21
  oil, 126
  price fixing and, 33–38 (see also Price fixing)
  railroads and, 16–18, 95, 112, 193–194, 211n44
  residual demand estimation and, 105–110
  shipping, 193
  steel, 112–114, 193–194
  telecommunications, 70–71
Information revelation problem, 24–26
Innes, R., 188
Insurance industry, 191–192
Internet Explorer, 135
Interstate Commerce Commission, 4
Inverse demand functions, 86
Investments
  buyer, 184–185
  competition reduction and, 167–175
  complementary effects and, 192
  empirical analysis of, 188–197
  equipment and, 179, 192
  exclusive contracts and, 171–175
    (see also Exclusive contracts)
  noncontractible, 180
  precompetitive justfications and, 178–188
  protection of, 178–188
  relationship-specific, 179, 182, 184, 187
  seller, 183–184
  training and, 179
  welfare effects and, 185–188
Iron industry, 193–194
Iron Law of Consulting, 86

Jenny, F., 40, 71–72
Johnson, R. L., 212n53
Joint payoff, 153, 168–169
Joskow, A. S., 212n53

Kaimen, M. I., 75
Kandori, M., 25–26
Kaplow, L., 183, 185
Kaserman, D., 36
Kelley, D., 39, 41–45
Kennedy administration, 193
Kessides, I. N., 76, 213n55

Index

Kihlstrom, R., 24
Kim, E. H., 117–119, 124, 126–127
Kindahl, J. K., 31
Klein, B., 179–180
Knock-out auction, 36
Koyak, R. A., 35–36
Kwoka, J. E., Jr., 36

Leasing, 193–194
Legal issues. *See* Antitrust law
Leonard, G., 89, 101
Levi, E., 134
Levin, D., 62
Levinsohn, J., 87–88, 90, 131
Lichtenberg, F. R., 128, 130
Longitudinal Establishment Data (LED), 128, 130
Lysine cartel, 36–38

McAfee, R. P., 24, 62, 111, 155
McCall's, 190
McCutcheon, B., 32
McGuckin, R. H., 128, 130
Mackay, R. J., 75
McMillan, J., 24
Magrane-Houston, 136–137, 169, 189–190
Mankiw, N. G., 16, 18, 74
Marathon oil, 126
Marin, P. L., 193, 220n50
Market definition, 77–79, 99
 econometric approaches to, 84–93
 event-study approach and, 110–114
 merger simulation and, 100–105
 residual demand estimation, 105–110
Markets
 beer manufacturers and, 194–197
 Canada's Competition Act and, 83–84, 199n6
 capacity limitations and, 82
 collusion and, 81–82 (*see also* Collusion)
 competition reduction and, 167–175
 concentration levels and, 79–81, 93–99
 defining relevant, 84–93
 demand elasticity and, 86–93
 durable goods and, 72–73
 ease of entry and, 83
 efficiencies and, 83–84
 exclusive contracts and, 136–139, 155–167 (*see also* Exclusive contracts)
 foreclosure and, 136
 Herfindahl-Hirschman Index and, 68, 80, 96
 Independence of Irrelevant Alternatives (IIA) and, 88–89
 input, 167–171
 mergers and, 100–105 (*see also* Mergers)
 multimarket contact and, 76–77
 performance evaluation and, 82
 precompetitive justifications and, 83–84
 price fixing and, 41 (*see also* Price fixing)
 purchase delays and, 72–73
 residual demand estimation and, 105–110
 structural factors and, 81–82
 substitution patterns and, 82, 90–91
 symmetry and, 176–177
 triangular structures and, 175–178
 Williamson trade-off and, 58–62
Marshall, R. C., 204n21
Marvel, H. P., 179, 182, 184, 189–192, 195
Mas-Colell, A., 74
Mason, C., 76
Masten, S. E., 179, 183–184

Mathematics, 2
Matsushima, H., 25–26
Mercedes, 89
Mergers, 1, 3
  aggregate effects and, 62–71
  consumer surplus and, 101
  cost reduction and, 73–74
  durable goods and, 72–73
  dynamic environment and, 71–77
  efficiency and, 73–74, 127–131
  endogenous, 75–76
  entry and, 73–74
  event-study approach and, 110–114
  examining actual results of, 114–131
  exclusive contracts and, 133–197 (*see also* Exclusive contracts)
  horizontal, 114–131 (*see also* Horizontal mergers)
  product changes and, 127
  profits and, 73–74
  purchase delays and, 72–73
  repeated interaction and, 71–72
  scale technologies and, 74
  simulation of, 100–105
  Williamson trade-off and, 58–62, 70
Microsoft case, 135, 214n2
Miller beer, 194, 196–197
Monetary damages, 9–13
Monopolies, 6, 53, 209n16
  AT&T, 71
  competition reduction and, 167–175
  durable goods and, 72–73
  exclusive contracts and, 152–178 (*see also* Exclusive contracts)
  externalities across buyers and, 144–151
  railroads and, 16
  retail competition and, 155–167
  Western Electric, 71

Motta, M., 216n17
Mullin, G. L., 112, 192–194
Mullin, J. C., 112, 192–194
Mullin, W. P., 112, 192–194
Multibuyer models, 175–178
Multimarket-contact effects, 76–77
Multiseller models, 175–178

Nash equilibrium, 21, 40
  demand elasticity and, 91
  merger simulation and, 102–105
National Beer Wholesalers Association, 195
National Industrial Recovery Act, 204n21
Neal Report, 53
Netscape, 135
Nevo, A., 88, 90, 101
New York Times, 1
Nguyen, S. V., 128, 130
Nold, F. C., 28, 30
Northern Pacific Railway, 211n44
Northwest Airlines, 115–118
NOW accounts, 124

O'Brien, D. P., 155
Offer game, 156, 167–168
Office-supply superstores, 94–95
Ohio, 33–35
Oil industry, 126
Oligopolistic competition, 17
  buyer externalities and, 144–151
  coordination problem and, 21–24
  durable goods and, 72–73
  Herfindahl-Hirschman Index and, 80
  information revelation problem and, 24–26
  new product development and, 76
  price fixing effects and, 26–38
  Williamson trade-off and, 58–62
Olley, G. S., 70–71, 130, 131
Ornstein, S., 219n48

Outside parties, 152–153, 170
Ozark Airlines, 115–118

Pakes, A., 130–131, 201n3
  dynamic-oligopoly model and, 76
  market definition and, 87–90
  telecommunications industry and, 70–71
Palfrey, T., 24
Panetta, F., 124, 126–127
Pautler, P. A., 126
People Express, 104–105
Perry, M., 176–177, 187
Per se rule, 15–19
Pesendorfer, M., 131
Peters, C., 102–105, 119, 123, 212n53
Petrin, A., 131
Phantom bidders, 49–51
Philappatos, G. C., 31
Phillips, O., 76
Porter, R. H.
  firm behavior and, 47–52
  price fixing and, 33–36, 40, 47–52
Posner, R. A., 4, 53–54, 134
Prager, R. A., 123–124
Prat, A., 218n40
Precedent effects, 111
Precompetitive justifications
  aggregation and, 83–84
  exclusive contracts and, 178–189
  investment protection and, 178–188
Price fixing, 205n28
  administration costs and, 18
  aggregate surplus and, 17
  agreements and, 20–21
  Archer-Daniels Midland (ADM) and, 9
  ban effects and, 20–38
  behavioral evidence and, 45–52
  bid rigging schemes and, 49–51, 201n1
  Block-Nold-Sidak model and, 28, 30
  cheap talk and, 21–24
  cheating incentives and, 40
  communication and, 17, 20–26, 38–39, 45–52
  coordination problem and, 21–24
  costs of, 41–45
  D.C. real estate case and, 36
  detection of, 38–52
  determining, 19
  enforcement actions and, 28–32
  estimating likelihood of, 39–40
  exclusionary behavior and, 42–43
  future play mechanisms and, 25
  game theory and, 40
  incentive problem and, 21
  information revelation problem and, 24–26
  lysine cartel and, 36–38
  market size and, 41
  per se rule and, 15–19
  phantom bidders and, 49–51
  potential gain and, 41
  procurement auctions and, 33–38
  regression analysis of, 28–38
  risk in, 31–33
  sanctions and, 8–13
  school milk case and, 33–35
  sewer construction case and, 36
  Sherman Act and, 6
  social benefits and, 16, 32
  structural evidence and, 39–45
  tacit collusion and, 52–55
  theory of, 20–26
  Trans-Missouri case and, 16–18
  U.S. Sentencing Guidelines and, 45
  U.S. Supreme Court and, 16
  welfare and, 16–18
Prices, 1–3
  aggregate surplus and, 17
  airline mergers and, 76–77
  Bertrand model and, 72

Prices (cont.)
  capacity limitations and, 82
  cartel's expected profit, 11
  Clayton Act and, 8
  concentration levels and, 93–99
  demand elasticity and, 87–93
  demand function and, 17
  endogeneity of, 85–86
  event-study approach and, 110–114
  examining actual mergers and, 115–127
  exclusive contracts and, 136–151 (*see also* Exclusive contracts)
  farmers and, 4
  first-mover models and, 140–151
  hold-out problem and, 75
  Independence of Irrelevant Alternatives (IIA) and, 88–89
  market definition and, 87–93
  merger effects and, 62–71, 115–127 (*see also* Mergers)
  monetary damages and, 9–13
  predatory, 6
  purchase delays and, 72–73
  railroads and, 4, 16
  SSNIP test and, 78
  steel, 112–114
  welfare effects and, 62–71
  Williamson trade-off and, 58–62
Procurement auctions
  D.C. real estate case and, 36
  frozen perch case and, 35–36
  lysine cartel and, 36–38
  phantom bidders and, 49–51
  school milk case and, 33–35
  sewer construction case and, 36
Protectionism, 144
Punishment. *See* Sanctions
Purchase delays, 72–73

Railroads, 211n44
  Burlington Northern, 95
  exclusive contracts and, 193–194
  Great Northern, 193–194, 211nn44,45
  horizontal mergers and, 95, 112
  Santa Fe, 95, 98–99
  Southern Pacific, 95
  Trans-Missouri case and, 16–18
  transportation costs and, 4
  Union Pacific, 95, 98–99
Ramseyer, J. M., 144, 152, 176
Rasmussen, E. B., 144, 152, 176
Ravenscraft, D. J., 128, 130
Regression analysis
  airline industry and, 115–123
  banking industry and, 123–126
  Block-Nold-Sidak model and, 28, 30
  concentration levels and, 93–99
  examining actual mergers and, 114–127
  firm behavior and, 45–52
  frozen perch case and, 35–36
  hospitals and, 126
  least squares, 97
  oil industry and, 126
  price fixing and, 28–38
  school milk case and, 33–35
Republic Airlines, 115–118
Resale-price-maintenance agreements, 6
Research & development (R&D), 62, 76, 97, 102
Residual demand estimation, 105–110
Retail competition
  bargaining process and, 156–162
  bidding game and, 156, 166
  bilateral contracting and, 160
  competition reduction and, 171–175
  exclusive contracts and, 155–167
  offer game and, 156

Third Court of Appeals and, 167, 217n30
Rey, P., 40, 72, 214n1
Richard, J.-F., 204n21
Roberts, K., 24
Ross, D., 43
Rule of reason approach, 7, 16, 136
Rustichini, A., 218n40

Sacher, S., 126
Salant, S. W., 10
Salop, S. C., 201n4
Sanchirico, C., 25
Sanctions, 25
 Clayton Act and, 10
 criminal penalties and, 8–9
 equitable relief and, 8–10
 monetary damages and, 9–13
 prosecution probability and, 11
 Sherman Act and, 10
Santa Fe Railroad, 95, 98–99
Sass, T. R., 194–197
Sauerman, D. S., 194–195
Scale technologies, 74
Scharfstein, D., 111
Scheinkman, J., 40
Scherer, F. M., 43, 128, 130
School milk case, 33–35
Schwartz, M., 155
Schwinn decisions, 194
Segal, I., 192, 216n23
 bargaining process and, 156
 buyer externalities and, 144, 151
 multiseller/multibuyer models and, 176
 precompetitive justifications and, 179–180, 183
Sewer construction case, 36
Sexton, R. J., 188
Shaffer, G., 155
Shapiro, C.
 durable goods and, 72–73
 endogenous mergers and, 75–76
 entry effects and, 73–74
 horizontal mergers and, 62, 65–76
Sherman Act, 4–6, 9–10
 agreements and, 20–21
 communication and, 20–21, 32
 coordination problem and, 21–24
 effects of, 26
 horizontal mergers and, 57
 limiting application of, 52–53
 Standard Oil case, 7
 U.S. Supreme Court and, 16
Shipping companies, 193
Shleifer, A., 70
Sicotte, R., 193, 220n50
Sidak, J. G., 28, 30
Siegel, D., 128, 130
Simplicity Pattern Company, 189–190
Simpson, J., 216n17
Singal, V., 117–119, 124, 126–127
Snyder, E. A., 179, 182–184
Southern Pacific Railroad, 95
Sproul, M. F., 27, 29, 32, 203nn14,15
Spulber, D. F., 206n5
SSNIP (small but significant and non-transitory increase in price) test, 78
Standard Fashion Company v. Magrane-Houston Company, 136–137, 169, 189–190
Standard Oil case, 7
Steel industry, 112–114, 193–194
Stefanadis, C., 216n17
Stigler, G. J., 18, 31, 40
Stillman, R., 110
Substitution patterns, 82, 90–91
Summers, L. H., 70
Sylvania decision, 194
Symmetry, 97–99, 176–177, 187

Tacit collusion, 21
 antitrust policy toward, 52–55
 multimarket contact and, 76–77

Taylor, C. T., 126, 204n21
Telser, L. G., 179
Thrifty, 126
Ticketmaster, 187
Tirole, J., 40, 155–157, 165, 171, 214n1, 218n40
Total-factor productivity, 128, 130
Trans-Missouri Freight Association, 16–18
Trans World Airlines, 115–118
Triangular market structures, 175–178
Turner, Donald, 53

Union Pacific Railroad, 95, 98–99
United Shoe Machinery Corporation, 179
United States Steel, 112–114, 193–194
United States Tobacco, 135
University of Chicago. See Chicago School
U.S. Census Bureau, 128, 130
U.S. Civil War, 4
U.S. Congress, 5–6, 193
U.S. Department of Defense, 35–36
U.S. Department of Justice, 7–10, 28, 39, 53, 187
  Antitrust Division budget and, 30
  collusion and, 81–82 (see also Collusion)
  concentration levels and, 79–81
  defining relevant market and, 84–93
  endogenous mergers and, 75–76
  entry effects and, 74
  firm behavior and, 47
  Horizontal Merger Guidelines and, 77–84
  market definition and, 77–79
  market factors and, 79–83
  precompetitive justifications and, 83–84
  price fixing and, 42
U.S. Sentencing Guidelines, 9, 45
U.S. Supreme Court, 193, 200n10, 202n6
  administration costs and, 18
  agreement and, 20
  Conwood v. United States Tobacco case, 135
  decrees and, 9
  Microsoft case, 135, 214n2
  price fixing and, 16
  rule of reason and, 7
  Schwinn decisions and, 194
  Sherman Act and, 16
  Standard Oil case, 7
  Sylvania decision and, 194
  Trans-Missouri case and, 16–18
  United Shoe Machinery case, 179
  U.S. v. Dentsply case, 135, 166–167
  U.S. v. Visa U.S.A. case, 135
U.S. Third Court of Appeals, 167, 217n30

Vertical mergers, 8, 133–134. See also Exclusive contracts
Visa U.S.A., 135
Vita, M. G., 126
Vives, X., 24

Wall Street Journal, 1
Washington, D.C., 36
Welfare
  aggregate effects and, 62–71
  durable goods market and, 72–73
  endogenous mergers and, 75–76
  entry effects and, 73–74
  exclusive contracts and, 185–188
  external effects and, 66–71
  Herfindahl-Hirschman Index and, 68
  hold-out problem and, 75
  horizontal mergers and, 62–74
  Trans-Missouri case and, 16–18

Werden, G. J., 35–36, 70, 73, 101, 212n53
Western Electric, 71
Whinston, M. D., 176, 216n23, 218n39
  anticompetitive exclusive dealing and, 152, 156
  bargaining process and, 162, 166–167
  buyer externalities and, 144
  horizontal mergers and, 74, 76
  investment categories and, 192
  precompetitive justifications and, 179–180, 183, 188
  price fixing and, 16, 18
White, L. J., 37–38
Wickelgren, A. L., 216n17
Wiley, J. S., 144, 152, 176
Williams, M. A., 62, 111
Williamson, O. E., 58–62, 70

Yi, S.-S., 75
Yugo, 89

Zang, I., 75
Zona, J. D.
  firm behavior and, 47–52
  price fixing and, 33–36, 47–52, 89, 101